Depression Economics in the 21st Century

Ma Lieguang
Translated by Wang Wenying

Paths International Ltd

中国社会科学出版社
CHINA SOCIAL SCIENCES PRESS

Preface

In real economy, there appear new situations that the mainstream (i.e. popular) economic theories cannot explain. For example, economic growth stagnates while debts mount up to a huge level, followed by some worrying phenomena in "a depressed era" coined by me. "A depressed era" means the world economy enters an era when long-term stagnation and high debts coexist. Implementing the easing policies in each country becomes normal actions. The money supply is sufficient, but economic indicators present unusual or even abnormal variations. The economic growth lacks momentum. A series of depressed economic situations that worry us come into existence, including large money stock, a long-term low inflation rate or continuous deflation, high unemployment rate, and so forth.

The connection between economic indicators also changes. The relation between the money release and the price level, and the relation between employment and price level both change. Banks have a large number of deposits. The monetary base is sufficient, but the price index is not high. Deflation is more likely to take place than inflation. Some developed countries endure both deflation and a high unemployment rate. In contrast, some countries experience an economic downturn but the unemployment rate is not high. In this case, the economic policies that take as double targets the adjustment of price index and unemployment rate are outdated.

Currently, the economic scale and supply become the main factors affecting inflation. The money issuance of central banks and fiscal deficits may not result in higher inflation. Some countries were once swept by hyperinflation, mainly because of huge changes in the economic situation. Factors, such as epidemics, wars, domestic turbulence, significant natural disasters, etc., lead to insufficient supply so that hyperinflation is induced. On the contrary, when the political and economic situations are stable, a high inflation rate is mainly a result of the relatively small economic scale. At that time, the economy experiences greater fluctuations. It is easy to incur relatively great waves of the economic growth rate that synchronizes with the inflation rate. For example, in the 1990s when China had a small economic scale, China also witnessed an inflation rate as high as 24%. When the economic scale reached a higher level, the inflation rate went down as the money amount and government spending increases.

The current cyclic fluctuations of economy have apparent distinctions from the past. The cycle of prosperity and depression once belonged to the cycle of growth, which means the economic growth of developed countries was in continuous growth. After each depression, the economy was welcomed by a further development. However, the situation changes now. Due to the incapability of solving the huge debts, both prosperity and depression are in a cycle of economic decline. The depressed economy becomes a long-term phenomenon. Many developed countries witness a continuous reduction of the economic magnitude.

As a system, the market economy has to improve and refines itself. This has no relation to whether the policies ought to intervene the market and whether the market is free or not. It is with regards to restructuring each competing unit and the competition order at the market. The free market economy can realize the proper allocation of resources and utilize social power with high efficiency to make the economy develop fast. But the market economy cannot automatically terminate the eternal strength of the most competitive participants. But it cannot solve the problems regarding uneven allocation of wealth and the debt accumulation. Though cyclical fluctuations of economy may result in the debt restructuring, it cannot automatically cut off the accumulation of debts.

The traditional economics fails to explain these entire situations. In front of reality, economics needs to make theoretical innovations. In the mansion of economics, there is no place to accommodate those escaping from the real world. Faced with the depressed economy and mountainous debts, we need to think about new approaches to coordinate economic issues. Economics also needs to modify itself in order to get adapted to changes and rebuild its theoretical system.

This book focuses on economic theories with regards to irreversibility, self-limiting and the multidimensional space. All these contents help with the interpretation of practical economic problems. Though theories regarding these topics still have flaws, I believe new theories will continue to perfect them, and a precise and cohesive system will be gradually built up.

The progress of thoughts is first manifested by the fusion of ideas. It does not only include the combination of theory and experience, the combination of mathematical models and big data analysis, but also the combination of different ideas, such as the combination of philosophy and economics, and the combination of physics and economics. Therefore, the book *The Economic Theory of Irreversibility, Self-limiting and Multidimensional Space* is just a preliminary attempt of concept innovation, combining philosophy, natural sciences, and economics, and expressing those broad and profound thoughts. Moreover, through the analysis of specific economic policies and characteristics of economic development, the creative ability and application effects of ideas are extended to their extreme, and the integration of parallel disciplines is promoted.

The mainstream economics has never been in such trouble of losing trust as it does today. From the liberal economic thought to Keynesian macroeconomic theory, the limitations of thought have been exposed more and more clearly in reality. Those determined liberals are the most disappointed by the decline of the practical value of theories. They have made attempts to modify old theories. But after repairing and making up, they found it meaningless, which worries and bewilders them.

Of course, I am not denying the great value of the achievements and inheritance of these ideas. No new theory can replace them and become a prevailing new consensus. At present, liberalism and Keynesianism in the mainstream economics are difficult to be replaced, and traditional thoughts have only lost some of the empirical foundation and its application value.

The progress of thoughts also starts from their dilemma. People with fewer burdens in mind can better understand the trend of the world. Those in pursuit of knowledge should give up their old ideas without hesitation. They would rather be a little naive and reckless than go back to the courtyard of old ideas. The gentle-touching spring breeze is already scenery of the past. Being too obsessed with the inheritance of the old would incur a heavy burden in mind. Guarding the gate of the school will never bring the defenders any respect. Persevering insistence and obsession in the tiny world of old thoughts run out of fun and delight.

If the book *The Economic Theory of Irreversibility, Self-limiting and Multidimensional Space* is only a comprehensive summary of previous views, an introduction of the learning experience, or a project focusing on application research, it may be just an ordinary book. When readers know a series of innovative ideas come into existence, what I hope most is that the readers are interested in the ideas in the book and think hard.

The beauty of thoughts is eternal. The huge ideological system has a rigorous structure, which indirectly hints the mystery of the free market economy. Modern people pursue the quintessence of these thoughts and will eventually maintain their admiration for rational thoughts. Respecting the laws of the market economy and studying how to strengthen the nation and better off the people are still the fundamental tenets of economics.

Contents

Chapter 1　Economic Reality in the Context of High Debt 1

1.1　Abnormal Swings in Economy 1

1.2　Diminishing Total Factor Productivity 12

1.3　Growth Aversion 19

1.4　The Disquieting Depression Era 22

Chapter 2　The Meaning of Random Disorder　30

2.1　Effective Mechanism 31

2.2　System Attribute 31

2.3　Natural Balance 35

Chapter 3　An Interpretation of Irreversible Changes 39

3.1　A Philosophical Introduction 39

3.2　Only Macro-systems Have Irreversible Phenomena 43

3.3　The Independency of Open Systems 45

3.4　The Law of the Development of Human Society 46

3.5　The Orderly Phenomena in Disorderly Systems 52

3.6　Energy Pyramid 56

Chapter 4 The Economics of the Irreversible Procedure 61

4.1 Three Basic Formulas of Macroeconomics 61

4.2 National income Multiplier Shifting from Lower Dimension to Higher Dimension 63

4.3 The Demonic S=klogY... 70

4.4 How Debts Accumulate? 75

Chapter 5 Common Trends of Market Economy 80

5.1 From Growth to Stagnation 80

5.2 The Common Trend of national income Changes 85

Chapter 6 The Principle of Irreversible Changes in Financial Theories 91

6.1 What is Money? 91

6.2 The Central Bank Have to Continuously inject monetary base to Sustain the Normal Operation of Commercial Banks 92

6.3 Why "Money Drought" Takes Place? 96

6.4 Excessive Issuance of Money is a False Proposition 100

6.5 High Investment Rate Is a Reflection of Mighty National Economic Competitiveness 106

6.6 The Key to Stimulate Economic Development is Loan Growth 107

6.7 Changes of Central Banks' Measures 111

Chapter 7 Phenomena and Principles of Self-limiting 117

7.1 The Definition and Phenomena of Self-limiting 117

7.2 The Theory of Self-limiting in Economics 122

Chapter 8 Demographic Crisis in a Depressed Era 128

8.1 The Current Situation and Problems of the Declining Birth Rate 130
8.2 Forecasts of Future Population 136
8.3 The Self-limiting Theories in Biology 142
8.4 Economic Theories Regarding Population 150
8.5 The Results of Self-limited Population Growth 156

Chapter 9 Theories of Multidimensional Space in Economics 164

9.1 Geometric Measure of Commodity Trading 164
9.2 Position, Distance and Behavior 172
9.3 The Spatial Relationships in Economic Phenomena 177

Chapter 10 Dilemma and Innovation of Economics 190

10.1 Dilemma of Economics 190
10.2 Defects of Traditional Theory 198
10.3 Equilibrium and Entropy Changes 205
10.4 Transcending the Conventional Paradigm 209
10.5 The Brief System of Economics 213

Chapter 11 Philosophical Economics 217

11.1 Philosophy, Science and Economics 217

11.2 What is Philosophical Economics?..221

Bibliography **230**

Postscript **233**

Table of Terms **235**

Chapter 1

Economic Reality in the Context of High Debt

In the cold winter, the water surface does not freeze.
The branches of the budding tree are slow to bloom.
Irregular weathers cause sudden abnormal season.
The economic indicators dropped unexpectedly.
People are not worried about food or clothing, but about jobs.
The past experience doesn't work, in this astonishing world,
to distinguish spring, summer, autumn, and winter. In a trice,
gold mountains have turned to mountains of debts.

——Ma Lieguang

1.1 Abnormal Swings in Economy

1.1.1 "Depression Era"

How should we describe the macroeconomic characteristics of this era? Can we use the term "Depression Era" to encapsulate the laws of entropy and economic phenomena which the monetary aggregate, inflation, and growth of national income follow?

In a rapid economic growth period with low per capita income, though there are debt crises, countries can solve the problem through a developing economy. To distinguish different characteristics of the process from the long-term growth to the long-term stagnation, the term "Depression Era" is used to indicate that each country's economic growth enters a phase of long-term stagnation and heavy debt.

The process of economic growth is the process of debt accumulation. Without debt accumulation, there will be no investment. The investment funds generate debts, and continuous investment accumulates debts. Besides, the process of economic growth is also the process of entropy increase. Therefore, the era of rapid economic growth and rapid entropy accumulation of national income is called the era of capital accumulation, while the era of stagnant economic growth and heavy debt accumulation is called the Depression Era.

The Depression Era is the post-era of capital accumulation. It first began in the mid-1990s when Japan stepping into a stagnant period and symbolized by the American financial crisis in 2008. During this period, the developed countries as a whole entered an era of high debt, relatively high unemployment, low inflation (or deflation), and long-term stagnation and decline of economic growth. This era is characterized by the increase of debt accumulation caused by the expansion of credit money, and the total amount of debt has reached an unprecedented scale.

The great economic crises in the 1930s and the 1970s did not involve government debt. So in these two crises, debt was not the major factor. In the 1930s, countries were in fiscal balance and did not have an excessive accumulation of sovereign debts. Fifty years later, in 1980, the total national debt of the U.S. was just $1 trillion. Countries could abandon the gold standard and pursued expansionary fiscal policies in the 1930s, and rely on stable money supply and sound fiscal policy in the late 1970s. But it is impossible to repeat the policies currently, because it was under these policies, the 2008 international financial crisis and sovereign debt crisis occurred. If fiscal and monetary policies alone can be applied to control the scale of debt, governments and central banks would have applied them long ago. Obviously, countries have failed in debt reduction.

The problem now is that the debt crisis is not only a sovereign debt crisis but also a crisis of credit money in the banking industry. If central banks shrink their supply of monetary base, commercial banks will be struck by “cash crunches”, and the financial industry will once again default on debts. In this case, when the crisis reappears, how should central banks and governments deal with it?

1.1.2 Statistical Analysis and Theoretical Explanation

In classical economics, the rising price is explained as a monetary phenomenon. If the supply and demand of commodities is balanced, the price will not increase. This point of view was so deeply rooted in people’s mind that European countries put forward a strategy in the 1990s for sustainable development: low prices, low growth, and low unemployment. They adopted monetary and fiscal policies that aim at tempering the business cycle to strictly control fiscal spending. Meanwhile, to narrow the gap between the rich and the poor, they also vigorously developed social welfare. In this respect, Europe has done better than the United States and the gap between rich and poor in Europe is also smaller than that in the United States. However, after the international financial crisis in 2008, the economic conditions of European countries deteriorated sharply. Among developed countries and regions such as the United States, Japan, and Europe, Europe had the highest unemployment rate and slow economic recovery. Failing in sustainable development, European governments squeezed spending, which first harmed the welfare of middle- and low-income families. The rise of the unemployment rate and reduction in government spending caused dissatisfaction among the people, who took to the streets to protest against the government’s austere economic policy.

In fact, there is just a correlating connection between rising price and currency issuance. There are both positive and negative correlations between currency issuance and the rate of inflation. When the economy develops to a certain scale, under the condition of sufficient commodity supply, the larger the amount of money is, i.e., the more money in the capital pool, the lower the incremental rate of price index will be. In other words, it seems that for economically developed countries the most effective way to prevent inflation eventually requires the issuance of more currency.

Another noteworthy phenomenon is the new relationship between debt and unemployment. In developed countries, government debt is inversely correlated with unemployment. The higher the government debt is, the lower the unemployment rate will be. On the contrary, the government debt is relatively low while the unemployment rate is relatively high. Besides, the greater the proportion of government debt in national income is, the lower the unemployment rate will be. For example, Japan's government debt reached 1,000 trillion yen in 2013, and its total debt amounted to more than twice of Japan's national income, but Japan's unemployment rate only stood at 4%. In contrast, the US government debt was 16.7 trillion dollars, which was twice as much as the national income, and the unemployment rate was 7.2%. For European countries, the average share of government debt in the national income of EU countries was only about 10 to 20 percent, but the average unemployment rate as high as 12%.

The heads of the Federal Reserve, during the financial crisis, released a large number of dollars into the market but were surprised to find that the currency in the capital pool was growing while the prices did not rise significantly. At that time, the inflation rate in the United States remained at a low level for several years. Therefore, the Fed used to buy treasury bonds every month and invested money into the capital pool with confidence.

There is also an inverse relationship between China's monetary aggregate M2 and inflation rate. In 2000, M2 was only 10 trillion yuan, while in 2013, it exceeded 100 trillion yuan. People exclaimed that the currency was over-issued and worried that the central bank would issue more currency, which would result in more serious inflation. However, the inflation rate kept falling. Since the reform and opening up, the most serious inflation occurred in the mid-1990s. In the second half of 1994, the consumer price index even reached a high level of 24%. But by January 2015, China's consumer price index was only 0.8%.

Some argue that statistics of China's inflation rate do not tally with facts. They cite the fact that China's housing prices have risen sharply in the past 10 years and therefore, it cannot be concluded that the more currency is issued, the lower the inflation rate is. There are some facts in this opinion. However, the calculation of the price index in economics is comprehensive. It refers to the average change in the price level of all goods and services in the same period, rather than to the single change in the prices of goods and services in a particular class or industry. When it comes to the calculation of the inflation rate, there are many indicators; among which the consumer price index (CPI) and the national income deflator are commonly used. In practice, although there are factors of underestimating the rise of housing prices or the rise of medical expenses, in general, both the price index calculated in the same sample and the deflator index reflecting the overall macro price level showed a fluctuating downward trend in the price statistics.

In short, the price index is a general indicator. Although prices in various industries could rise high or little, and even rise rapidly in some commodities, this independent change is not reflected in the national income deflator. At the macroeconomic level, the overall inflation or deflation is generally discussed instead of partial deflation and partial inflation; or structural inflation and deflation is used, so soaring house prices do not imply the excessively rising prices in all commodities.

Larger money issuance, however, is accompanied by a decrease in the inflation rate. This is a common phenomenon shared by many countries, especially the developed ones, in their economic development. The U.S. price index has kept falling, Europe is heading for deflation, and Japan has fallen into a long-term deflationary state since the 1990s. Since the beginning of the 1990s, due to the downturn of Japanese economy, the Bank of Japan has adopted a series of monetary expansion policies, not only pumping a large amount of monetary base into the market but also implementing a monetary policy of zero interest rate. Although during the two years from March 2006 to December 2008, the quantitative easing was temporarily withdrawn, and the base rate increased to 0.25%, after 2008, the zero interest rate and ultra-loose quantitative easing policies were reintroduced. By March 2013, the Bank of Japan had infused a large amount of monetary base, resulting in a total asset of 165.39 trillion yen, an increase of 90.81% from January 1999. In the same period, the balance of government bonds held by the bank of Japan reached 125.05 trillion yen, an increase of 153.51%. A large amount of the supply of monetary base did not cause the price index to rise. At the end of 1999, Japan's CPI was 104%, which is considered low inflation; in 2013, Japan's CPI was only 99.2%, a sign of deflation.[1]

To clearly demonstrate the relationship between monetary aggregate and inflation, we can make a graph of the relationship between China's inflation rate and monetary aggregate from 1991 to 2013 (see Figure 1-1), taking the year as the abscissa, the inflation rate as the left ordinate, and the monetary aggregate as the right ordinate. As shown in Figure 1-1, the inflation rises first and then falls, with a downward trend similar to hyperbola, and the monetary aggregate presents an exponential growth, showing that the amount of money grows exponentially, which constitutes a u-shaped graph. We can clearly see that when the monetary aggregate is small, the inflation rate is high, and when the monetary aggregate increases, the inflation rate decreases.

The traditional monetary theory can only explain the positive correlation between monetary aggregate and inflation. But what is new is that low inflation or persistent deflation under monetary inflation is a long-term phenomenon. This has been going on in Japan for more than 20 years, leading to stagnant economic growth, mounting national debt but low unemployment. Some American scholars wrote articles criticizing the Federal Reserve's plan to buy treasury bonds, believing that the Fed's continued purchase of treasury bonds and increase of

1 Guo Kewei, "Effects and Limits of Super Easing Monetary Policy in Japan", *The Banker*, 2013, Issue 6.

the supply of monetary base will lead to later inflation; others say that, on the contrary, the money supply causes deflation.

Does the increase in the money supply cause inflation or deflation, or neither? The relationship between the money supply and the price index is just a complex interactive relationship; it is neither a causal relationship nor the only positive correlation for the increase in monetary aggregate does not necessarily lead to inflation, and the changing trend of monetary aggregate and price index is essentially a reflection of the law of entropy change. Inflation is an increase in entropy, so the rise in the price level is a manifestation of the increase in the entropy of the economic system.

The so-called law of entropy change refers to the irreversible change of the macroscopic process. When external conditions are stable, the microscopic disorder in the macroscopic system tends to be maximized with the increase of macroscopic quantity.

The increase in the monetary aggregate and the growth of national income are also a natural macro process. Therefore, the changes in the monetary aggregate and national income follow the law of entropy. As the monetary base and total national income increase, their microscopic disorder tends to be maximized, and the growth rate of currency and national income gradually declines and tends to zero. Correspondingly, the inflation rate gradually decreases, changing from inflation to deflation; that is, in the long run, the increase in the currency will lead to a decline in interest rates, inflation rate, and long-term deflation. This statement is contradictory with the monetary inflation theory.

Macroeconomics has many explanations for the relationship between inflation and currency, such as monetary aggregate, effective demand, rational expectations, and so on. However, these theories have a basic premise: they are based on market-cleared commodity equilibrium. Therefore, these theories all agree that the essence of inflation is a monetary phenomenon. But in the author's opinion, there is no such essential relationship between inflation and currency. They both just follow the law of entropy change, and entropy change is only related to the scale of its own national income and monetary aggregate and has nothing to do with other factors. Other factors, such as interest rate regulation, demand management and similar fiscal and monetary policies are only exogenous factors. Keynesians generally assume that the velocity of money circulation is constant; and statistical analysis does not support the hypothesis that the velocity of money circulation tends to be higher. In the long run, with the increase of monetary base, the velocity of money circulation tends to be lower.

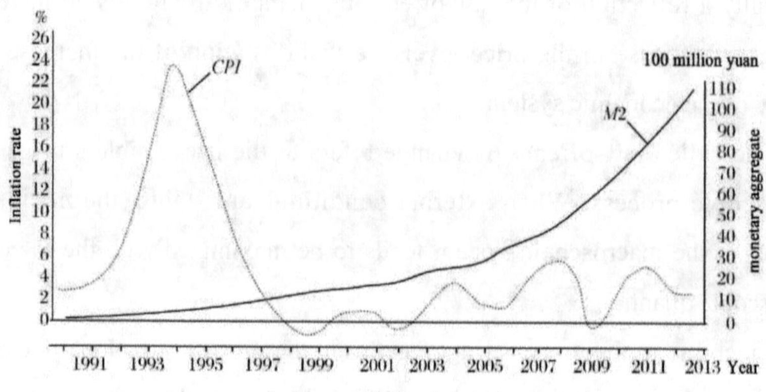

Figure 1-1 U-shaped Trend of China's Monetary Aggregate and Inflation Rate

Note: In 2013, China's money supply M2 reached 110 trillion yuan, while the inflation rate did not rise significantly.
Source: National Bureau of Statistics, China.

Inflation is defined as the continuous rise in commodity prices related to changes in national income. Inflation rate refers to the rate of increase in commodity prices, which can be expressed by the variables $\Delta P / P$. Capital P is the average price. Monetary aggregate and price level can be expressed by the monetary aggregate formula, which is the theory put forward by economist Irving Fisher in 1911. Modern economists modified the formula and changed the trading volume of currency on the left side into national income, so the mathematical formula of the relationship between currency and national income is as follows:

$$PQ=vM \tag{1-1}$$

The P in the formula represents the average price of national income,

Q represents the total quantity of commodities, v is the velocity of money circulation, and M is the monetary aggregate. This formula expresses a kind of correlation. Currency M is not a dependent variable of national income, and they have independent endogenous influencing factors respectively.

Next, we substitute the statistical analysis results of monetary aggregate M and commodity's average price P into this equation to find some new relations. The importance of mathematics in theoretical analysis lies in further exploring the laws behind the phenomena through mathematical reasoning.

Statistics show that after the economic development reaches a certain scale, under the condition of sufficient supply of commodity the inflation rate decreases with the increase of monetary aggregate, and as shown in figure 1-1, the changing track of the relationship between the two is a downward sloping hyperbola. So we can list the mathematical relationship according to the fitting trend diagram, using $\Delta P / P$ to denote the inflation rate and ΔP to represent the commodity price variable. For the purpose of easier analysis, we prescribe $\Delta P \geq 0$, and then there is a formula:

$$\Delta P / P \times M = k \tag{1-2}$$

In the formula, k is a constant and M represents a monetary aggregate. This relationship indicates that the product of inflation rate and monetary aggregate is a constant, the smaller the monetary aggregate is, the higher the inflation rate will be, just as the situation in China in the 1990s; the larger the monetary aggregate is, the lower the inflation rate becomes, as it has been since 2000. Furthermore, associating the relation $PQ=vM$ with $\Delta P / P \times M = k$ results in:

$$\Delta PQ=vk \tag{1-3}$$

In the formula, v is the velocity of money circulation and k is a constant. Because of the small change in the velocity of money circulation, we define vk as a constant. From the derivation, we can see that for inflation, the larger the total amount of commodities is, the less the price increases. The smaller the total amount of commodities is, the more the price increases. This relationship shows that the increase in the average price of goods is related to the total amount of commodities.

Since the inflation rate and the monetary aggregate change in reverse, and there are data suggesting the similar change in the increase of commodity price and the total national income then in practice, the inflation rate and the growth rate of national income should also coincide with each other, with a positive correlation between them. Statistical tests prove that the two are indeed highly correlated, which is manifested in the convergence of monetary growth rate and national income growth rate.

From the long-term trend, in the economic cycle, when the national income growth rate is high, the inflation rate is high; when the national income growth rate is low, the inflation rate is low. There is a positive correlation between inflation and monetary growth rate, but no direct positive correlation with the monetary aggregate (see Figure 1-2 and Figure 1-3). When the growth rate of monetary aggregate decreases as a result of its increase, the growth rate of national income tends to decline and so does the inflation rate.

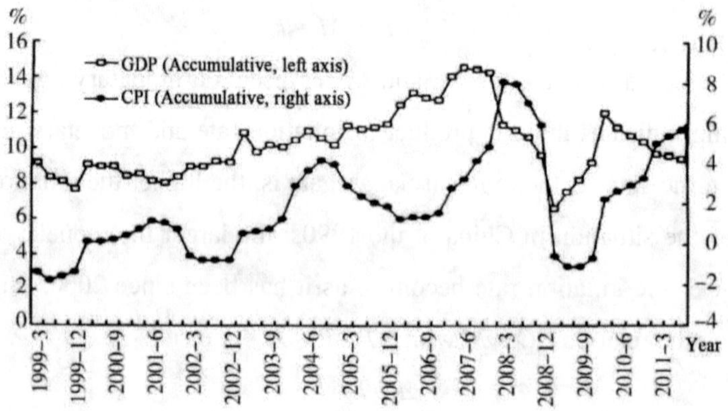

Figure 1-2 China's National Income Growth Rate and Inflation Rate

Note: The inflation rate is basically consistent with the fluctuation of national income. As long as there is economic growth, there will be inflation.

Source: Tang Duoduo, Zhang Xiaojing, Wang Hongju and Zhang Ping , *Keep Policies Stable and Concern about External Risks*, from *China's Economic Growth and Economic Cycles (2011)*, Economic Press China, 2012, p. 77.

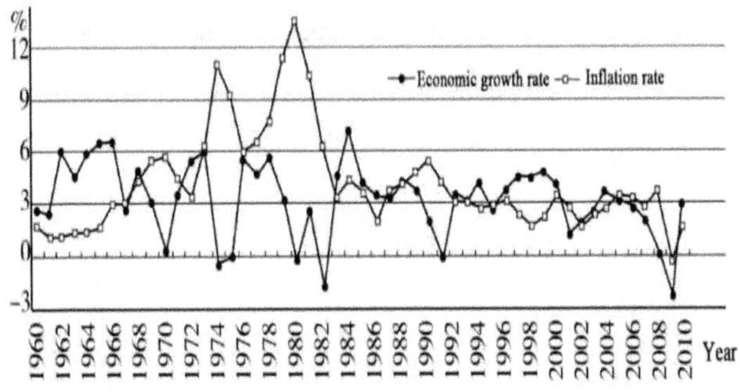

Figure 1-3 America's Economic Growth Rate and Inflation Rate

Note: The relationship between economic growth and inflation rate in the United States shows a consistent trend in the long run, especially after the year 2000, although there are short-term inconsistencies.
Source: Tang Duoduo, Zhang Xiaojing, Wang Hongju and Zhang Ping , *Keep Policies Stable and Concern about External Risks*, from *China's Economic Growth and Economic Cycles (2011)*, Economic Press China, 2012, p. 85.

Obviously, both national income and monetary aggregate have the same process of increasing entropy, which is called NI entropy and monetary entropy. What's more, their entropy values change in the same direction and tend to maximize.

Statistics show that there is consistency between prices and national income growth. Although the range of growth is different, the trend of change and fluctuation is basically the same. In this case, according to the results of statistical analysis, we can use a positive proportional relationship to describe the relationship between price rise and income increase, namely:

$$\Delta P = \alpha \Delta Q \tag{1-4}$$

In the formula, ΔP is the average commodity price variable and ΔQ is the commodity variable. Substituting the equation into the relation $\Delta PQ=vk$ obtains a new equation $\alpha \Delta Q \times Q = vk$, then there are:

$$\Delta Q = \beta / Q \quad \beta = vk / \alpha \tag{1-5}$$

Since v, k, and α are constants, β is also a constant. The relation $\Delta Q = \beta / Q$ indicates that when the national income commodities increase, its increment tends to decline. This relation explains why the larger the scale of national income, the growth rate of national income will decline with the increase of income scale commodities. It needs to be especially emphasized that this relationship can be tested by statistical data, and the economic development trend of various countries shows the characteristics of decreasing growth.

1.2 Diminishing Total Factor Productivity

The Industrial Revolution based on scientific and technological progress has completely changed human society and promoted the development of the global economy in leaps and bounds in just a few hundred years. In 1972, American sociologist Daniel Bell published *The Coming of Post-industrial Society*, which divides industrial society into pre-industrial society, industrial society, and post-industrial society. He believes that the post-industrial society is a society of knowledge, in which the economic structure has changed from a product economy to a service economy, and the share of industrial production in national income has declined while the proportions of knowledge-based services such as commerce, transportation, entertainment, and scientific research has increased. In a later period, with the rise of the Information Revolution in the 1990s, the society accelerated to enter the information society. The Internet has changed the traditional way of information transmission and triggered the knowledge revolution and information revolution. As a result, high-tech industry has developed rapidly, the proportions of both knowledge industry and knowledge workers have increased, and the contribution rate of knowledge and technology to economic growth has also risen.

In macroeconomics, passionate viewpoints about the scientific revolution and confident opinions on technological progress have also been proposed. Economists believe in general that the existence of capitalism is based on the full use of the results of technological progress to create wealth effectively through the market. They believe that technological progress will turn the world into one in which everyone has wealth.

Technological progress, like breeze and rain in spring, can melt the ice and snow in the winter-like session in economy and bring back the economic growth that is natural and balanced. However, research shows that the more advanced science and technology is, the lower the economic growth rate is. The decline of labor productivity is not the result of the change in economic structure, nor is it a manifestation of the decline in the overall technological level of the national economy. This is because the technical levels of all industries are improving, and no technological retrogression has ever occurred. The decreasing effect of technological progress on economic growth is exactly the major reason for the decline of total factor (manpower, capital) productivity.

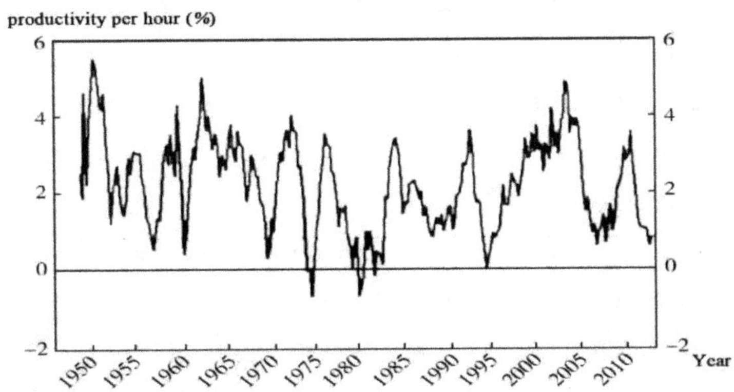

Figure 1-4 U.S. Productivity per Hour in Non-agricultural Fields (100 in 2009)

Note: according to Michael Fero, chief economist at JPMorgan Chase & Co, U.S. labor productivity has grown at an annual rate of just 0.8% over the past two years, the slowest pace since the World War . From the long-term trend described in this chart, it can be seen that productivity growth tends to decline.
Source: collated from United States Department of Labor Statistics, http://wallstreetcn.com/

Netizen 2013luan wrote in an economic website, namely bbs.pinggu.org, that China's total factor productivity (TFP) had increased from -1.9% before the reform and opening up (1952-1978) to 3.3% -- 4.6% between 1978 and1995, and its contribution to economic growth had reached 33% -- 47%. However, after 1995, TFP had shown a downward trend and fallen to 0.6% between 1996 and 2001. The author believes that the reasons for the decline of TFP in China are various, for example diminishing marginal return on investment, resource allocation of tangible capital distorted by measures such as tax exemption for foreign capital and low price of land, and actual loan interest rate that is much lower than the growth of wage. In addition, the author also believes that the low efficiency in the use of resource and the widening gap in national income will also reduce TFP.

The views of netizen 2013luan are fact-oriented analysis, not involving the main reason for the decline of labor productivity. Labor productivity in the United States is also declining. In spite of the increasingly higher technological base, why is the TFP in the U.S. declining as it is in China? The essential reason is that with the expansion of economy in scale, technological progress has played a lesser role in economic growth, and its driving effect on economic growth has diminished.[1]

Theoretical analysis: the contribution of technological progress to output decreases with the expansion of economy in scale. Under the condition of technological progress, the law of diminishing marginal product still exists.

Total factor productivity (TFP) refers to the rate of technological progress, first proposed by American economist Robert Merton Solow. He introduced the rate of technological progress, an exogenous variable independent of labor and capital, in the production function. Due to technological progress, it can offset the decline rate of marginal benefit in capital and labor input, resulting in an increase in output. In fact, however, the decline rate of marginal product still exists in the context of technological progress. When the output growth rate of dependent variables is lower than the growth rate of technological progress, technological progress makes a decreasingly less marginal contribution to output. A brief representation is as follows.

Assume $Q/L=T_{(t)}F(K/L)$, where $T_{(t)}$ denotes technological progress, t the time and $F(K/L)$ the production function of capital-labor ratio, and technological progress and capital-labor ratio are both factors affecting output. If the

1 2013luan, "Why TFP in China experiences a marked decline?", CRU Economic Forum, http://bbs.pinggu.org.

technological progress changes while K / L remains the same, the partial derivative of the output Y and the technological progress can be calculated under this circumstance. If the second-order derivative is calculated to be over zero, then the marginal benefit of technological progress on output decreases.

The law of diminishing marginal product can also be expressed as follows: suppose $Y = f(T, K, L)$, where T represents technological progress, K capital investment, and L labor input. The output is the function of T, K, and L. When T, K, and L all change, if and only if $g_Y < g_T$ (or g_K, g_L) (g stands for growth rate, g_r for output growth rate, g_T for technological progress growth rate, g_k and g_L for capital growth rate and labor growth rate respectively), T (or K, L) has diminishing marginal product.

More specifically, if T is a constant, the production function shall be $Y=Tf(K, L)$; if the capital input continues to increase while the growth of labor input slows down, then the diminishing marginal product of capital input shall be $g_K > g_Y$.

If L is a constant, the production function shall be $Y=Lf(T, K)$. If the technological progress increasingly grows while the growth of capital input slows down, then the diminishing marginal product of technological progress shall be $g_T > g_Y$.

In terms of the history of economic development, there would be no economic development to speak of without technological progress. Human beings are constantly improving skills for life and production technologies, accompanied by the development of the commodity economy and the changes in the social system. Fundamentally, the progress of human society is based on the accumulation of knowledge.

The Industrial Revolution has brought unprecedented prosperity to human society. In the 20th century, science and technology had pushed human economic activities to an unprecedented height. Because science and technology are closely related to economic development, the development of technology and related industries has a great impact on the overall development of the world economy. Especially when countries are experiencing low per capita income, the periodic changes of technological progress will have a direct impact on economic development.

As technological progress is ongoing (similar to corpuscular property in physics) and has the characteristics of periodic fluctuation (similar to physical wave)[1], the impact of technological progress on economic growth is also cyclical. Such a cycle is not disorderly nor unpredictable but sustained. The impact of technological progress on economic cycle is sustained and can be judged and predicted.

Technological progress is characterized by creation and technological renewal. Likewise, commodity production should also be based on technological renewal, with constant introduction of new products to meet the demands for social commodities. Corresponding to product renewal, market demand is also changing. Technological progress brings about new products as well as fresh demands. Since the changes of market demand are closely related to people's lives, the production of social commodities must adapt to the changes of market demand, indicating that the changes in the demand for commodity is the mechanism through which technological progress is related to commodity production.

Bacon's "knowledge is power" has called for generations after generations to struggle. The wave of science and technology is rolling forward. No one will listen to those who propagate that scientific and technological progress will stagnate or scientific and technological development is the "root of misfortune". Any doubts about scientific and technological progress will be marginalized by society. Feeble criticisms, some opinions and specific customs cannot change the widely acknowledged viewpoints, as people firmly believe that scientific and technological development has unlimited possibilities as well as its key role in promoting economic growth.

1 Not only does visible light have wave-particle duality, but also everything else implicitly exhibits this kind of characteristic, depending, of course, on how the observers see and express it.

However, with the increase of per capita income, the role of technological progress and scientific and technological revolution in promoting economic growth shows a decreasing trend. The main reason is that economic development has its own laws, and the cycle of technological progress is still an external factor. With the rising level of technology and social demand, the increasingly varied and abundant commodity, along with its increased total quantity, will inevitably lead to maximized microcosmic disorder in commodity market demand.

But the influence of technological progress on commodity production occurs at the micro level of enterprises and commodities, so the independence of individual entities and overall disorder in the market economy weaken the overall influence of technological progress on economic growth.

The microcosmic disorder of the commodity market tends to maximize with the increase of total scale, especially under the condition of technological progress. The law of irreversible change of monetary fund movement speeds up debt accumulation, and enables financial money to operate independently and massively. Technological progress leads to the expansion of production finance in equal proportion in scale, and the countervailing effect between each other weakens the direct influence of technological progress on the economic growth cycle. As a result, technological progress plays a decreasing role in economic growth. So it is inevitable that the productivity of input factors declines. It is found that despite the improvement of technology and management, output lags behind the growth of input.

The decline of total factor labor productivity shows not only the diminishing direct effect of technological progress on economic growth, but also the strong effect of another reason, namely the increasingly transparent limiting effect of microcosmic disorder on overall growth. The footsteps of disorder sounds noisier, the economic waves are shrinking, and the economic cycle is blurring. Stagnant economic growth, excessive supply, persistent deflation, debt accumulation, high unemployment and other upsetting depressing phenomena have replaced the booms represented by rising productivity, falling rate of unemployment, sustained growth and surging inflation in the past.

It is worth noting that if there are no significant changes in society and technological levels, these changes in the role of technological progress on economic growth are irreversible under the conditions of a market economy. Although in the long run, continuing economic deflation will not sustain and there will be a short-term recovery, economic growth is still depressed. It is not possible to automatically shift from stagnation to the long-term sustained growth in the past, nor will the accumulated debt be reduced on its own. In the face of such a change, the theory of technological progress in the past is out of date. The theory is not only of no guiding significance for the correct understanding of the economy, but will also lead to sad ignorance if it is blindly adhered to. Debt accumulation is determined by the law of monetary movement. Technological progress promotes production development, and debt increases correspondingly in the market economy when wealth is accumulated. Existing technological progress has a diminishing effect on economic growth, so it is not feasible to rely on technological progress to overcome both economic stagnation and the debt problem.

Technological progress has led to overproduction and rising unemployment. In the environment of global trade liberalization, hardworking Chinese sell cheap goods to people in every corner of the world. As a result, the manufacturing industry in developed countries is shrinking day by day. But science and technology have increased the per unit area yield of agricultural products worldwide. For example, China's grain output had kept increasing for 10 years in a row by 2013, exceeding 600 million tons.

Bumper agricultural harvest is achieved every year, with the increased unit yield playing a major role. It is because of the oversupply of commodities in the world that the price of products has not risen sharply. Moreover, people doubt the viewpoint of limited resources because the supplies of commodities and energy are sufficient, believing that there will be no crises of overpopulation or shortage of resources in the history human development. What current situation is the debt crisis has emerged before the population crisis and resource crisis arrive. Under the condition of technological progress, people need not worry too much about the shortage of resources. Quantum mechanics tells us that matter contains endless energy. A small stone, in the state of motion, spends the energy far greater than the total amount of energy that has been consumed by humans in the past hundreds of thousands of years. The outstanding economic problems are not the shortage of resources, but environmental pollution, stagnant economic growth, rising unemployment, declining population growth, aging population, and debt crisis.

1.3 Growth Aversion

"It's not because I don't understand, but because the world is changing so fast." Compared with the first 30 years of the planned economy, China has experienced another 30 years of reform and opening up, and the economy has undergone earth-shaking changes. In just a generation, the country has become affluent. No one knows why a kind of aversion is bred after all these exciting achievements. Economic growth immediately turns into a boring topic. It not only destroys the environment but also wastes resources. Perhaps it is because we used to believe too much in growth that we have lost our way. It seems that every kind of effort to save the economy will elicit skepticism and cynicism. Is it a mistake to be busy?[1] All of a sudden, there were scenes of exhaustion in the wake of economic development at all levels of society.

Happiness is proportional to utility and opposite to desire. Utility refers to the degree of satisfaction brought to consumers by goods, while desire is the strong need for goods. When the utility of goods is unchanged, the greater the desire is, the less happy people feel. Chinese people's sense of happiness from economic growth could be analyzed in line with this theory. When people are less satisfied

1 Wolf Lepenies, *Qu'est-ce qu'un intellectuel européen? Les intellectuels et la politique de l'esprit dans l'histoire européenne*, translated by Li Yanming, Guangxi Normal University Press, 2011.

with economic growth, their desires for material increase, and their sense of happiness deminishes with the decrease of utility. Economy grows every year, so no freshness can be found in these monotonous years. Who would have thought that now taking growth as the right path would trigger resentment 30 years back?

People in developed areas are less likely to be optimistic than those in less developed areas. People in small cities and rural areas yearn for large cities and developed areas, and they cram into these places, not only promoting the development of these cities and regions, but also, bringing some problems like road congestion, environmental pollution, and uncontrollable uncivilized behaviors. No more romantic reminiscences in the crowd, but annoying commotion and noises. The development has annoyed us so much.

It is not only the environment that is polluted, but also the thoughts. Facing all kinds of slanders, the thinkers are as dull as the populace. The familiar theories of economic growth in the past are disappointing as the economic growth has not developed towards the intended goals. Doing research turns out to be nearly a failure for those people like me who have been thinking about the economy throughout all their lives. After a plenty of failures, I have gradually become depressed. I have studied Western economics for decades and it is till now that I've begun to understand that much of the macroeconomics of the past has lost its value in practical applications.

With growth aversion, people's memories weaken, making them forget what poverty is. Barren hills and torrential rivers fade into haze-free green mountains and blue waters. The age, in which bicycles run all over the street, seems healthier when the shortage of materials is replaced by spiritual richness. Despite their depression and misfortune, what are pictured in people's brain crammed with memories about the past are still leisurely idyllic scenes.

When the belief in growth becomes an outdated symbol, growth aversion becomes a mental illness in the time of depression. I once argued with netizens on the topic of growth aversion on the Internet and find that aversion is an emotion that is irrationally vented out. So do not reasons to people with aversion, reasons incur disgust from people as well.

The best cure for aversion, it seems, is not economic growth and prosperity, but recession and depression, and returning to poverty is the most effective way to clean up mental illness.

It is economic growth that has lifted us out of poverty. Growth is not only about creating jobs but also about helping people get rid of poverty and turning China into a strong nation. As the saying goes, you shall know how to cherish your loss and tell what it is when you have lost it. After growth stops, we shall know what prosperity is; after getting rid of debt, we shall know what wealth is.

A Hundred Flowers Blossom

The famous verses in the poem,
Like a ripe apple,
That everyone wants to bite.
The repeatedly chanted verses are,
As ordinary as talks,
Beautiful but unimpassioned.
Tired of the blooming of a hundred flowers,
Then take an emotional explosion or go into the distance,
For cold winter will pay a visit to your home.

——Ma Lieguang

Growth aversion is Chinese people's discomfort in the face of rapid change. How to adapt to great changes is a big problem. History tells us that individuals, businesses, thoughts, cultures, and spirits will eventually be marginalized and replaced by the fittest if they cannot adapt to the changing circumstances of the country.

Many examples of the changes in human society show the one-way path that has no turns for getting back. When the Chinese give up a way of life, they can no longer regain it. For example, after urbanization is realized, people will not return to the life of countryside, and most people who have a car to drive will never ride a bicycle again just because of the haze in the city. Anyone contemplating a return to the past would better give up the thought as society cannot afford to risk going backward.

A large number of facts show that the market economy is efficient; its operation can make the social economy prosperous and people rich. In this way, through the comparative analysis of both positive and negative aspects, China, without hesitation, has chosen the system of market economy as the orientation for its reform of the economic system.

The aforesaid paragraph is written by Chen Taifu in his *Reflections on Economic Philosophy*[1], which reflects the consensus among the political and economic circles in China in the 1980s and 1990s. Mr. Chen's book was published in 2005, shortly after which the world has taken a new visage. In today's academic circle, who would mention these thought-provoking words again?

1.4 The Disquieting Depression Era

"The rich die in trust, the middle class die in stock speculation, and the grassroots die in P2P. There is always a specific trick for you." Words like this are both a joke and a fact.[2]

Can the market economy solve the debt problem on its own? The answer is a "No".

A free market economy itself is a mechanism that generates debts. Without the market economy, how can there be debt? Without debt, how can there be wealth? Debt accumulation is determined by the law of capital movement, and it is also the product of the market economy itself. The debt problem does not temporarily

1 Chen Taifu, *Pondering Upon Economic Philosophy*, China Social Sciences Press, 2005, p. 6.

2 zounghy, "Troubleshoot Fund-raising Risks Under Strict Orders", Macroeconomics on CRU Economic Forum, *Caixin Weekly,* January 16, 2016.

exist for the time being but exists in the company of the market economy. But macroeconomics is so over-confident in technological progress, resulting in a lack of a correct understanding of the fatal defects of the market economy and the ignorance of the law that should have long been noticed. This law is that with the expansion of economy in scale, the micro disorder will lead to stagnation of the overall growth and irreversible debt accumulation.

When economic growth stagnates, the debt crisis will suddenly become palpable. After the economy recovers, the debt problem seems to have disappeared and then will come back in repetition. It will become more and more serious, indicating that the debt will not disappear on its own. The debt crisis in the United States in 2008 put an end to the myth that the market economy solves its debt problems through automatic adjustment, and at the same time raised the question of whether the market economy will destroy itself. What are we supposed to do? We have no other choices than the market economy, as it is the most efficient system in modern society, and no other systems have more economic freedom and public welfare than the market economy. In the past, people used to believe in a utopian system in which property is shared and everyone is equal. Such a society is beautiful, but not yet a human world. There is a great distance between ideal and reality.

Ideal and Reality

Believe it or not,
Heaven and earth share the same ideas,
But still have different circumstances.
Freedom and equality are in heaven,
And non-freedom and inequality on earth;
The truth is in heaven,
While we live on the earth.

——Ma Lieguang

It has to be admitted that the market economy has lost its luster, but it is not lifeless yet, because people have not yet found a more glorious replacement for it. We, of course, do not blindly believe that the end of the market economy is the beginning of another great era. Since we firmly believe that the market economy is the most appropriate economic system for human beings, there are only two ways ahead: stick to the development of the market economy until all efforts within the existing system and rules fail and it can no longer be sustained, or — destruct everything we have to dissipate wealth and debt in an attempt to initiate an endless circle with a completely fresh new start.

The risk of self-destruction of debt cut-off on our own is too great to advocate. Just as everyone has to prolong their life by curing diseases, they will not refuse to cure them because they will eventually die one day and thus give up a healthy life. When the economic crisis comes, refusing to try to neither save the banks nor alleviate the debt problem is tantamount to choosing economic suicide. If some natural disasters and wars happen, the situation will be even worse. The dictators will rule again until after a great failure, society rekindles hopes for wealth accumulation and resumes the old path of the market economy to restart the circle of debt accumulation and the reappearance of the debt crisis.

When economic growth stagnates, there is a feeling of sorrow over the past and prosperity in society. Over time, people will resent stagnation and demand a change. It is difficult for them to feel happy even though they stay well-fed. The atmosphere of optimism will fade away. Afflicted by the agony of melancholy and worry, people will start to yearn for the unknown age. It is because they do not know how to break out of the debt chain that melancholy and worry will lead them to weariness of the world and despair. Coupled with a rising tide of boredom, nationalism, bellicosity, war, and upsetting disturbing slogans, local wars between nations will become inevitable.

For the developed countries, the biggest puzzle is that fiscal and monetary policies are becoming ineffective. Japan has been floundering for two decades, but the prospect is still bleak. After the Second World War, the Japanese economy has always been dominated by the government, and the central bank of Japan has kept maintaining a loose fund supply for commercial banks for years that most of the funds of Japanese companies come from bank loans, while just a few generated through market-based financing such as stock and bond financing. Since the 1990s, the Japanese economy has been in a sustained downturn. The Japanese government has always adhered to a loose policy, issuing a large number of government bonds and expanding public spending. The central bank has adopted a low interest rate policy to support key industries and stimulate economic growth. The interest rate of the central bank of Japan is almost zero, which makes the interest rate completely lose its role of regulating the money supply. Judging from this, it can be seen that the Japanese government is the most active government to intervene in the economic operation. In 1996, the Hashimoto government introduced six major economic reforms in governmental administration, finance, fiscal system, economic structure, social security and education respectively, as well as the so-called "Big Bang" financial reform to relax foreign exchange controls. In 2013, the Administration of Shinzo Abe again vowed to lead Japan out of the long-term economic downturn, and implemented substantially loose economic policies in fiscal, monetary, and foreign exchange aspects simultaneously. However, it ended in a struggle with little hope. The future is not optimistic, as Japan's economic downturn would still continue.

Under the influence of neoclassical macroeconomic theory, the United States has been adhering to a neutral monetary policy since the 1980s, taking curbing inflation as the basic policy. But the international financial crisis in 2008 declared the failure of neoclassical macroeconomic theory. The Federal Reserve completely changed this traditional policy and carried out quantitative easing monetary policy instead to directly export money to the market by purchasing treasury bonds and lending money to commercial banks. Now, it seems to be a right approach. The US economy is recovering and the Dow Jones Index is rising to a new record. Many experts estimate that the US economy will continue to improve. But how long the upturn will last remains in doubt, since stagnation of economic growth will be a long-term phenomenon and debt is still mounting. A temporary recovery is just the last transient boom before the final recession. Each short prosperity is followed by a more serious and longer recession.

The situation in Europe is even more worrisome. Now Europe basically implements tight fiscal policies and loose monetary policies, resulting in a contraction in its economic aggregate as well as a disastrous unemployment rate. "The unemployment rate among young people in Greece, Spain, and Croatia is as high as 50%, and in Europe, there are large regions with an unemployment rate of 25%." Austerity in Europe has not led to a reduction in debt, with European governmental bonds and bank liabilities continuing to rise. Bank deposit rates have been falling, and the European Central Bank has begun to gradually pursue a negative interest rate policy. Some consider the policy as a plunder of assets, a violation of the sanctity of private property, and a challenge to capitalist ideals.

To reduce social debt, we have to cut off the savings of enterprises and residents, and the reduction of debt can only be achieved through the bankruptcy of commercial banks in a wide range. Neoclassical economics used to believe that the Great Depression is a "good" thing as only depression could forever bury the old values and expectations, and clean up the abnormal process of the economy[1] to help economy enter the next development stage. There is some rationality in this thinking, but the consequences of great economic depression disturbing. The Great Depression of the 1930s proved that a hands-off economic crisis would threaten the capitalist system, and the Hitler regime emerged after the Great Depression. Additionally, even if capitalism as a whole is overthrown and reconstructed, social debt will accumulate again. This is because debt and wealth are two sides of the same process, living and dying together: Social debt keeps low when the country is poor. When there is an adequate supply of social goods, the amount of both debt and wealth will stand as a sign of the country's affluence.

1 Joseph Schumpeter, *Theory of Economic Development*, translated by Zou Jianping, China Pictorial Publishing House, 2012, p. 234.

The question at present is how to deal with the rich debt crisis, which, with no theoretical explanation in the past, has become so unfamiliar that people have no consensus. Europe's debt crisis, for example, is said to be the result of highly welfare that has led its citizens to work less hard, but the hard-working Japanese have taken on more debt. China's exports are also regarded as the culprit of a downturn in other countries' economies, but the Chinese economy is also on the same path toward a high level of debt accumulation.

Facing China's social debt accumulation and economic slowdown, some people stress the need for reform, insisting that "sacrifice the growth rate to some extent in exchange of the room for reform" and that only reform can bring us a future. There was a TV special that reviews the history of reform since 1978. Several old scholars told their experiences, which made people clearly understand the obstacles and achievements of the reform and opening up. It is an indisputable fact that without the reform and opening up, there would have been no such great achievements in China's economic development.

Here is the problem at present. What will China's development rely on in the next few decades or an even longer period? We will continue to pursue reform and opening up, respect entrepreneurs, and strengthen the legal system. But the economic problems we face are no longer those of the 1980s and 1990s. They are the problems of stagnant growth or a growth next to stagnation, debt accumulation, and high unemployment that countries advocating the rule of law and human rights have to face altogether. These problems are ones of a free-market economy with a sound legal system. More importantly, in the aspect of the market economy, the degree of marketization in China has greatly improved. New economic reform measures will bring about problems associated with diminishing benefits for economic growth, poor effectiveness and the failure in further marketization, and will even play a negative role in the worst case. If reform is not conducive to economic development, it only causes regression.

The reform of the economic system cannot solve the debt problem, especially the liberalization reform in the financial field. Although the development of micro credit, financial innovation, the invigoration of finance, and the facilitation of financial payment are beneficial for the channeling of savings and the acceleration of the flow of funds, they also spread the debt risk. When the financial crisis occurs, small banks, small loan companies, online lending platforms, trust and loan money funds, compared with traditional savings banks, are the weakest in bearing financial shocks, and their investors face a greater risk of failure as they are the ones that collapse first. The online lending industry has witnessed crises. A large number of P2P online lending platforms have a difficulty satisfying the demand for money withdrawal which leads to the investors' run on the platforms. A large number of microcredit companies emerged in the reform wave have difficulties of operation in their future development. In the boom of financial innovation, if Internet finance is further developed and enlarged in scale, the promise of the Internet financial empire will be broken at the onset of the crisis. Fortunately, it has just started now and risks can be controlled. As for Internet finance, there is still a problem that loans cannot be fully recovered as the loans are transferred to income savings. The more loans and the larger the loan scale there is, the larger the loan repayment gap will be. Internet finance blows up an expanding bubble again, and the online lending platform will finally face the fate of collapse.

> Peer to Peer, namely online lending, refers to the direct financing between individuals through online platforms...This concept, born in the UK and the US, has put forth a different "flower" in the soil of China. To solve the financing difficulties of small and medium-sized enterprises, small and medium-sized enterprises are the major borrowers in the P2P market...Bosses, liars, elites, grassroots, and everybody are engaging in P2P. What is exactly hidden in this basket? [1]

Like the developed capitalist countries, China's economic development will eventually enter the era of depression. As of 2012, the current national debt to

1 Zhang Yue, "P2P-Licking Honey at a Knife-Tip", *Southern Weekly*, July 31st, 2014.

GDP ratio had been about 20%, a figure not high, and the government debt was estimated to account for 53% of GDP in 2012 with the local government debt included.[1] At present, China's economy still has a certain room to grow. The economic level of China's big cities has reached that of moderately developed countries, but the rural areas are still very backward. So China needs to realize modernization in its agricultural sector and accelerate the development of small and medium-sized cities.

Fiscal policies and the central bank's monetary policies still have room to stimulate economic growth in comparatively effective way. At present, the key issue is what economic theories can be used to guide the formulation of policies. If the monetarist principles are still abided by to strictly control the release of money, it is tantamount to the creation of a crisis on our own, just like the "money shortage in June" of 2013 we experienced. When China's economic growth continues to decline, tightening the money supply will not only miss the opportunity to revitalize the economy, but also hinder the flexible use of monetary policies, making it difficult to change the accelerated trend of economic decline.

Although we advocate the continuation of the loose fiscal policy and monetary policy to save the economy, economic policies are not a panacea, which cannot save the economic depression in the Depression Era in the end. Even the countries with a developed market economy have to face the great depression of the market economy, which is one of the outcomes of the Depression Era. In this regard, we should not be too pessimistic, because the Great Depression has a reason to exist, and it is also an inevitable stage that the market economy has to undergo in its long-term development.

1 Li Yang and Zhang Xiaojing, *China National Balance Sheet: Theories, Methods and Risk Assessment (2013)*, China Social Sciences Press, 2013.

Chapter 2

The Meaning of Random Disorder

When we look at the ever-changing nature of metropolises, we will fall into deeper confusion. Buyers, sellers, authorities, streets, bridges, and buildings are all changing constantly. It seems that the coordinated operation of a city is inseparable from the ceaseless flow of people and the various structures they form. Like waves in front of a reef in a torrent, cities stay in a dynamic pattern. None of its components can be independently preserved without change, but the city itself survives.

What enables cities to operate harmoniously despite constant disasters and the lack of central planning? In fact, they haven't yet solved the puzzle. We could say, for instance, that it is Adam Smith's "invisible hand" or people's sociability, or customs that keep the city operating in harmony. However, we must go further by raising another question: How does it make it?[1]

1 John H. Holland, *Hidden Order: How Adaption Builds Complexity*, translated by Zhou Xiaomu and Han Hui, Shanghai Century Publishing (Group) Co., Ltd., 2011, p. 1.

2.1 Effective Mechanism

The "invisible hand" is a metaphor for the market for its role of promoting the development of the whole society through the automatic adjustment of commodity supply and demand by and the pursuit of personal interests.

The competition for survival among creatures is bloody and predatory, and a fight of survival or death. This is because creatures don't have the wisdom to use limited resources to create new resources that are beneficial for their survival. Unlike the species' competition for survival in nature, goods are produced and consumed through exchange in the market economy, so free competition is the best way to improve production efficiency.

A free market economy is inherently a mechanism to ensure the free movement of individuals in the least restricted space. This kind of mechanism shows that individuals maintain overall harmony through "niche" balance, repeated trial-and-error function and the principle of minimum distance[1]. In doing way, individual changes will automatically tend to overall balance. In the absence of central planning, this is the key factor to know how a city functions.

2.2 System Attribute

From the aspect of the internal relationships of a system, the random disorder of a microcosmic individual in motion is the basic condition for its spatial order and equilibrium distribution.

Spatial order can be divided into two types: one is the consistent relation due to the correlation between individuals at the micro-levels. The difference between the order and disorder of the microcosmic system is mainly manifested in the correlation and consistency of the motion between the systems.

The other is the relation without consistency in which the individuals at the

1 Niche, trial-and-error, and minimum distance principle are related to space theory.

micro-levels do not have any connection. The order inside the non-consistent relation is displayed as the organized even distribution in space and the microcosmic kinetic energy.

The spatial uniformity of the microcosmic system means that each microcosmic system has its own independent space. Moreover, in the state of disorder, the interaction force between the systems is the smallest or the mutual influence is the smallest if the space size is assumed to be uniform.

The connections between systems are short-range, represented by boundaries. The boundary of a system refers to commonness, and commonness means consistency. However, consistency is just a kind of attribute, which does not only refer to the positive correlations such as harmony, similarity, and linkage, but also the negative correlations such as conflict, opposition, collision, and so on. The boundary is the set of all the identical attributes of the system.

Micro connections have their limitations. The same microform cannot connect all macro systems infinitely for there are many forms of micro connections among macro systems. For multidimensional space, only Brownian motion has been proved to be able to pass through it freely, which is also the reason for the universal randomness of the motion of the microsystem.

If the motion of the system is confined to its own dimensions, then the motion in the multidimensional space will be completely enclosed in its own space and will not extend outward. If there is no free movement of the microsystem inside the macrosystem, the macro-system itself will lose its stability and adaptability to the external environment, resulting in the collapse of the system. More likely, in addition to the variables of the microsystem that can be viewed as a constant, there is a state of random motion within any macro-system.

Due to the lack of correlation of individual motion in the system, the orderly motion of correlation is avoided. The kinetic energy of internal disordered motion is microcosmic, the correlation of behavior between micro individuals is small, and the state of spatial equilibrium within the system tends to be maximized, so as to maintain the internal stability of the system. Moreover, an independent microsystem is the most dynamic and freedom often brings efficiency, which can improve the efficiency of the individuals to the greatest extent.

The orderly motion of internal correlation has relatively high dynamic energy, which is easy to cause the conflict of internal relations and abnormal disorder, and thus harm the safety of the system. The orderly system will also lead to unnecessary waste of kinetic energy. Some turbulence and changes within the system are insignificant for the stability and development of the system. The orderly motion is often a waste of kinetic energy, and the internal consistency restricts the independent vitality of the microsystems. So, the micro order is not the best state of the system.

A large number of physical phenomena have proved that the microsystems inside the system have a random disorder and are randomly distributed uniformly in the space, each of which has independent space for free movement. For example, the air in a room is evenly distributed, with roughly equal amounts of oxygen particles being evenly distributed everywhere, and the water molecules are also evenly distributed in a glass that is steadily placed flat on the table.

Pedestrians in the street have their destinations to go and they all abide by the traffic rules, but they have little correlations and are almost unconnected. If they walk in the same rhythm, their simultaneous treads will make the ground tremble.

In the market economy, everyone's economic behavior is purposeful, rational, and prudent, reasonably arranged. People, enterprises, and transactions are carried out independently. Although there is an interactive relationship, every expenditure is determined alone, each demand is different. Subjects of market economy behavior have their own ideas and make decisions independently and carry their own risks.

There are many reasons why the market economy is efficient and successful in the rational allocation of resources. The most important one is that individual independence and differences lead to the coexistence of comparative advantages and comparative disadvantages, and free competition enables market individuals to give full play to their comparative advantages by making the best of their strengths and avoiding their weaknesses.

At the same time, free competition at the micro-level harmonizes supply and demand for goods, as Hayek put it, “Because everyone knows so little...And we rarely know which doors we know are the best, so we believe that through a lot of independent competitive efforts we can channel what we want when we see it.” [1]

A free economy is not only full of vitality but also order, without chaos, and efficient operation. For example, shopping malls open for business normally every day, the shelves are neatly placed with a variety of goods. The workshop is neat and orderly, busy but not messy. The flow of people in and out of the luxurious bank is relatively stable, not very crowded, and the banking business is handled in an orderly manner. Although financial markets are sometimes unstable, they remain largely stable for most days. The economic indicators that reflect the economic situation change relatively steadily, with few big ups and downs.

It is because of individual independence that economic behaviors are decentralized. If a group acts in concert and customers go to the mall to buy goods at a certain moment, the goods in the mall will be snapped up by customers. If a large number of people go to the bank to withdraw money together, there will be a crowd run on the bank, which will empty the bank’s cash. Only by making individual economic behavior independent, it will not appear crowded situation, ensuring the normal operation of the mall. Bank depositors go to banks to deposit and withdraw money at different times, making it easy for banks to cope with daily cash transactions and to use the extra money to make loans.

The orderliness of the market economy depends on the dispersion and disorder of micro individuals. Disordered behavior refers to the independent and dispersed activities of individuals that are contrary to consistent collective behavior and is not based on the certainty and commonality of the collective. In the whole system, the individual disorder appears as a random state. Buying and selling stocks is a

---

1 Vernon L.Smith, *Rationality in Economics: Constructivist and Ecological Forms*, translated by Li Keqiang, China Renmin University Press, 2013, p. 31.

random behavior, every deal is a rational choice, but each decision has nothing to do with others' ideas or interests. Bullish and bearish investors have different reasons, but if investors buy stocks or sell stocks in large numbers together, they will impact the financial market and their runs will lead to the closure of the market and the collapse of banks.

A planned economy is an organized and orderly economy. Within the planning system, the micro basis is the enterprise. Their production and sales are carried out according to the plan. The enterprise lacks autonomy, and the production is highly consistent in political and economic through administrative means. Although this organized system can promote the recovery and development of the national economy in a short time, it has seriously restrained the enthusiasm and creativity of the enterprise, resulting in low economic efficiency, a great waste of resources, weak competitiveness, and incomplete and imbalanced development of the overall economy.

2.3 Natural Balance

A random change is a manifestation of the natural balance within the system. Economic efficiency is based on the natural balance. In the economy, micro individuals exceed the overall average, sometimes resulting in a waste of resources. Similarly, if a country's wealth is concentrated in the hands of a few people, it is not a really rich country. Here's a good example of how maximizing production efficiency depends on some kind of natural equilibrium.

Ford, the car tycoon, commissioned a survey of waste car stalls in the United States to find out if the T-Ford had any part that had never been damaged. The investigators returned and reported that almost every part was damaged: the axle, brakes, pistons, and so on. However, there was only one exception that caught their attention. In these damaged cars, all the steering shaft sales can be used for many years, without exception. As a result, Ford concluded with ruthless logic that the quality of the main pin of the steering shaft of the T-car exceeded the requirements, and ordered that the main pin produced in the future should be reduced by a grade.[1]

This story was "invented" by the British psychologist Nicholas Humphrey, who used it to show that efficiency is often based on the average and that it is a waste on the whole for an above-average individual within a system, unless the whole system is aligned to this higher level so that the quality of the system reaches a higher level. However, any more advanced system tends to a state of natural balance, which is the most efficient state.

More importantly, a free market economy automatically tends to balance in order to maximize efficiency. The system tending to balance is a natural process, after the balance is reached, the overall growth of the system will be in a state of stagnation, and once the balanced relationship is broken, the system begins to change again, and automatically tends to balance until a new balance appears.

Micro disorder and randomness is an efficient system. This is why all macro systems have the process of transformation from order to disorder, which is the natural selection of the system itself. When the external conditions are certain, the system will tend to the maximum disorder according to random changes. In this process, the system itself has also been developed.

But surprisingly, once the disorder is maximized, the system stops developing. This is the content to be introduced in the next chapter--while improving the overall efficiency, the micro disorder will also lead to the stagnation of total growth, which is a phenomenon to be explained by the irreversible theory.

For a growing and changing system, their initial size is relatively small, the internal disorder is relatively low, the spatial distribution is not balanced, some places are very crowded, and some places are very sparse. In this case, the system is unstable. In a market economy, small systems sometimes exhibit dramatic changes.

1 Richard Dawkins, *River Out of Eden: A Darwinian View of Life*, translated by Wang Zhihua and Yue Renfeng, Shanghai Scientific & Technical Publishers, 2012, p. 97.

With the increase of the internal micro disorder, the larger the system size is, the more stable the system will be. For example, if a country is in the early stage of economic development and the scale of a national economy is relatively small, the growth rate of total income will fluctuate more wildly. With the expansion of the scale of national income, the fluctuation of the growth rate decreases gradually. When commodities are not abundant, the commodity price index fluctuates greatly, and when commodities become abundant, the fluctuation of the commodity price index decreases. If the stock market scale is small, the stock market fluctuation will be relatively great; if the stock market scale is large, the stock market fluctuation will become relatively small.

It is the individual disorder that ensures the balance of the whole. The stability and balance of the market economy depend on the state of the micro disorder of a system. The higher the degree of micro disorder is, the more balanced the economy will be; on the contrary, the lower the degree of micro disorder is, the greater the system will change and the more unstable the system will be. The order and balance of various economic orders are based on microcosmic disorder. Random changes build the basis of some economic relations. Without the randomness of micro individual behaviors, there are no economic relations, nor even the economic system.

All activities in the market economy, including those that reflect changes in economic indicators, should reflect the respective characteristics of different scales. Quantitative indicators, although with different fluctuations, are subject to the spatial and random distribution mechanism of micro individuals, and with the growth of the total, the spatial distribution of micro individuals tends to the maximum balance.

If there is no significant change outside the system, the system will gradually calm down. The maximum cost of individual freedom is to make all spontaneous connections in more inconsistent states, without spontaneous regathering of kinetic energy to form ordered connections.

Liberalization itself is also the result of forces within the system tending toward disorder rather than returning to order. The trend towards liberalization makes it impossible for the system to automatically shift from disorder to order. When micro individuals are separated from their relationships with other individuals, it can be a laborious task to re-establish relationships. Physically speaking, the transition from disorder to order requires additional energy input into the system, which requires more energy input from the outside world. For example, the evenly distributed air in a closed room does not circulate automatically. To get the air in a room to flow again needs to inject energy into the indoor air from the outside, or open doors and windows for the wind to blow in, or burn a stove in a corner where the heat of the fire allows the air to form an orderly cycle.

The interior of the room is layered. The large room is made up of divided smaller rooms. So the injection of external air or the use of heated air to circulate indoor air is hindered. Generally speaking, for complex systems, layering is the basic structure. Moreover, after layering, the system becomes more closed so that the microsystem becomes more independent. Layering generates internal stability of the system and weakens the influence of external factors on the system.

Individual freedom is conditioned by closure, although there are external connections, due to the macro system is layered, so it is relatively closed to the outside world. In this case, there is inevitably an irreversible change process in the macro system.

If the system is finite, the limit of its change and growth will be reached when the micro disorder within the system reaches its maximum.

The theory that describes this change in the system is the law of entropy, which was originally the second law of thermodynamics. Later, it was found that the second law of thermodynamics also applies to all macrosystems and entropy is a measure of the micro disorder within macro systems.

Chapter 3

An Interpretation of Irreversible Changes

3.1 A Philosophical Introduction

3.1.1 The Macro-system and the Micro-system

The macro-system in this book refers to "a system in which the individual does not conform to the whole", while the micro-system is "a system with consistency" featured by "knowing one individual, knowing the whole". Therefore, only the macro-systems have irreversible processes.

In philosophy, the macro-system and micro-system differ from their counterparts in physics which usually defines any spaces no bigger than 10^{-10} meters as the micro-world.

The macro-systems and micro-systems in philosophy are distinguished, instead of the size of the system, according to the opposite law of macroscopic and microscopic. So this definition is more general and abstract. Both the macrosystems and micro-systems consist of many sub-systems.

At the same time, the macro and the micro views stand for two different visions respectively. Systems change due to vision alteration.[1]

3.1.2 Closed and Isolated Systems v.s. Bounded and Independent Systems

The perception of the irreversible procedures stems from thermodynamics. When a heating experiment is taking place in a closed system, the irreversible procedure of thermal motion is displayed. Based on the verification of physics experiments and daily experience, it is accepted that the existence of entropy is subject to the closed and isolated system.

A system always has boundaries and its own space-time attributes. There is no completely open boundless system on earth.

Similarly, there does not exist any system that is absolutely closed nor isolated from the surroundings. The closure and isolation of a system are in comparative terms. A system is always prone to be affected by the surroundings. But the outside effect is relatively so weak that it fails to change or reverse the spontaneous irreversible procedures of a system.

Considering the relationship between a system and its surroundings, it is admitted that the term of a bounded independent system can serve as a more appropriate illustration. A system exists on its own. It must have boundaries. A system without boundaries does not exist in the world.

To clarify the relationship between the system itself and its surroundings in a more appropriate manner, a bounded independent system is a better definition than a system that is absolutely closed and isolated. The former is more accurate and generalized for understanding the theory of irreversibility. Meanwhile, it avoids confining the irreversible procedures to a specific, experiment-oriented physical system.

1 Ma Lieguang, *The Space and Principles of Thoughts*, Economic Press China, 2012, p. 289, p. 301, p. 309.

All minor systems inside a giant macro-system are bounded and independent. For example, human organs and cells are bounded and independent systems. So are the stars at night, the solar system, the earth, and everything on our planet. Machines, nations, social organizations, families, corporations, markets, and so forth are all considered bounded and independent systems, of course.

3.1.3 The Space-time Quality of Irreversible Procedures

System alterations and motions have their own space-time structure and tendency. In spite of its current status, every system changes in compliance with the law of irreversibility implicitly. These features are manifested in their space-time relationship. The directionality of time, the homogeneity of spatial distribution, space size, dimension, and time duration all reflect some properties of a system.

Therefore, the study of irreversible procedures is supposed to take into consideration the entropy of independent variables, as well as a series of definitions regarding space and time, such as spatial micro-status, distribution, direction, dimension, and so forth.

The finiteness of a system refers to its finiteness in space and time which, together with its finiteness in function, size, and existence duration, gives rise to the phenomena of appearance, disappearance, growth and destruction that keep happening all the time. It reveals an undeniable fact that depression and destruction, rather than endless prosperity, are in the wake of flourishing.

3.1.4 Highlighting the Math Formulation to Avoid Vague Definitions

Almost all movements and alterations inside a system are irreversible. Therefore, the entropy theory evolves from a part of physics to a systematic science, and is further applied in almost all subjects including cosmos, information, ideology, meteorology, geography, demography, medical science, economics, management, psychology, and politics.

To avoid confusing definitions and vague descriptions, it is of vital importance to strictly apply math formulation. In other words, math formulation is indispensable in entropy theory. Because concepts defined in mathematics are not only accurate and logic, but also calculable. More importantly, despite different contents of different subjects, the result data worked out with the probability method is supposed to be the same. As described in 5.3 in this book, Boltzmann entropy, information entropy, and NI entropy share the same value. The same outcome obtained by different objects and different systems demonstrates that different systems comply with the same law and share one unique and definite value.

3.1.5 Energy Conservation, Entropy, and Perception

Energy conservation and entropy are the two famous theories in thermodynamics. Then what does perception mean?

Everything can perceive. Unlike the perceiving abilities of living creatures that are admitted by all, the counterpart abilities of matters is not yet defined in science. However, it becomes understandable based on the interaction theory, also a fundamental theory, in physics. All matters interact with and move around each other. The mutual perception between matters correspondingly echoes the perception between living creatures.

Since all things and all systems change in line with the rule of irreversibility, then face the reality and live with a peaceful attitude towards death. In this process, nature upgrades depending on two kinds of power: kinetic energy of matters and the interactions among the systems, and the perceiving abilities of all things.

A system comes into being, changes, and eventually perishes, but matters will stand forever. Correspondingly, everything has the perceiving ability. This lays the foundation for the motion, revival, and development of all things, and makes the evolution of the universe and all things happen.

3.1.6 The Eternal Stone

In the face of death,
The sages stood helplessly.
Though making every effort to stop it,
They watched the stone rolling down from the top of the hill,

Insurmountably.
The only choice,
Is still to roll it up along the hill path,
One attempt after another,
Only proved their repeated futile efforts.

——Ma Lieguang

Note: The Eternal Stone. Sisyphus in Greek mythology was punished by Death Thanatos to pay for his refusal of death. He had to lift a giant stone from the plain to a high hill with all his might. Every time he accomplished the mission, the stone would roll tumbling down from the hilltop, and Sisyphus had to lift it again. Even though Sisyphus is an unyielding hero, his effort in resisting death still proves futile

Without flowers in full bloom all over the plain in May, what meets the eyes, instead of a vast stretch of red, is only the green of the grass. Technological advancements stir small ripples only, just like the joy of nobodies spreading from the corners. There are no responding echoes from the far distance, not to mention the applause and cheers of the world in agreement.

The rocks get weathered, and the iron gets rusty as well. The ending stage of the market economy is rather insipid. Though some bubbles keep appearing to claim their existence, such a bustle is nothing but trivia. In depression, any angry roars will overwhelmingly be replaced by resigned sighs in the end. When the harmonious symphony starts to play again, all the chaos will give way to tranquility.

3.2 Only Macro-systems Have Irreversible Phenomena

Irreversibility means the alterations of a macro-system are directionality-oriented. A procedure can neither take place in the opposite direction nor repeat back and forth. For bounded and independent systems, with the expansion of the system, their internal procedure from order to disorder is called irreversible procedure if all other conditions remain unchanged.

The definitions of a system's reversibility and irreversibility are not absolutely fixed since they are determined from the observer's perspective. Changes of a system are reversible if it is classified as a micro one. The changes can repeat back and forth and happen in endless cycles. If the system is classified as a macro one, its changes are irreversible. Furthermore, macro-systems automatically stop growing because of the disorder of their micro components.

Many repetitive phenomena exist in nature. For instance, the sun rises in the east and sets in the west. Other examples include the alternations of the sun and the moon, the four seasons, as well as the regular daily life of people such as taking the subway on time. However, these system changes are relatively simple without other complex relations being considered. Meanwhile, their microsystems do not have space expansion or a tendency towards disorder. Generally speaking, it is acceptable to regard a repetitive event as an independent micro-system.

Irreversibility is the basic rule for changes inside macro-systems. For a system under observation, if a magnitude of changes of its micro-components must be considered, then its changes as a macro-system are irreversible.

There are colossal micro-changes inside a macro-system, due to the influence of which and dimension augmentation the macro-system experiences space expansion. Consequently, multidimensional expansion is also irreversible.

Ideological space is multidimensional which its form of existence is. Human ideology, in which the theory of irreversibility works, can be regarded as a macrosystem. Irreversibility that was originally found in thermodynamics also applies to spirit and ideology, the development of which is also irreversible. Spirit and ideology are not bound by laws in physics and chemistry, but the thoughts change in line with the rule of irreversibility in ideological space.

The Ratcheting Effect in economics refers to the irreversibility of consumption habits once they are formed. It represents the irreversibility at the spiritual level. Consumers tend to spend more money with the increase of their income but have difficulties in cutting off the expenses when their incomes drop. So, it is easy to increase the expenses while hard to cut them down.

In the following sections, we will, based on the states at the micro-level, talk about the irreversible attributes in changes of economic systems, and build up the model of the economic theory of irreversibility. This is the key part of this book, laying the theoretical foundation for the discussion of real economic problems included in the depressed era economic.

3.3 The Independency of Open Systems

The Second Law of Thermodynamics formulates the phenomenon of irreversible heat transfer in a closed system. Heat in a closed system always transfers from high to low temperature, never otherwise. In other words, internal heat movement has a direction to follow. From order to disorder, heat equilibrium within a system will be eventually achieved.

What the Second Law of Thermodynamics describes can apply to all movements at the micro-level inside a macro system for the micro-systems move from order to disorder. Therefore, a large number of disorderly movements can be described through the probability theory. For example, the highest probability can be used to calculate the maximum value a disorderly movement tends to reach, and the maximum value is entropy.

In reality, there is no absolutely closed system. Every system interacts with the outside world, even man-made air cylinders and sealed containers cannot be completely closed from the outside world without connections. Meanwhile, the airtight closed and isolated system is too special to be a general representation of all systems. As for absolutely closed systems, they only exist as a concept and cannot be found in reality.

All systems in the world are open systems inside which large numbers of micro-level movements are irreversible. The irreversible procedure is illuminated as follows: As the macro-system expanses in scale, disorder at the micro-level approaches its extreme. This irreversible procedure can also be formulated by the probability theory.

Why do open systems also have irreversible procedures in accord with those in closed systems? This is because macro-systems are bounded and independent, relatively independent of the outside world despite their connections with the surrounding environment. This kind of relative independence assures the in-system stability.

Most in-system movements are determined by the system's structure and immune to external influences. For example, the human body interacts with the outside world through five sense organs limbs, and skin. We can feel and think. In addition, our respiratory system, digestive system, blood circulation system and immune system, instead of being controlled directly by the outside world, have their own independent operational mechanisms to follow. Only when all parts of our body function independently on their own, can the body work with normal body temperature and blood pressure and guarantees us a good appetite, normal excretory function, good sleep, and a life of quality.

The market economy is an open economy. It is not only open between its sub-systems (e.g. economic behaviors of corporations and individuals, as well as product trade and investments between nations) but also has a close connection to nature. However, the economic system is layered, and individual economic entities are independent with boundaries. As a result, the market economy is also relatively closed and isolated. The influence of nature upon the market economy decreases as the market economy expanses in scale.

Irreversible procedures exist in a relatively closed and isolated system. As the economy expands in scale, the external factors will exert a weakening impact on it. At the same time, its internal disorder at the micro-level will maximize, eventually resulting in growth stagnation of the economic system.

3.4 The Law of the Development of Human Society

First of all, the market economy is taken as a macro-system composed of independent consumers, investors, corporations, governments and social organizations. Resource allocation and capital accumulation are realized through currency and commodity exchanges.

Secondly, the market economy is multidimensional due to its flexibility and elasticity. It grows in the multidimensional space and follows the law of irreversibility.

3.4.1 Irreversible Change is the Prerequisite to Unbound the System from the Outside Environment

The macro system's tendency of becoming disorderly is a result of the "instinct" movements of internal micro-systems to achieve maximum freedom.

Inside the macro-system, states of order and disorder coexist. When the influence on the system from the outside world is fixed, the system will automatically approach disorder and this process is irreversible.

A refrained system without freedom has no free spaces and is controlled by external forces. If the increased degree of freedom inside the system is taken as development, then such a development presents, in essence, a procedure. It means the internal and external environments gradually come to a balance where the net energy from the outside reduces until it ceases to do so. The automatic balance between the internal and external forces is a basic requirement for the existence of free spaces.

For a system with continuous development and self-expansion, its development leads the system to disorder instead of order. As the system grows larger as a whole, its internal sub-systems gradually approach disorder. This irreversible procedure is a law followed by biological beings and human society.

Based on this definition, if we apply the law accordingly to the development of human society and economy, it is natural to make such a conclusion that a free market economy is an economic status where equilibrium is achieved between the outside world and the economic system. Meanwhile, the orderly status (limited freedom) is transitioning to the disorderly status (minimum freedom).

The social economy experiences accumulative development in the context of the free market economy. Development and freedom are closely related to each other. An economy with incomplete free competition would face low efficiency and the waste of resources, not to mention the slow-down of technological advancements. In culture, economy, politics, and other fields in human society, freedom is the civilized flag of sound development.

3.4.2 Historical Evolution of Mankind is a Process of Maintaining Balance with Nature

The market economy may have only been in existence for thousands of years if it is counted from the appearance of division of labor and free trade. Compared with the hunting history that had lasted for hundreds of thousands of years, free capitalism has a much shorter history. The market economy since the start of industrialization only has a history of hundreds of years. Only in the process of industrialization did the free market economy get the chance to realize full development.

Then, what stands for the external power outside the market economy? It is supposed to be the power of nature. Ever since human beings came into existence, this mysterious power keeps infusing energy into human society that is equal to the energy human society exports to nature. Technological advancements not only bring out sharp increases in capital and labor but also augment the energy from nature. With increasingly refined labor division, participants from all walks of life get connected through the market. Not until human society develops into a certain scale by accumulating power is it able to enter the state of the free market economy.

A review of the history will facilitate people's understanding of the changes in energy accumulation of human society. Before the Industrial Revolution in Great Britain, the power for production in Europe in the Middle Ages was generated by wind, water, and animals, as well as the crude and simple machines powered by it. Sparsely populated European society in the early Middle Ages saw self-contained farms as major production organizations, and "almost 90% of the people live on planting and grazing".

"Continuous population increase is the main impetus for the prosperous economy and development of the Middle Ages. Therefore, despite the simple technologies at that time, the relatively fertile lands and other natural resources could guarantee a productivity rate higher than that required for sustaining a normal life for people."[1] The growth of population and trade promoted labor division and professionalized production. More towns appeared and prospered to become business centers alongside the waning feudalism and manorialism. National states like Great Britain and France were established one after another.

The emergence of the first steaming engine stands for the start of the Industrial Revolution. Science and technology grant people more advanced measures to tap into and utilize natural resources. Labor division became more refined, products were more abundant, and population and economy both grew at an unprecedented rate. Free philosophical thoughts infiltrated into every field of ideology and the domain of politics. After political revolutions, economic and political systems of free capitalism were eventually established.

From the history of Europe in the Middle Ages, it is known that the power accumulated in human society is characterized by population growth. Advancements of thoughts and production technology brought about the abundance of man-made articles (products). The accumulation of population and man-made articles is the result of energy transfer from nature to human society in essence. Once the population and products reached a high level in amount, the market economy and political regimes would come into being. This is a procedure that cannot be reversed. Modern and contemporary history of mankind is a history of how the market economy has been developing. The British free market economy has become followed all over the world.

Wealth accumulation comes as a result of the operation of the market economy. The demand for products declines as the population decreases. Demographic and

1 Douglas C. North and Robert Paul Thomas, *The Rise of the Western World,* translated by Li Yiping and Cai Lei, Huaxia Publishing House, 1989, p. 39, p. 45.

economic crisis lead to the collapse of wealth.

If the market economy suddenly shrinks in scale, which leads to the change in its energy and channels, the turmoil in human society is likely to affect the status of the market economy that has become uniquely influential in the world. Consequently, a new order will appear and govern inside the economy of society, and new constraints will influence the market economy to weaken the freedom in it. Poverty and autocracy will appear in a constrained economy with less freedom. The economy will not revive until the population growth and market prosperity recover.

3.4.3 Spiritual Irreversibility

An article of an anonymous writer on the Internet named "Spiritual Irreversibility and Pursuit"[1] clearly summarizes the relationship between spiritual irreversibility and human progress. The passage is quoted as follows:

Automatic irreversible procedures exist in physics. Such physical phenomena, as I notice, are also common in the field of human social psychology. A proverb says "a man struggles for higher goals, while water falls downwards". But no proverbs reveal what will happen if a man aims for lower goals. The personal situation in society and life may encounter irresistible changes, some of which take place by leaps and bounds. If such changes are against people's will, they will resist the changes and become unadapted to them. I call such a phenomenon "Spiritual Irreversibility".

Generally speaking, there are several typical situations representing a man's struggle for higher goals: promotion in work, enlarged power, increased wealth, and greater reputation. Amongst them, reputation (or being respected or in attention) is the most important one. When people possess a position, power, or wealth satisfying them, they will pursue reputation. In a culture in which commodity economy is the mainstream value, whoever takes the spiritual

1 magic/tp, "Spirit Irreversibility and Pursuit", cited from CRU Economic BBS/ philosophy and psychology, http://bbs.pinggu.org.

improvement as a target to pursue will undoubtedly be mocked as an idiot or a psycho...

Spiritual irreversibility is a mental law that no one can resist. It drives us to continuously pursue and strive for higher goals and brings us endless fear and pain. People in higher positions are likely to face more fear and pain because the probability for them to trip off from that position is higher. Recently, I read about an article in which a foreign psychologist finds out that modern people's sense of happiness differs little from that of those living dozens of years ago. This reveals that social development, technological advancement, and improved living conditions fail to make more people feel happier.

I reckoned, why could Germany and Japan in the 1950s quickly recover their economy and develop at a fast speed regardless of the fact that they had started from the same starting point as China and many other countries did? For this question, spiritual irreversibility must be considered. The German and the Japanese regained their prewar living habits very soon. They even maintained their mysophobia while living on ruined lands. Such a feeling of perfection and "mysophobia" (referring to habits in decorations, bathing and hygiene) urged them to improve the quality of their products to an advanced standard almost at a fleeting rate. In contrast, a large number of products we have today are not qualified. We cannot rely on the people who furnish their residences in a perfunctory attitude to manufacture high-quality industrial products. I once mentioned that I would first take a look of a machine producer's residence before deciding whether or not to hire him or her.

People's knowledge and sense of beauty will never reverse once they reach a certain level. This is because spiritual stuff like these is not completely based upon approval from other people or objective materials. Neither depression nor destruction in external world can reverse people's self-awareness.

People are in pursuit ceaselessly until they exert themselves or touch the limit of capability, after which they start to fall back. Therefore, managing to postpone the peak-like moment in one's life is an important law for mental games.

People's spiritual pursuit can improve cultural and moral standards of society, delight people spiritually, and harmonize their relations. In this way, people get adapted to new imbalances resulting from material production and affect in turn the means of material production. I do not know whether people are spiritual pursuit is endless or not. Or is it some kind of religious belief, *qigong*, or other special realms in life. I believe that dreams, illusions, and intoxications are part of this. But I am not quite sure why this kind of spiritual state can bring people the sense of happiness, which seems to be the ultimate target that people pursue in spirit.

3.5 The Orderly Phenomena in Disorderly Systems

Biological evolution reveals the principle that beings evolve from lower levels to higher ones. Similarly, technological advancements propel the development of human society and culture, helping them gets rid of primitive ignorance. Are both biological evolution and social development signs of orderly progress or paths leading to a disorder end? No consensus has been reached yet for this issue. Some consider the former as the orderly process and deny the theory that alterations of macro-systems will lead to ultimate disorder.

Judging from the stages of birth, development, growth, aging and death in life, it is true that the whole process of life complies with *the Law of Irreversibility* because a man cannot live perpetually. However, from the perspective of a population, there seems to be an orderly connection. In other words, individual members in a population continuously get refreshed in loop as the sun rises and sets day after day. As a result, the population as a whole keeps evolving.

Human society progresses like other beings. It realizes the evolution of the whole through the withering and refreshing of individuals. Furthermore, the accumulated knowledge of mankind frees human society from the constraints of nature to a civilized society featured with higher wisdom and ability of self-control.

However, we cannot separate the orderly phenomena in biological evolution and social development from the irreversible procedures. In biological evolution and social development, freedom is a generalized and fundamental status instead of an outcome designed in the course of evolution and in the aspect of wisdom. It is a natural law. The independence of beings, as well as the space for the expansion of freedom, is the prerequisite for both biological evolution and social development. Once independent individuals, free spaces and feasible worlds coexist, the irreversible procedures come into being as a matter of course.

Evolving from order to disorder is a fundamental process that all beings and human societies have to experience in the course of their development. Treating beings and human society as a whole, it is reckoned that the whole evolution process must consist of the four stages of orderliness, cycling, development, and stagnation. With the enlargement of the whole in scale, individuals tend to approach the maximum disorder.

For example, in the feudal society at the beginning of the Middle Ages, Europe was sparsely populated. People were bound to tillage. Who are freer? The modern people, or the medieval residents? In ancient times, people were strictly restricted by nature. Their daily life and work were rather plain and simple, following the schedule that the sun follows. Their life was poor but regulated. Modern people enjoy diverse lifestyles, which makes disorder a more common phenomenon in all walks of life in society. In other words, compared with the orderly life in ancient society, human society has evolved from simplicity to complexity and from order to disorder.

So never consider biological evolution and social development a progress against disorder. The examples of orderly developments are just specific representations for specific stages in the course of their evolution. Every orderly process is just the prelude and local phase of the movement of disorderly evolution. The orderly events are partial, only serving as supporting elements that add to the whole process from order to disorder.

The Belgian scientist Llya Prigogine once proposed the "Dissipative Structure

Theory". He thought that order and organization could be generated from disorder and chaos through a self-organized process. However, he disapproved that spontaneous order at the micro-level would lead to order at the macro level. Nor did practical experiences support any spontaneous process heading for an orderly status. However, the alteration from disorder to order mentioned by Prigogine does not deny the irreversible process. What he specifically pointed out is that the phenomena as part of the irreversible procedure or at the micro level cannot reverse the system's movement as a whole. For example, when the flowing velocity is low, the fluid flows with distinct layers; when the velocity starts rising, wave-shaped ripples appear in the layers; when the velocity is much higher, the ripples give way to tiny eddies in the fluid, the distinct layers start to mix, the fluid move irregularly, and turbulences appear in a motion pattern different from that of the fluid. At the micro level, the turbulence is highly organized. "The multi-layered space and time dimension correspond to relevant movements of hundreds of millions of molecules. In this way, the transition from lamellar flow to turbulence is a self-organized process."[1]

In practice, within the disordered systems, there exist orderly phenomena similar to turbulence. This complies with the opposite law of macroscopic and microscopic. namely the individual order within the disorder of the ensemble. If the earth is an orderly isolated island in the disorderly universe, it could be said that we live like one of the hundreds of millions of molecules in a self-organized manner. But our future is not optimistic, as the orderly "turbulences" of earth will eventually disappear in the rapid torrents of the universe in its course of evolution.

3.6 Layered Systems

Now we have known macro-systems' tendency towards disorder and supposed

1 Ilya Prigogine and Isabelle Stengers, *From Disorder to Order, A Dialogue Between Human and Nature*, translated by Zeng Qinghong and Shen Xiaofeng, Shanghai Translation Publishing House, 1987.

the reason is that individuals are prone to become disordered and result in disorder at the micro-level. In other words, the macro-system's tendency toward disorder is the result of its micro-systems' "instinctive" movements for the purpose of maximum freedom. However, freedom and equality are neither the same properties shared by micro individuals nor the interdependent results that are destined to happen among them.

Or convergence, the definition used to describe equality, can be applied to represent the accordance of the micro-systems at the same hierarchy. Since macrosystems are layered, convergence mainly exists in different layers between which convergence is not involved.

From the perspective of the layered relationship, subsystems compose a new system. Once a layered relationship is formed, the importance of components in subsystems is weakened compared with the newly formed system. The reason is that layers in the new system block the interaction among different layers. The value of a bounded and isolated system is determined by its position in the system. If it is alone in a certain position, then it possesses the whole world. If it is just part of a community in a position, it becomes less and less important as the number of its peers increases.

Every subsystem has its own space in which system elements and micro statuses coexist. The micro statuses embody many probable forms of changes, laying the foundation for the independence and freedom of the elements in the system and assuring subsystems' adaption to subtle changes in the outside world.

Materials, organisms, and social organizations are featured with layered networks. The bottom layer is the foundation, consisting of atoms and molecules which also serve as the fundamental materials of plants and animals. Materials make up macromolecules, further constituting solid, liquid, and gas. Beings, from small ones to large ones, compose a pyramid-like network, with small-sized ones in the bottom layers and large ones in the upper layers. There are more materials in the bottom layers while fewer in the upper layers.

On earth, the number of electrons weighting 1 gram is 1000 times larger than that of the suns in the cosmos (Astronomers estimate that the cosmos may have one hundred trillion suns, i.e. 10^{14} stars.).[1]

The following is an example of ecology.

3.6 Energy Pyramid

The sun continuously provides new energy for the food chain. Without sunshine, most lives on earth will fail to sustain themselves. The sunshine offs energy to producers like plants for their photosynthesis, and then energy is transferred from one living body to another. For example, after a locust eats grass, it captures the energy of the grass. After a bird eats the locust, it obtains energy from the locust. Likewise, energy flows into the eagle after it eats the bird. The higher hierarchy a living body is in, the less energy it will get. The energy pyramid clearly portrays how energy reduces as the level of consumption becomes higher. Approximately only 10% of energy from the lower layer can be transferred to the higher one.[2]

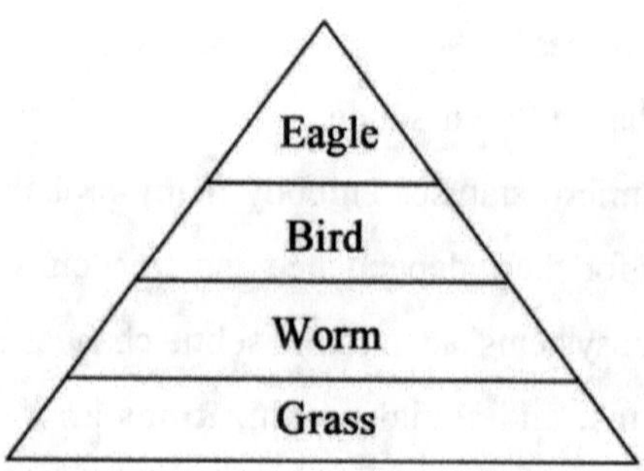

Figure 3-1 Energy pyramid in the chain of biological energy

Considering the ecology is a system, it is hierarchic with the lower layers

1 Graham Bateman, *Atoms, Molecules and States of Matter*, translated by Lin Na, Posts & Telecom Press Co., Ltd., 2013, p. 21.

2 Zhiqu Information Technology Co., Ltd., *Ecology*, Publishing House of Electronic Industry, 2013, p. 13.

having much more elements than the higher ones. Each layer is independent with separate subsystems and micro statuses. The world seems to be like a net made up of chains that constitute elements of hierarchies. Subsystems in different layers absorb different influences from the outside world. There is no open structure shared by all systems.

Macrosystems in human society and nature have internal hierarchies. Materials consist of atoms and molecules. Systems have thermal motion, particle movements, energy conversions, and chemical reactions. The foundation of living bodies is also composed of materials such as atoms and molecules. However, living bodies can grow and develop on their own from a small size to a big size, from embryo to a being with various functional organs and circulatory systems. Such a phenomenon cannot be attributed to any physical or chemical principles as it is the natural property of hierarchic living bodies. Therefore, despite the same micro-foundations, beings and the material system do not converge. They have significant distinctions.

Human society and the economic system also experience the progress of spontaneous growth and developments. In the progress from a small size to a large size, there appear labor division, professionalization and multi-layered structure. The market economy also derives from labor division and professionalization. Though the market economy is embedded with full competition and equal opportunities, the economic structure and the levels of economy are distinctively hierarchic. Moreover, with the expansion of the market, economic structures, financial relations, and management regimes tend to become more complicated.

Individuals, families, corporations, social organizations, and governmental departments altogether make up a complex social structure. Individuals are the footstone of economic and social organization. Families, the "social cells", are the basic units of the social organization. Because of the layered relations in social economy, an individual plays different roles in his or her family, corporation or working place.

In family, every member matters. An intact family includes the father, the mother, and their kid or kids. Relatives and the family's social relations are hierarchic relations deriving from the family. For everybody, their family is the most important organization. "In your family, you really matter. But in your workplace, you are just nobody."

Layered systems have boundaries between each other. It is due to the layered relation that the microcosmic statuses keep transitioning. So the space has a chance to change, and the world becomes richer and more colorful. If systems are not layered, everyone becomes equally important to his or her family, working place and society. At that time, the society, working place, and family will consequently lose their importance, and society ceases to exist.

In the market economy, per capita income differs among different industries, classes, and nations. However, unequal income is widespread in all countries. In 1897, the Italian economist Pareto found the "80/20" phenomenon. At that time, most of the national wealth in Great Britain was held by 20% of the people in society. Although a century has passed, the "80/20" phenomenon still exists all over the world. There is also an "80/20" phenomenon in other economic fields. For example, 80% of the products may be produced by 20% of the corporations in the market, or 20% of the consumers purchase 80% of the goods, or 80% of the profits are generated by 20% of the staff.

In the market economy, information distortion in the process of transfer is inevitable due to social hierarchy. This phenomenon is called the "Beer Effect".

> Professor Sterman in MIT made a renowned experiment...Suppose 7 steps are needed before a product is completely finished. The production requires seven upper-stream suppliers to provide raw materials and accessories. In the first month, the client places an order of 100 products. To avoid the risk of short supply, the company orders materials enough for the production of 105 products from the upper-stream supplier who, intending to avoid the same risk, asks its upper-stream supplier to provide materials for the production of 110 products. In this way, the supplier at the last layer of the supplying chain may have to prepare materials for the production of more than 200 products. 10 months later, with the passing of

the time and the accumulated materials by all the suppliers in the hierarchy, the products required might be far more than those needed in practice, causing the supplier at the last layer to suffer a loss 100 times more than the actual cost.[1]

With the specific contents of living bodies and social economy being removed, the system's hierarchy can be simplified through a layered network (See Figure 3-2). Layers only connect to their adjacent upper or lower layers, and to the systems at the same layer or in the same category. Connections to the system with one layer in between or other distant systems become lesser and lesser and even disappear.

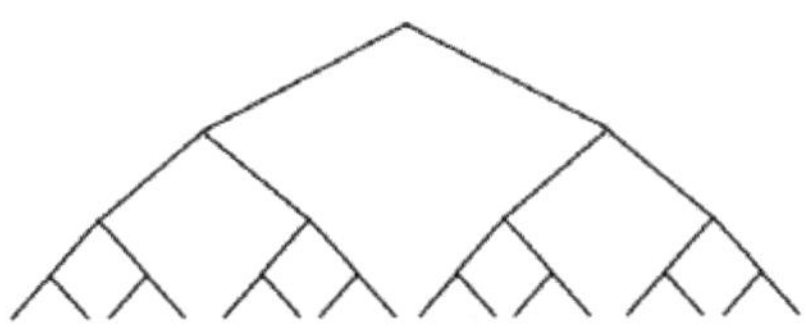

Figure 3-2 Layered Network

Note: This is a random binary tree that is layered from bottom to top. Its subsystems are layered in the same way. Micro-subsystems at the lower layers are more than those at the upper layers. In a standard binary graph, the number of subsystems at each layer differs according to 2^n, representing the nth layer, increases in natural numbers one after another. The subsystems in each layer increase exponentially.

Because of the system's hierarchy, subsystems in each layer tend towards maximum disorder. Because of the same reason, the disorder in micro-systems in each layer is independent of each other with limited mutual influence. Since the micro subsystems in each layer change from order to disorder independently at different speeds, each layer as a whole enters a different status. Because of such differences among individual layers, the macro-system ultimately presents a disorderly status.

If some rule(s) and power reappear to stop the irreversible procedure, it is tantamount to constrain the freedom of micro-systems. Such constraints or

1 Huang Xiaolin and Huang Mengxi, *The Most Magical Principles of Economics*, New Century Publishing House, 2010, p. 74.

bindings require energy from the outside into the inside of the system. If the system as a whole tends to become disordered, the energy from the outside has a diminishing effect on the system. And if the power from the outside is not great enough to alter the internal structure of the system, it fails to change the disorder of the system.

Chapter 4

The Economics of the Irreversible Procedure

Great theories are usually simple just like Darwin's Evolution Theory. Natural selection interprets the brilliant and seemingly complicated nature in a clear-cut way without too many hypotheses. Even sophisticated mathematic formulas are unnecessary. Simple expressions and one or two mathematic formulas are enough for the generation of poetic and picturesque beauty.

4.1 Three Basic Formulas of Macroeconomics

The income multiplier formula is :

$$\Delta Y_t = \frac{1}{x^i(1-x)} \Delta Y_0 \qquad (i = 0,1,2,3,\cdots,n) \qquad (4\text{-}1)$$

ΔY_t represents the incremental national income at period t. ΔY_0 represents the initial spending at the current period, indicated by previous income. x is the marginal propensity to consume, i the exponent represented by natural numbers,

And x^{i} the multiplication of the marginal propensity to consume. The value of i represent i types of distribution of savings in the spending and re-spending circulation process of national income. If i=1, the formula $\frac{1}{x(1-x)}$ is called the structural multiplier. If i=0, the aforementioned structural multiplier is in the form of Keynes multiplier.

The second formula stands for NI entropy:

$$S=\log_2 Y \tag{4-2}$$

S stands for entropy. Y is the national income.

The third formula indicates the theorem of debt formation:

$$\Delta D=\Delta S \tag{4-3}$$

ΔD represents the increment of unpaid debt during a certain period, and ΔS represents the increment of residents' savings during a certain period.

The first formula is a nonlinear income growth model. The variables in the formula can be extended and connected to theories of investments, consumption, and savings, such as the Multiplier-Acceleration Principle. Meanwhile, the formula also involves nonlinear economic theories like the chaos principle and the period-doubling theory in the distribution of savings and marginal propensity to consume.

The second formula reveals that it is inevitable for national income to go through the circle from growth to stagnation. The variables can be extended to the aggregate supply of currency and the theory of inflation. The formula is connected to disorder at the micro-level of the free economy, as well as the equilibrium theory of commodity supply and demand.

The variables in the three formulas are not directly generated from empirical induction but are gained through mathematical formula derivation based on empirical induction. All the variables are quantifiable. The three formulas are not only outcomes through logical inference but are also the knowledge that can be analyzed and verified with data.

It is said that the Babel Tower only has three floors in total. Maybe the same number will suffice for the building of economics.

4.2 National income Multiplier Shifting from Lower Dimension to Higher Dimension

4.2.1 A Conversation Between Keynes and I

Thoughts can travel through time. At dawn, our conversation began before the sun was about to rise and birds started to sing.[1]

Keynes wrote down a mathematical formula on paper: $Y = [1/(1-x)]\ I$, and asked his student, "Do you know what this means?"

The student answered, "Yes. Y stands for national income, I for investment. x is the ratio of marginal propensity to consume to marginal national income. Substitute $1/(1-x)$ with λ. If x is smaller than 1, then λ is bigger than 1."

Keynes: Think about it. If a company invests 100 dollars, the income from it would be greater than 1 after multiplying it with λ. That's why λ is called the multiplier. If someone spends 100 dollars, amongst which 80 dollars is used for consumption and 20 for savings, then the ratio of 80/100 equals to x.

The student: It is understandable.

Keynes: Income and spending are in a cycle. In other words, one's spending will become another person's income. Can you analyze what will happen next about spending?

The student: Yes. Suppose I get an income of 80 dollars. According to the ratio of x, 80% of it would be used for consumption, and 20% for savings.

Keynes: This process can continue till the income is fully used up. The total income is the sum-up of income of those that are part of this cycle. Then could you calculate the total savings in the cycle?

The student: 100 dollars.

Keynes: Now you understand that the 100 dollars as savings equals to the 100

1 Ma Lieguang, *The Space and Principles of Thoughts*, Economic Press China, 2011, p. 233.

dollars as investments. Therefore, investment is equal to savings.

The student: What if the investment is also in a cycle, Mr. Keynes?

Keynes: What are you talking about? I have no idea.

The student: If the money for investment also runs in a cycle, then the investment turnover will also result in a multiplier, won't it?

Keynes: I haven't thought about that before.

The student: If a person spends more than 100 dollars, amongst which 20 are used for investment and 80 for consumption, he or she, after receiving an income of 20 dollars, would continue investing in a 2 to8 proportion. If the income is 80 dollars, he or she would spend 80% of it for consumption and 20% for savings in the aforementioned ratio of x. In this case, we have both investment turnover and consumption turnover.

Keynes: Your idea changed my assumptions. My theory did not include re-investment.

The student: I only changed one condition with others remaining the same. However, the conclusion of the theory is quite different. Following your calculation method for consumption and spending, I calculated the spending for investment. The corresponding formula of income multiplier is obtained: Y=[1/ 好 (x(I-x)]y. The variables in the formula are the same as yours. The only variation is that ex-ante income y substitute's ex-ante investment I.

Keynes: Does ex ante income y equal to savings?

The student: Yes, savings = ex ante income.

Keynes: (In a loss for words).

The conversation ended with the sun still down the horizon and the birds in silence.

The new income multiplier in the conversation has one more dimension than Keynes income multiplier. The Keynes multiplier is uni-dimensional, namely 1/(1-x), while the structural multiplier is bi-dimensional, namely 1/x and 1/(1-x). This is because the process of investment and re-investment are added for the structural multiplier, while the Keynes multiplier doesn't consider it. In addition, more information is included. If the exogenous variables, such as the investment I (or the ex ante income y), is fixed, the different distributions of savings in the process of spending and re-spending of national income will determine the value of the income multiplier and the amount of national income.

Credit currency can be introduced for the concept of ex-ante income to specify that credit currency eventually turns into other people's income or savings through the process of spending and re-spending of national income.

NI multiplier is mainly used for investment analysis or estimating how much national income can be generated through investment and consumption. This is determined by three factors: the amount of investment, the proportion of investment or consumption to the total national income, and the distribution of savings in the process of spending, which is represented in different forms of the multiplier model, such as the two forms of multipliers in the conversation. Meanwhile, the formula in the conversation can be used to represent the flowing of credit currency and the formation of income and savings.

Like flowers in nature, the thoughts in economics can grow and bloom on their own without borrowing elements from others. Marxism is a paradigm of Marx. Keynes has his own system. Osmanthus can never be sunflowers and both blossom with their unique traits. The NI multiplier theory inherits and develops Keynes's thoughts, whenever new methods are applicable, thoughts will naturally evolve in the empirical direction.

4.2.2 N-dimensional Multiplier

We can compare the relations between currency turnover and national income to the water pipeline network.

Commodities are defined within the framework of national income. The amount of commodity is calculated based on the trading volume in the average unit. Currency is calculated in its average unit. "Water pipelines" are made up of unit commodities. Since national income equals to spending in investment and consumption, the "pipeline" should have two separate branches. This kind of binary "pipeline" shows that each spending has two channels for investment and consumption respectively that are open to selection. Some small holes randomly scatter along the "pipelines", each representing one unit commodity. This represents that funds flowing into the pipelines through the small holes are not used in re-spending. Therefore, a binary network with small holes is formed.

When currency flows like water into the "pipelines", it moves and ends up flowing out with nothing left in the "pipelines" due to the existence of those small holes. The area that the water passes by is the national income, while the water leaking out of the "pipeline" is the money used for savings. National income has nothing to do with the size of the "openings on the pipeline". The currency amount is not included in national income if it does not touch the pipe wall. The amount of national income is decided by the area that the infused monetary aggregate flowing in the pipeline covers and the randomly scattered small holes. This pipeline model is a multiplier model for national income.

National Income Multiplier[1]

Investment and consumption are randomly distributed in the process of spending. The initial income can multiplicatively increase national income after the re-spending in investment and consumption. But the multiplier is decided by the random distribution of savings rather than that of investment and consumption.

Figure 4-1 is a branching Figure with fine rules. In the diagram, the left-pointing arrow represents investment. The right-pointing arrow refers to consumption. Apart from the directions specifically regulated, both investment and consumption are random variables. Savings are randomly distributed in the process of spending. In the diagram, ΔY_0 stands for the income of the previous stage or initial income. x is the marginal propensity to the consumption of stage t. The big circle " ○ " is the savings point. The concentric circle " ◎ " is the overlapping point or crossing point of savings and investments (or consumption).

1 Ma Lieguang, *A New Discussion of Economics: Multiplier, Statistical Entropy and National Income*, Economic Press China, 2006, p. 20, p. 43.

The small circle "∘" is the spending point of investment and consumption on the joint assumptions of Keynes multiplier and structural multiplier. The black circle "●" describes all the possible spending points in the spending tree.

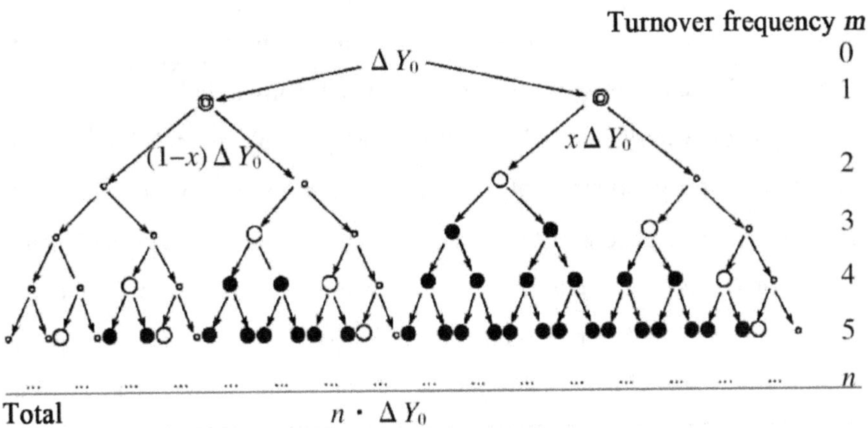

Figure 4-1 Turnover Frequency

The binary tree of spending in context of randomly distributed income

When calculating the income at stage *t*, if the turnover of income re-spending does not generate savings, the total income of all the spending points equals to:

$$\Delta Y_t = n\Delta Y_0 \qquad n = 1,2,3,\ldots,m$$

where *n* stands for the turnover number of the initial income . The variation of total income ΔY_t equals to the amount that the initial income times turnover number. If no income re-spending occurs, the sum-up of spending at all overlapping points "◎" is:

$$\Delta Y_t = \Delta Y_0$$

The initial income ΔY_0 turns into savings only after one spending. The variation of total income at stage t, ΔY_t, equals to the initial income ΔY_0. According to Keynes' assumptions of savings, in which investment equals to savings, the add-up of the income at the overlapping point "◎" and income at big and small circles deriving from $x\Delta Y_0$ is equivalent to the Keynes multiplier. That is,

$$\Delta Y_t = \frac{1}{1-x}\Delta Y_0$$

$1/(1-x)$ in the formula above is in the form of Keynes multiplier. x is the marginal propensity to consume. The reason why the Keynes multiplier is in this form is that it assumes investment to be an exogenous variable. So, in the process of income re-spending, investment does not have any re-spending chain. The savings from income after consumption equals to the investment. It is an idea about equilibrium instead of some fact based on empirical induction.

In Keynes Binary Tree of Spending, the spending in each layer in a cycle diminishes at a geometric rate as the turnover number n increases. It has a fundamental difference with the formula $\Delta Y_t = n^* \Delta Y_0$. When the initial income ΔY_0 is fixed and n is a big number, the total income variation, having nothing to do with n, is subject to the proportion of savings $(1-x)$.

In practice, spending in investment also has a chain. If savings are supposed to be equal to the investment split from consumption, then the sum-up of incomes of all the circles in the tree is:

$$\aleph Y_t \quad \frac{1}{x\ddot{u} - x} \quad Y_0$$

The multiplier is the structural multiplier, And $x\,(1-x)$ is a binomial expression.

More generally, without restraining the paths of investment and consumption and only in the context of randomization, using the distribution of micro components, we can deduct a simplified formula that includes both the Keynes multiplier and the structural multiplier.

$$\Delta Y_t = \frac{1}{x^i(1-x)} \Delta Y_0 \qquad (i = 0, 1, 2, 3, \cdots, n)$$

$1/x^i(1-x)$ above is the income multiplier model on the condition of the distribution of maximum probability. Obviously, the random distribution of savings determines income if ΔY_0 is fixed. The exponent i stands for the savings of group i. When i=0, $1/x^i(1-x) = 1/(1-x)$, which is the Keynes multiplier. When i=1, $1/x^i(1-x) = 1/x(1-x)$, which is the structural multiplier.

i is an exponent. The formula is deducted using stochastic formulas, equivalent to a Markov chain. The random distribution of savings determines the form and value of the multiplier. The Keynes multiplier is just a special example for the lowest dimension—when *i* is 0 dimension.

From 1 dimension to 2 dimensions, the multiplier theory embraces a new vision. This is a good start. Following this concept, the multipliers at *n* dimension appear as a matter of course. This alteration is also a change in spatial form from low dimensional space to a higher one. Multi-dimensional variables can be expressed in a simple mathematical relationship.

Multidimensional space is not only space in math but also can be perceived and "seen" just like a 3-dimensional space. Space is the form of the existence of materials or an assembly of variables. In economics, the alteration of the form of something suggests the variation of its spatial dimension. The formula $1/x^i(1\text{-}x)$ has many variations, indicating that multidimensional space also exists in the economic system. If it is to add a floor or a window as we do in 3-dimensional space, the formula keeps its consistency in multidimensional space. But the essence of a function changes if the variable is multidimensional. When i=0, the first variation is the Keynes multiplier.

From the perspective of the space theory, the nature of the system changes if its spatial size does not match its dimension. In physics, Erwin Schrödinger's Cat is a good metaphor to explain the complete space and the physical changes caused by space collapse. If the box is not opened and keeps intact in form without damage, the cat inside is both alive and dead at the same time; if people attempt to open the box to observe what happens inside, the status of the space inside the box will change no matter what instruments are used in such observation. Then there are only options for the cat, to be alive or dead. In daily life, spatial changes mean the changes of the properties of things. If a piece of paper is cut into halves, it will shrink by half. Its space decreases exponentially, and that piece of paper no longer exists and is replaced by a set of atoms. Similarly, a drop of water occupies a very small space, but an overwhelming wave will form if thousands of drops of water are gathered together. The market economy is a free economy with independent individual activities. The individuals actions in line with their own purposes, and are free and independent of each other. However, inside the economic system exists a multidimensional space. If all the individuals act together uniformly, the market economy will become a 1-dimensional system. No matter what is done, the system will collapse. For example, if people withdraw money from the banks at the same time, the bank will go bankrupt; if people go shopping at the same time, the mall has to shut up.

So the high dimensional systems are utterly different from the low dimensional ones, so are the high dimensional functions from the low dimensional ones.

4.3 The Demonic S=*k*logY

In ancient times, when a host of demons running wild, God was the very guide leading people to fight. In a contemporary society filled with chaotic economic activities, people groan and quarrel in disappointment. They could do nothing but sigh to relieve their feelings after complaining and swearing. In the face of depression, our "God" is our rational thinking. The call for theories is like ancient people's ardent longing for God's guidance.

4.3.1 The entropy of national income (NI entropy)

On Boltzmann's tombstone is carved the simple equation $S{=}_{k}\log W$. It links two fields seemingly irrelevant to each other. One is thermodynamics, and the other is information theory, both of which have been widely accepted. However, there is another area still unknown to the public. It is economics. When $S{=}_{k}\log Y$[1] was created, it does not predict a promising future for economics but a rather dim prospect just like that for the thermodynamics and information theory. "Demons" run wild here.

Y is defined according to the definition of spending and income. So is its process of analysis. The free market economy expands with the increased scale of economy. The disorder at the micro-level leads to the tendency of long-term stagnation of national income. S stands for the degree of disorder, namely

1 Ma Lieguang, *The Great Collapse of Capitalism*, Economic Press China, 2012, p. 23.

the entropy. Y is national income. The entropy approaches its maximum as Y increases.

We can also substitute Y with $Y=vM$. Then $S={}_k\log_2 vM$. M is the currency, v is the velocity of currency circulation. From the relationship, it could be known that the money supply also has growth stagnation.

Every system, be it an open system such as living creatures and formation transfer in a system or a bounded independent system like the air in a bounded independent experimental container, can be measured by entropy as long as it has the disorder at the micro-level. The principle of maximum entropy tells the fact that disorders at the micro-level approaches its maximum. In thermodynamics, the amount principle of maximum entropy is expressed as The Second Law of Thermodynamics. However, since the disorder at the micro-level exists in all systems, the entropy formulated through probability theory is established. And it is in full accord with the Second Law of Thermodynamics.

Science is not always in prosperity. Tragedies happen now and then. Boltzmann received more criticism than praise after publicizing this formula. In the afternoon of September 5, 1906, when his wife and daughter were happily drifting and paddling on a boat in the famous coastal resort city Duino, Astro-Hungary, Boltzmann ended his life. He tied one end of the short rope to the wood window frame, looped the other roughly around his neck, and hanged himself. It is his daughter who found his body.[1]

Shannon was born in Michigan, the United States, in 1916. Thirty-two years later, he came up with the formula of information entropy. At that time, he also felt confused why his formula looks the same as Boltzmann's? What was behind the two identical formulas? When he publicized the Theory of Information Entropy, Shannon did not expect such a widespread effect it would bring to the world.

In 1948, when Shannon's formula was announced, entropy still looked like

1 Charles Seife, *Decoding The Universe*, translated by Sui Zhumei, Shanghai Scientific and Technological Education Publishing House, 2010, p. 19.

a mystery to people. No probability axiom about entropy had ever been put forward. Shannon himself was also not sure about the relation of his formula to Boltzmann's— Boltzmann summed up his formula by analyzing a container filled with air. Though Shannon's colleague helped with the invention of the name "entropy", Shannon himself did not dig deeper into the relationship between Boltzmann's thermodynamic entropy and the entropy he found. However, Shannon was lucky to be born in a nation in the worship of rational thinking which always inspires people. Therefore, scholars at Shannon's era continued the study of entropy, extended their knowledge about it, and eventually figured out what entropy is. With the development of the information theory and the probability theory, people found that the two formulas share the same meaning. Entropy is a measurement of disorder at the micro-level. Both thermodynamic entropy and information entropy are specific representation of such measurement.

Regretfully, the proposition of NI entropy encountered quite a cold welcome. But surprisingly, the economy is speeding up on the way to disorder.

4.3.2 Why Boltzmann entropy, information entropy, and NI entropy are the same?[1]

As everyone may wonder at the first sight of the formula, why thermodynamics and information are mixed with national income? However, in fact, as long as the mathematical derivation is correct, the three concepts of entropy are so closely related that the closeness of their relations is beyond our imagination.

Boltzmann put forward the formula $S=k\log W$. S is entropy. W represents the sum-up of micro status. Shannon's formula is $S=-\sum Pi\log Pi$, Pi stands for the probability of a specific piece of information amongst a series of possible information sent from a single information source. $\sum$ is the total of all the possible

1 Hermann Haken proposed a more generalized deduction about the identical entropy formulas of the Information Theory and Thermodynamics in *Information and Self-organization*. More details can be explored in "Information Entropy is a Measurement of Order", Zhao Wentong and Zhao Peizhang, cited from *The Great Debate- The Third National Symposium Collection of Papers in Entropy and Interdisciplinary Sciences*, p. 142.

information items. The NI entropy is expressed as $S=\log_2 Y$, where Y stands for the national income in the context of the possible maximum total number of transactions.

Now we analyze the outcomes of entropy calculated through the three formulas respectively with the example in which the same way is adopted. For example, four identical glass balls are thrown into a box. The bottom of the box has two small slots. The balls have an equal probability to fall into either the left or right slot. After countless trials, the most frequent situation is that two balls fall into the left slot while the other two fall into the right. Then how to calculate the entropy of this system?

Since W in Boltzmann's formula stands for the maximum probable number, then consider the number for different situations when 2 balls fall on each side. The maximum number for such situations is 6. This is because the probable combinations for the 4 balls falling on the right cover the following situations: 1 and 2, 1 and 3, 1 and 4, 2 and 3, 2 and 4, 3 and 4 respectively. Therefore, the entropy is $S=k\log 6$.

Elements in Shannon's formula are information instead of the glass balls. But we may change the way of expression. For example, numbers 0 and 1 can be used to substitute the left and right slots. 0 indicates that the glass ball falls on the, 1 the right. As for the situation of putting balls into the box, we can use bit information to enumerate all the possible combinations: 6 situations that are most probably to occur, namely 1100, 1010, 1001, 0110, 0101, 0011.

Every piece of information has an equal chance to "fall" either on the left or right, so they have equal probability, i.e. every piece of information has 1/6 of the chance to "fall" either on the left or right. In other words, $-\sum Pi\log Pi$ has 6 items. Each piece of information stands for one item, and each P_i, namely each formula, has a chance of 1/6 to occur. Therefore, $S = -\sum Pi\log Pi = -\sum P_i \log_2(1/6) = \log_2 6$.

National income differs from glass balls, too. If it in the monetary base is used to substitute the glass balls, one currency unit represents one glass ball. For instance, suppose four 1-yuan notes stand for one unit, the box the market, and investment and consumption the two slots in the box. The market economy is free, and each expenditure is conducted independently. With no confinement, if the probability P_i of choosing either investment or consumption is unknown, then using four of 1 yuan notes in either investment or consumption is of equal probability. The probability theory can prove that the maximum number for the ways of combination of investment and consumptions, N, is the same as the entropy obtained by Shannon. It is $S = \log_2 N = \log_2 6$.

Investments plus consumption equal to national income. The maximum probable national income is gained by multiplying the times of expenditure by the amount of currency in each transaction. Y=Ny, where y represents the 1-yuan note. So Y=Ny=6 yuan. The number of slots, 2, is the base number of the logarithm log. So it goes this way:

$$\log_2 Y = \log_2 N + \log_2 y \qquad (4\text{-}4)$$

In this example, 1 yuan stands for 1 glass ball, so y=1, and $\log_2 1$=0. Since $S = \log_2 N$, $S = \log_2 N = \log_2 Y = \log_2 6$.

Then, where is k in Boltzmann entropy? This is due to different base numbers of the logarithm. 2 is the base number of the logarithm, and only the expression form of constant k is altered. Based on this, k=1.

In the example above, more glass balls can be used in the test, such as 4, 40, 400, ..., n balls. In addition, the number of slots can be extended to 3, 4, ..., m. As long as the glass balls remain independent variables, the outcomes calculated with the three formulas will not vary. The three formulas are completely identialy. The NI entropy is the Boltzmann entropy, the Second Law of Thermodynamics at the same time, and is the information entropy when it is expressed with information.

Let's study the NI entropy separately. In the market economy, national income at a certain stage is so large that it would not be generated without numerous transactions. That is to say, the number of transactions is also very big, compared with which the average amount of each transaction is too small to be worthy of any attention. So the number of transactions is in place of the amount of national income, and thus the NI entropy is represented by number.

The secret of nature is hidden in tranquility. Great power always exerts in silence! Entropy is irresistible. Great thoughts have an overwhelming power whether the readers believe it or not!

I believe the principle that reveals everlasting increase of entropy is supreme. If someone points out to you that the cosmic theory you worship is out of accord with Maxwell formula, then nothing would be worse for the latter. If your theory is found to be inconsistent with observations, then the experimentalists might do something wrong. However, if you find your theory is contradictory to the Second Law of Thermodynamics, then I could give you no hope; it has to be overthrown with no other options.[1]

——A.S.Eddington[2]

4.4 How Debts Accumulate?

Residents put their money in banks, which is called a deposit. Banks lend the money out. Then loans are created. Banks record deposits as liabilities and loans as assets. Deposits are the commensurate liabilities shared by banks and depositors.

Have deposits and debts been clarified clearly? Wait a minute. If we want to know where the deposits come from, the causal relationship shows it seems to be the residual of labor payoffs, investment returns, and other incomes after being used in expenditure. But credit currency is originally from banks, and banks lend money out as loans. Then how are bank loans related to incomes such as labor payoffs and investment returns?

Though deposits and loans are mingled and share some overlaid properties, they still differ from the circular relation of chicken and eggs because chicken

1 Ilya Prigogine and Isabelle Stengers, *From Disorder to Order*, translated by Zeng Qinghong, Shanghai Translation Publishing House, 1987, p. 283.

2 A.S.Eddington (1882-1944), A astronomer, physicist, and mathematician of Great Britain.

is chicken and eggs are eggs. The connection between deposits and credit loans resembles more the quantum entanglement or quantum superposition. An electron and a photon in an experimental box penetrate two different cracks and run along two separate paths at the same time. The experiment result shows the interference phenomenon. For monetary capital, if deposits are considered as one path and loans the other, then a fund is both a deposit and a loan at the same time.

The most magical thing about quantum mechanics lies in the following fact: If a piece of observing equipment is placed in the box to light up the path and observe the movement of the electron, then the superposition will disappear and the electron will run on either path *A* or path *B*. It will not run on two paths simultaneously. The interference phenomenon disappears as well.

A similar phenomenon occurs in banks' monetary capital. Banks are like the experimental box, and money deposited in them possesses dual characters: It is both deposit and loan at the same time. Residents and borrowers are like the observing equipment. When printing the transaction notes, they get one result only- the money is either deposit or loan. Double-entry bookkeeping is like Erwin Schrödinger's Cat that is also both alive (debit) and dead (credit) at the same time. Once the status of each fund is observed clearly, the cat (money) is either dead or alive. Therefore, economics should develop from double-entry bookkeeping with it as its mark.

The following 6 steps clarify the accumulation process of residents' deposits and debts. The theory is simple and easy to understand.

1. Companies and the public make up the fundamental economic units in the market economy and financial system. The savings during a certain period refers to the balance of companies' and the public's monetary incomes after spending during the current period, which is shown as follows:

$$\Delta S = Y - Z \quad (4\text{-}5)$$

ΔS in the formula shows the new incremental savings at the current stage. Y stands for the monetary income at the current stage. Z is the monetary expenditure at the current stage. The public has a strong desire to deposit. Statistical data shows total deposits are greater than loans despite that lending is a common phenomenon among the public. Therefore, the savings of the public are positive. As revealed by other statistics, the savings of the public increase faster than the expenditure with the rising income of the public. The savings-to-income ratio of the public also increases with the rising income of the public.

2. Companies have difficulties in satisfying their needs of investments in the process of expanding their businesses. Even though they can often maintain a positive amount of savings, their borrowings are greater than their savings.

3. From the perspective of loan-to-deposit relation, loans (D_d) = borrowings (J_j). It shows that the money lent out equals to the money borrowed in. When a bank issues a 10-trillion-dollar loan, it means that the borrower borrow a 10-trillion-dollar fund from the bank. In this chapter, when we discuss the amount of funds, we confirm that the borrowing amount and the lending amount equal to each other in amount, i.e. L=B. So there will be no more explanations of it in the following chapter.

4. Suppose the monetary fund only circulates among the companies within the country, the public and commercial banks. When the public's deposits from income increase, a gap between the loans issued by commercial banks to the companies and the public and the repayments from the borrowers will appear, this is equal to the savings from income and is expressed as follows:

$$\Delta S = \Delta Dd - \Delta Hh \tag{4-6}$$

ΔD_d stands for bank loans at the current stage. ΔH_h is the varied amount of repayments from companies and the public. Repayments refer to the repayments from credit loans and income at the current stage. Based on equation (4-5) and (4-6), the following equation is obtained:

$$Y - Z = \Delta Dd - \Delta Hh \tag{4-7}$$

The equation above shows that current income minus current expenditure equals to new loans during the current period minus varied amount of repayment during the current period.

5. According to the relation on the right of the equation, we know that:

① If the new loans equal to new repayments, then the savings during the current period is zero, indicating that there is a change in the savings that were deposited in the bank in previous periods.

② If new loans are more than new repayments, then the savings during the current period increase. So does the aggregate savings at the current stage.

③ If new loans are less than new repayments, then we need to reduce the savings deposited in previous periods. For example, people can withdraw money from their savings account to repay the bank the loans they have borrowed.

Though situations expressed in (4-5), (4-6), (4-7) may all exist in reality, the right-side relation is bound by the left-side one. From the macro perspective, the positive savings of the public means there is always a part of loans being deposited into banks as the balance of income. That is why repayments may be less than loans.

In the situation where savings increase, there exists a gap between loans and repayments. As the funds in saving augment accumulatively, the gap becomes bigger and bigger. After the amount of repayments is deducted, the current outstanding loans in banks equal the deposits from income savings in the amount.

6. To better understand the equal relationship between each other, the current-period repayments can be set as the possible maximum repayment (maxΔH_h, max means maximum). The possible maximum repayments refer to the funds retrieved from both the commodity market and the financial market by borrowers to repay bank loans as much as possible on the condition that all loaned money has been used for spending. Explained in another way, the possible maximum repayments refer to the repaid loans plus the loans that might be repaid in the future.

Current-period outstanding loans (ΔD) equels to Varied amount of current-period loans (maxΔH_h) minus Possible maximum repayments (maxΔH_h) equels to current-period new savings (ΔS)

$$\Delta D = \Delta Dd - max\Delta Hh \qquad (4\text{-}8)$$

$$\Delta D = \Delta S \qquad (4\text{-}9)$$

This formula shows that new increments in outstanding loans equal to new savings. Funds flowing out as loans turn over through re-spending. Money loaned to borrowers turns into savings of the public. Savings are both the loans that have not been retrieved by banks and the debts not yet repaid by the borrowers. In this book, such a situation is described as "double-debt", which means the borrowers' debts to banks and the banks' liabilities to depositors.

This shows that the savings in the bank stem from bank loans. The savings turn into incomes of companies and residents after the process in which the money is loaned for re-spending in investment and consumption. After the turnover of loans, the ownership of funds changes and the loaned money becomes the savings of companies and residents.

Considering that the gap between loans and repayments is the savings of residents, there is no way for the bank to generate profits. The profits of the bank are made and displayed in a set of statistical statements, in which the savings are just liabilities of the bank that are excluded from revenue accounting. Therefore, commercial banks are always capable of fabricating satisfactory profit statements.

Chapter 5

Common Trends of Market Economy

5.1 From Growth to Stagnation

Surrounded by the prosperous phenomena created by the Industrial Revolution, the majority of people hold an optimistic attitude towards economic development. In spite of the world economic crisis, post-crisis prosperity indulges people in sustainable developments in the long term. When it comes to "the long-term trend of the economy", people's minds are loaded with beautiful words, such as growth, development, and prosperity. Very few realize that, in the future, the probability of the occurrence of long-term depression will be greater than that of long-term prosperity. The long-term depression, rather than sustainable developments, as formulated below by the author, is the long-term trend of the economy which is determined by its own course.

At a certain stage, if the growth rate of economic magnitude remains constant, then the economic magnitude will grow exponentially. For example, at a stage, the average growth rate of national income is constant, and then the total national income increases at an exponential rate. The price level and the credit fund scale experience an exponential increase on the horizon axis of time. Even the population, energy consumption, new technological state, industrial and agricultural output presents the same trend.

Figure 5-1(a) displays a positive growth, showing a trend of an accelerating increase with no restriction. Malthus introduced the exponent into economics because, as he supposed, the population would grow limitlessly when the birth rate is greater than the death rate.

Figure 5-1(b) displays a negative trend in which the economic variable decreases at a higher rate until it approaches zero or the minimum value.

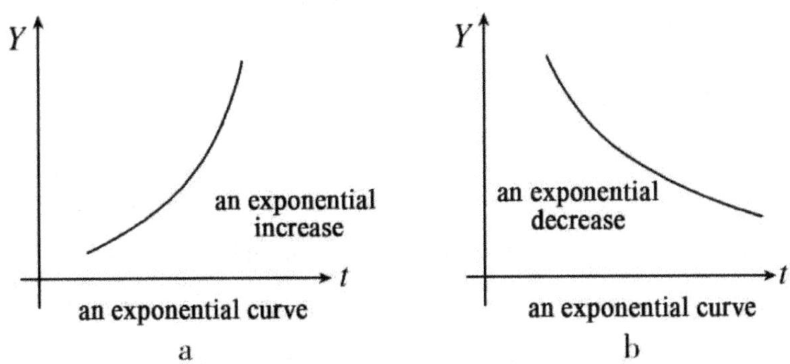

Figure 5-1 exponential growth

Note: the two diagrams are usually used to display the accelerated changes of economic variables.

One typical example includes the accelerating decline of the stock market index. And another is the biological extinction led by the death rate higher than the birth rate.

One feature of exponential increase is that the magnitude doubles even though the growth rate increases only a bit. If measured by the passage of time, the magnitude doubles within a much shorter period. Take the annual growth rate of national income as an example. If the growth rate is 2%, it takes 35 years to double the national income; if it is 4%, then it takes 18 years; if it is 7%, it takes 10 years. In 2013, China's GDP based on US dollars was 9400 trillion. Suppose that the national economy in the next 10 years grows at 7% annually, given that the RMB-to-USD rate remains unchanged, then our GDP would reach 18,800 trillion.

People were once worried about the outcome brought by the exponential increase since a small change in power will incur a significant difference in the magnitude. If variables, such as population, economic magnitude, resource consumption, and environmental pollution, all change in an exponential manner, it is impossible for nature to endure such unbounded and magnificent changes.

Unlike the exponential increase, the logarithmic rise is restrained by stagnation after the magnitude reaches a limit. In nature, the exponential increase is confined to a specific period because nothing in nature has ever experienced an unbounded growth yet. Following the logarithmic rule, everything evolves. The Second Law of Physics is a law expressed in a logarithmic form. As time passes by, it is noticed that all the macrosystems will increase logarithmically as long as the disorder at the micro-level exists.

An economic system is a macrosystem at each level, such as the production cycle in factories, industries and economic magnitude, the price level, the credit loan scale, and the changes in population magnitude, and so forth. In other words, almost all economic activities in human society ultimately become logarithmic shaped in the long run. (see figure 5-2)

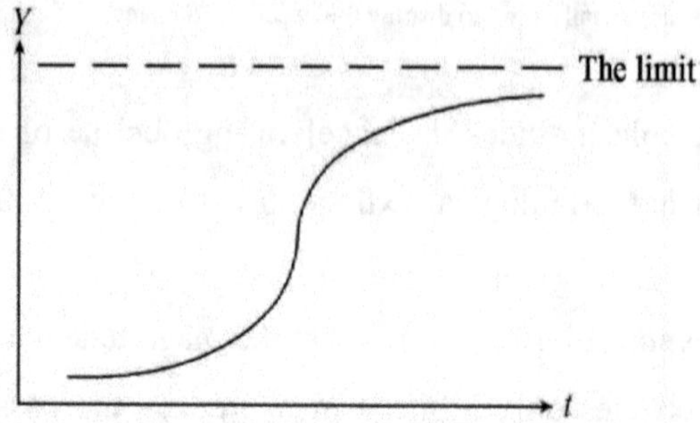

Figure 5-2 The logarithm curve for economic activities

Note: the vertical axis *Y* is the variable. The horizontal one is time. At the initial stages, the variable changes exponentially. In the long run, the growth rate gradually decreases and approaches zero-growth.

The 20th century saw rapid economic development all over the world. The economic magnitude reached an unprecedented level with almost all gross indicators displaying an increasing trend at a rising rate. In the short term, they complied with the features of an exponential rise.

However, another feature was observed at the same time. The growth rate increased as the gross indicators decreased. As for the population, aggregate social products, national income, the monetary aggregate, and the price level, the decreasing growth rate became a common feature.

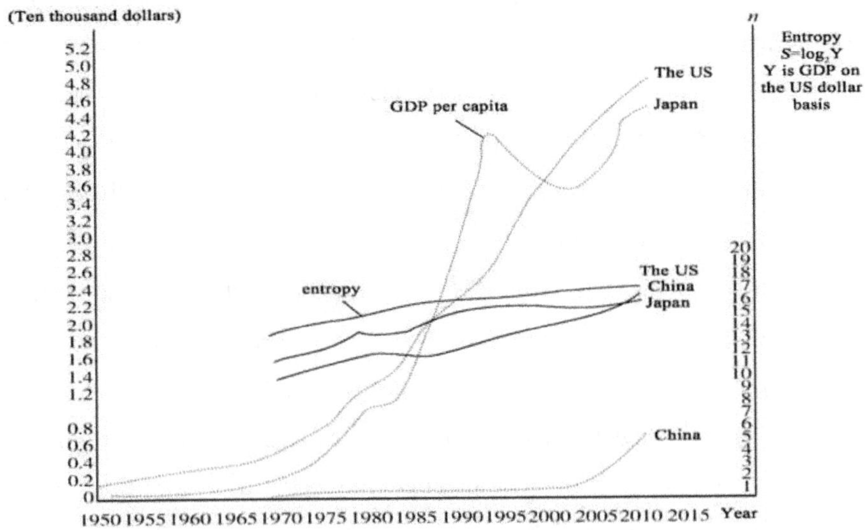

Figure 5-3 Comparison of NI entropy of China, the US, and Japan

Note: the vertical axis is derived from equation $S=n=\log_2 Y$. S is entropy. n is the number of times It is the scale of NI entropy with a meaning equivalent to the turnover frequency of ex-ante national income being allocated in national income spending and re-spending. Actually, n is an entropy scale.

Take the national income as an example. The US takes the logarithmic form of the magnitude, setting it on the vertical axis and time on the horizontal axis. Then some trends show up on an annual basis. As shown in Figure 5-3, from 1950 to 2015, the national income of China, the US, and Japan, all on the US dollar basis and in the logarithmic form, display their trends comparatively. The national income of Japan and China experience a greater fluctuation than that of the US.

One reason is related to the currency exchange rate, the fluctuation of which affects the shape of the curve. Another is the fluctuation of the annual growth rate of national income in each country. A greater fluctuation incurs greater curve flexibility. As shown in Figure 5-3, China has a much steeper curve than the US and Japan. Japan has a relatively flat curve, while the national income of the US still shows a slight rise. This indicates that, in China, the national income will persist to grow at a higher rate than that of the US and Japan.

This Figure also displays the national per capita income in the three countries, which also explains why the logarithmic curve of China's national income is much steeper and upward. A country with a lower national per capita income has a much higher growth rate of the national economy. It is located on the lower band of the S-shaped logarithmic curve, or the middle band. Meanwhile, a country with a higher national per capita income is located on the upper band of the S-shaped curve which is also much flatter.

Particularly emphasized, with other conditions unchanged, the logarithmic curve represents the long-term trend. And it is irreversible. Also, it excludes the probability of perpetual growth and cyclical fluctuation. It tends to have unalterable growth stagnation. If the economy remains unchanged, it will enter long-term stagnation once the global economy reaches a certain level. At first, the developed nations with higher national per capita income will firstly go into the long-term stagnation in which a depressed economy, a growth slump, and a high unemployment rate accompany each other. Then, nations with relatively low national per capita income are divided into two groups-one with an accelerating development and the other falling behind in the long term with a weakening economy impaired by political turmoil and wars. Over a long period, nations with rapid developments will own a decreasing growth rate. And eventually, since the advancements of technologies lead to a greater commodity supply than the demand, the global economy will enter the era of deflation.

5.2 The Common Trend of National Income Changes

From 1978 to 2012, with the increase of aggregate national income, China's GDP fluctuated less and the growth rate of the economy tended to fall. Why Chinese economic growths also tend to fall? Because China has been practicing the market economy likes foreign countries since the reform and opening-up. Therefore, economic growth reflects the properties and limits of economic rules with no exceptions. Before 1978, our country implemented a planned economy but received an unsatisfying outcome. At that time, the products were lacking in varieties. The foreign debts did not exist. There did not exist a gap between the rich and the poor like nowadays. However, the unemployment rate was high and our economy lacked competitiveness. After the reform and opening-up, the economy becomes more market-oriented and liberalizes the productive forces. Within only 30 years or so, China quickly grew into a great power with a leading economic magnitude all over the world. Restrained by the law of entropy changes, our economic growth becomes slower after the expansion of the economic scale. The law of entropy changes only relates to the scale of the market economy. Though the national conditions differ, the discrepancies between national cultures, political regimes, geographical locations, and natural resources cannot result in changes in the law of the market economy.

As shown in Figure 5-4, with the economic expansion, the zenith of GDP growth rate declines annually. The economic growth rate displays a downward trend. From 1980 to 1990, the fluctuation was great, while years between 1991 and 2013 saw a gentler fluctuation with a declining general trend. Apparently, taken 1953 as the starting point, the fluctuation during 1980 to 1990 can only be regarded as smaller ones, as shown in Figure 5-5.

From Figure 5-5, it is apparent that in the 1950s and 60s the growth rate of GDP fluctuated in a relatively violent manner. A similar feature reappeared at the end of the 80s and the beginning of the 90s. However, generally speaking, the fluctuation of the growth rate became flatter. Obviously, the growth rate is directly related to the scale of the economy. The smaller the scale is, the greater the fluctuation will be; the larger the scale is, the smaller the fluctuation will be. In the long term, with the expansion of the economy, the growth rate became smaller and smaller.

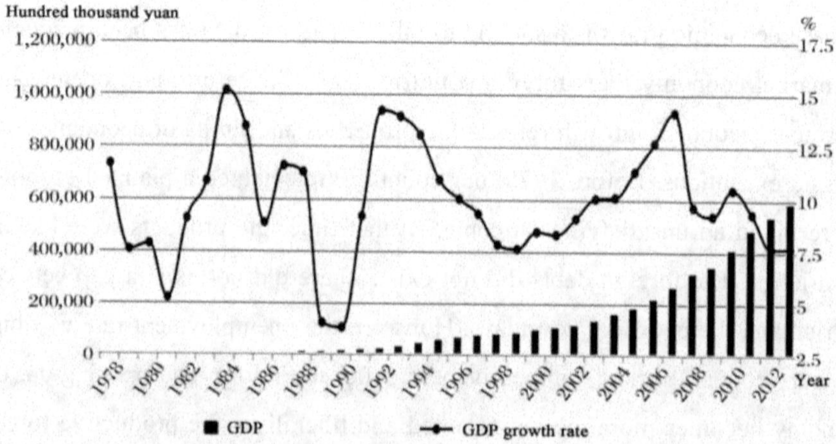

Figure 5-4 China's economic magnitude and the fluctuation of growth rate

Note: from 1978 to 2012, the economic growth rate was in a declining trend as GDP rose.
Resource: National Bureau of Statistics of China

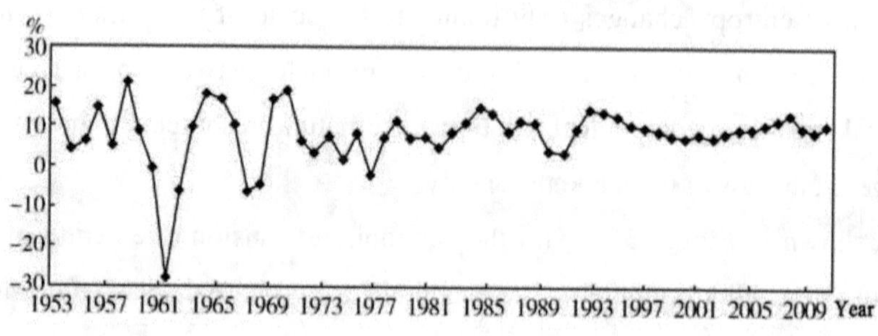

Figure 5-5 The trend of China's national income fluctuation

Note: The fluctuation of China's GDP tends to be flat and declines annually[1]

The statistical materials show, countries which implemented the market

1 Cai Zhizhou, "Analyze China's Economic Growth from the Penetration of the Ultimate Demand", from *China's Economic Growth and Economic Cycles (2011),* Economic Press China, 2012, p. 280.

economy are apt to be in the same situation where the economy stagnates, debts accumulate and indicators, such as money supply and inflation rate tend to be the same. In other words, their market economies share the same features. For example, from Figure 5-6, from 2001 to 2002, each economic entity endured a slight fall. From 2003 to 2008, each country enjoyed a rising trend before a significant slump was later induced by the Financial Crisis in 2008. After 2009, China's economy bounced up much vigorously but still fluctuated in a trend similar to that of other nations. Meanwhile, the economic growth rate in each country all displayed a downward feature.

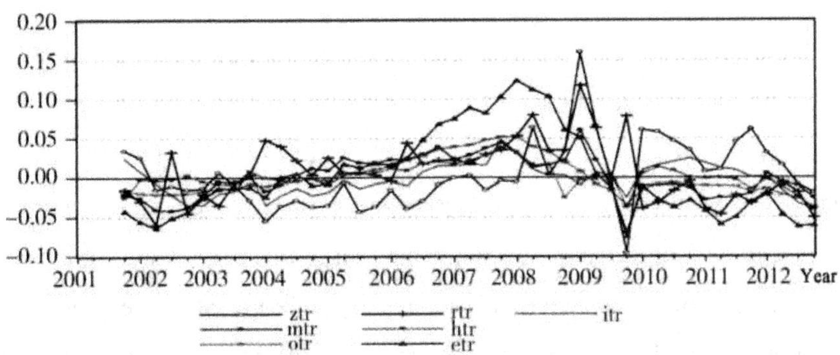

Figure 5-6 The fluctuation of GDP in some countries and regions

Note[1]: ztr, mtr, otr, rtr, htr, etr, itr in the Figure respectively represent the common graph of the economic growth in China, the US, the EU, Japan, South Korea, Russia, and India

Figure 5-7 testifies the factual convergence of economic trends all over the globe. Though the world economy kept growing, the growth rate declined from 1971 to 2008. The comparison amongst different resources reveals that higher national per capita income comes with a lower growth rate and thus the fluctuation is smaller. Changes of the market economy are apt to be in accord, which means the market economy has its own rules that are not affected by different national

1 Ouyang Zhigang, "The Economic Growth Trend and International Synergistic Work During Economic Fluctuations", *Economic Research Journal*, 2013, Vol.7, p. 40.

conditions.

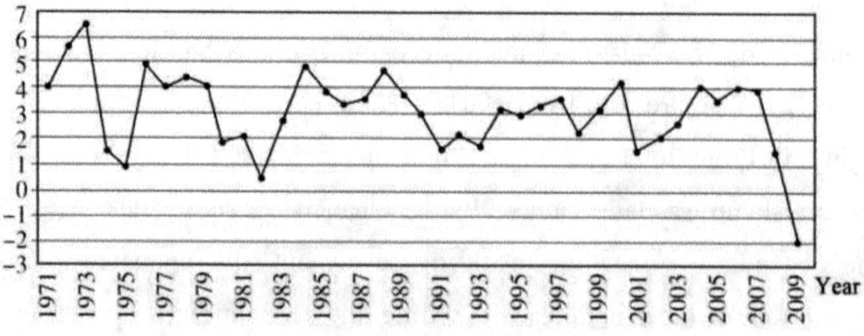

Figure 5-7 Trend of the world-average real GDP

Note[1]: from 1971 to 2009, the growth rate of the world real GDP presented a downward trend generally.

Economics initiates from the study of economic growth. In *Wealth of Nations* by Adam Smith, it is acceptable to say that economics bears the same meaning of economic growth.[2] Classical economics also covers some assumptions and arguments of economic growth "convergence". But in neoclassical economics, "convergence" has a different meaning from that in this book. Here, convergence refers to a series of phenomenon of homogenized indicators: the phenomenon that the economic growth goes down and stagnates as the national income increases, the common feature that the price index is positively or negatively related to the money supply, the diminishing effects of technological advancements, the declining total factor productivity, and the rising inflation rate.

In classical economics, "convergence" means "the tendency that income gap between countries or regions narrows as time elapses". In neoclassical economics, "convergence" is based on the neoclassical model, arguing that "the economic growths in different countries converge to the path to steady or balanced growth"[3].

1 Li Xiaoxi, *On Discussing the Cycle of World Economy, from China's Economic Growth and Economic Cycles (2011),* Economic Press China, 2012, p. 351.

2 Deng Xiang, *The Theory of Economic Convergence and Economic Gaps in Different Regions of China*, Southwest University of Finance and Economics Press, 2006, p. 1.

3 Ibid, p. 23.

Thanks to the convergence of economic growth, poor countries grow quicker than the rich, and both head for the "same" level of economic performance.

In the past, the macroeconomics did not include the theory of entropy changes and had difficulty in clarifying the phenomenon that the national income growth decreases while the economy magnitude increases. A group of theories burgeon. The theory of sustainable development in Europe insists that the market economy will automatically come down to balance by adjusting the economic growth and smoothing out the economic cycle with fiscal and monetary policies. How optimistic! Who has ever thought of the lines "falling down all of a sudden like a mansion collapsing, and ending up in gloom like the shadowy candlelight crushing out". The free market economy does not head for the equilibrium but for the entropy changes.

In 2006, I wrote a book named *A New Discussion of Economics: Multiplier, Statistical Entropy, and National Income*, in which I mainly introduced the theory of entropy changes of national income and the thought of non-linear multipliers. Then I talked with some netizens. At that time, some people took the introduction of entropy theory as a mechanical application of physics. They argued that it sounded like human beings ending up in death ultimately. Everybody agreed, but death was far away from now. Such a theory of entropy changes of national income bore no meaning. However, the unfortunate thing happened. The financial crisis swept the world. Some were mocking and swearing, while others were enduring and suffering. Conventional theories met their Waterloo, neither explaining why the debt crisis took place nor clarifying the relation between money supply increase and continuous deflation. Macroeconomic theories were also in a crisis, a crisis of trust, and received a load of criticism. Lacking feasible theories, people did not know how to tackle the crisis. Disputes were basically more than agreements. Endlessly, groups of people took turns to shout out their assertions. Such overwhelming chaos vaporized the enthusiasm. The position was lost. Such a bleak phase was covered by extra melancholy like dust and fog veiling an already-shabby premise. So it is-

Lonely rivers flow towards the east

One is shouting, the other is blaming,
Nothing is received but vaporized enthusiasm,
And submerged position,
A bleak phase wears another layer of dust,
Bears extra melancholy in a smog.

Sadness fills the mansion, even God envies me.
Sighing in a humble cabin, whose thoughts twist?
The loneliness of a wild goose flying, the coldness of the moon hanging,
Winds and rains sweep night by night, so does my distress.
Whoever takes the jade bowl as a pottery pot,
A rough twig pulls out
A stack of trash.

——Ma Lieguang

Chapter 6

The Principle of Irreversible Changes in Financial Theories

6.1 What is Money?

Some say money is the medium of exchange. Some say money is a commodity in exchange for other products. Others say money reflects the value of labor embedded in a commodity. All the views highlight some features and functions of money.

However, in fiduciary standards, credit money is guaranteed by state credit. Money is issued by the central bank and further created by the commercial banks by expanding credit. Credit money is worth a strict definition and displayed in a math formula based on the principle of debt formation, as shown below-

$$\Delta D = \Delta S \tag{6-1}$$

ΔD is the outstanding loan at a given stage. The outstanding loan is both the debt and the credit money. ΔS is the new increment of savings at a given stage. S is the income held in the residents' pockets, and it comes from working and investments.

This principle tells us that the more money saved by the residents, the larger the outstanding loans are. Of course, the debts are greater.

We can use the induction method to define "money" according to its properties and features. The induction method is widely used in philosophy and social sciences, such as defining "money" as the medium of exchange for commodities. However, in natural sciences, we apply a math equation to define a concept. For example, Newton defined the interaction forces by introducing the formula $F=ma$ where F is the interaction force, m is inertial mass, and a is the acceleration. Also, in physics, time is defined by the distance (s) and the velocity (v), shown as $t=s/v$.

The best way to define "money" is to use measurable variables instead of describing "money" in abstract words and concepts because the latter may cause unnecessary misunderstanding and controversy. In the meantime, economics prefers practicability. Practicability means advancements. For example, for an old theory and a new one, though both of them are self-consistent, it is still hard to decide which one is more advanced if they lack practicability. Maybe neither of them lives up to the standard of an advanced theory. Therefore, the mathematical formula in defining a concept can not only reveal the relation between the concept and other variables, clarifying its properties but also quantify the concept, making the ordinary definition a precise concept.

6.2 The Central Bank Have to Continuously Inject Monetary Base to Sustain the Normal Operation of Commercial Banks

Popular financial theories in modern times suppose loans issued by commercial banks can be repaid in equal amounts. If so, there must be an equal relation between loans of commercial banks and repayments. Despite of losses caused by bad loans, commercial banks generally gain profits, for the interest income and other incomes are greater than the losses. Otherwise, commercial banks are unlikely to expand and develop.

In the theory of money multiplier, loans = repayments are fully expressed as follows-

Loans issued by commercial banks = monetary base issued by central bank × money multiplier

Loans recovered by commercial banks = monetary base shrinking from market × money multiplier

Bank reserves are the monetary base that can be managed by commercial banks in practice. The monetary base refers to the original deposits that the commercial banks use to issue original loans. Original deposits stem from the money that comes into banks in a variety of ways, including personal cash deposits, loans issued by the central bank, the net inflow of foreign currencies, and so forth.

Since the loans issued have the same multiplier as the loans recovered, when the monetary base is equivalent in amount, loans = repayments. Based on formula (4-7) in Chapter 4, such opinion can be further illustrated as follows-

If the change of loans (ΔD_d) = the change of repayment (ΔH_h), then income (Y) = spending (Z), and the increment in savings (ΔS) is zero. Considering the income of commercial banks, sometimes repayments are greater than loans. In other words, on the right side of the equation is the negative value of the repayments ($-\Delta H_h$), while on the left side is the negative value of the money spending ($-Z$). Commercial banks generate profits from negative repayments ($-\Delta H_h$). The part of the public that has not borrowed spent more than their income at the current stage. Therefore, they need to withdraw deposits at previous stages to cover the gap of the negative repayments ($-\Delta H_h$).

The perception that loans equal repayments is not in accord with the trend of the income growth of the public in reality. At the micro-level, this perception suits the case of repaying a small number of loans, but, fails to explain the situation at the macro level. The deposits of the public are positively related to their income. The increase of deposits is due to the net outflow of the funds of borrowers, as the unequal relation $\Delta D_d - \Delta H_h > 0$ (see formula (4-7) in Chapter 4). The net outflow is other depositors' money of the bank that cannot be repaid by the borrowers.

Owing to the income savings, the money creation of commercial banks is not equivalent to the money recovered. The loans recovered are smaller than the loans issued. Therefore, the money multipliers on both sides are not equal, either. We could not determine the money recovered simply based on the principle of a money multiplier.

When the outstanding loans are in the relation $\Delta D_d - \Delta H_h > 0$, borrowers have three ways to solve the financial gap, roughly listed as: (1) gaining income at the commodity market to repay the loan; (2) gaining income from the financial market to repay the loan; (3) apply for a new loan from the bank to repay the old one.

Money from the commodity market or the financial market is unlikely to pay off the loans, logically speaking. Firstly, the process of spending the borrowed funds is not equivalent to the process of repaying the loans by selling commodities. To put it simply, spending is much easier than recovering. There is always part of the funds having to be occupied for a long time, or turning into bad loans due to bankruptcy. Secondly, the public has a strong desire to deposit. Usually, they deposit part of their income and avoid draining up all of it. Consequently, this part of the loans that turn into the income of the public never flows back to the banks as repayments.

Borrowers repay the loans by selling financial assets, which is also susceptible to the financial market, so they cannot fully pay off the loan by making a balloon payment once and forever. Though the financial market has a considerable scale, for example, the market value of stocks even surpasses GDP, the fluctuation of such a great market value totally depends on thousands of millions of small-amount tradings and most of the stocks do not participate in the transactions at the same stage. As a result, in prosperous periods, repaying debts is much easier, while in depression, it is harder to do so because dumping stocks drags down the stock price, incurring a stock price even lower than the initial purchasing price. Greatly increased loans borrowed in prosperous periods are unlikely to be fully repaid by selling out financial assets in depressed ones.

Therefore, the borrowers who fail to pay off loans in the way (1) and way (2) have to apply for new loans to cover the old ones.

Repaying old loans by taking out new loans is of vital importance to the development of the financial system. The new loans sustain the well-functioning fund-debt chain between the borrowers and the commercial banks, making sure that borrowers who can maintain normal operation do not go into bankruptcy due to the insolvency of old debts.

At the same time, banks can gain more interest income from the new loans. After the expansion of credit, loans are issued more frequently and the volume of each loan also becomes greater. As a result, the risk of insolvency of a certain loan declines. For example, suppose a large bank and a small bank both faces a bad loan. The former is more likely to tolerate it than the latter.

More borrowers appear with the expansion of credit. Funds flow among the borrowers and this broadens the living space for them, making it easier for borrowers that are trapped by old debts at previous stages to get rid of the financial burden.

For commercial banks, pay old loans by issuing new loans leads to debt accumulation, though this is a critical way for banks to exist and develop. To sustain the corresponding relation between money borrowing and repayments by issuing new loans is indeed a loan extension through which the commercial banks can manage to keep the cycle of funds flowing between loans and repayments. However, an extended loan is owed to a changing group of borrowers instead of one fixed independent borrower. Therefore, paying off the old loans with the new ones is a roll-over of debt, which gives rise to an increasing amount of debts.

When we notice that the outstanding loans equal savings, this amount has become far beyond the capital and profits of commercial banks. The outstanding loans, therefore, have to be included in the loss of commercial banks. Also, we ought to realize that commercial banks are only capable of sustaining the loan scale by issuing new loans in terms of the magnitude rather than retrieve those loans that have already turned into savings.

The financial theory about "loans = repayments" is by no means enough to encapsulate the case of the loan loss due to the passing of title. As for individual borrowers at different stages, "loans = repayments" establishes itself at the theoretical level. But for all the borrowers as a group, the fact is always true that loans are greater than repayments. In other words, it is accessible for commercial banks to recover loans at the micro-level, but unrealizable at the macro level.

For the reasons above, the central bank has to inject monetary base continuously to sustain the normal operating of commercial banks. Otherwise, the commercial banks do not have extra money to issue new loans.

6.3 Why "Money Drought" Takes Place?

How to solve the excessive accumulation of debts? Is it solved after the economy develops? Not the case. Because the process of economic development is also a process of debt accumulation. In theory, if the government does not intervene in the economy unduly, the government can make ends meet. However, commercial banks and corporations may continuously accumulate their debts due to the growing savings of other corporations and residents. The deposits in commercial banks are the asset accumulation of corporations and residents. In other words, the assets of some people are the debts of some others.

Deposits are the result of the capital movement of commercial banks. As explained in previous chapters, monetary capital is used in investments and consumption, and part of the credit capital ultimately turns into the monetary income of residents after spending and re-spending. The residual of monetary income after spending becomes deposits. So a fund gap between loans and repayment appears.

The growth of deposits incurs the growth of debts of commercial banks. Banks lend the new deposits to companies and individuals. Correspondingly, banks own a larger amount of assets. They then generate profits from the interest gap between loans and deposits. Meanwhile, those companies and residents borrowing loans from banks become debtors. Take the society as a whole and we can notice that assets equal debts. Wealth means debts. For banks, the number of their assets equals their debts.

Anyway, loans need to be paid off. Savings grow with the increase of residents' income. Supplemented money only comes from the central bank which continuously injects monetary base to commercial banks. And the latter spends it on government debts or issuing new loans. New loans are used for filling the gap between the old loans and repayments. This gap comes from the existence of savings.

In short, by increasing the issuance of monetary base, repaying old loans by borrowing new ones is a way to sustain the capital movement of commercial banks. If the central bank enacts a tight monetary policy, or the supply of monetary base is not enough to sustain the capital movement, the commercial banks will be trapped by "money drought" due to the failure of loan recovery. They have to reduce loan issuance, or even cease it. Within a short period, the short-term inter-bank rate will soar up. If the central bank cannot increase the issuance of monetary base in time, the tightening-up of funds in the banking industry will eventually bring about money drought in the whole financial system. A shortage of money can easily make a financial crisis in the wind.

That I say commercial banks are short of money is from the perspective of fund supply. All money in the world is deposited in banks. How come banks are short of money? The appearance of "shadow deposits" actually means the diversion of the deposit usages. It increases fund supply. But this is not the reason why banks have no money to lend. The main reason for the failure of loan recovery is not the loan loss, because the loan loss will not surpass the book profit of banks. Compared with the increasing amount of credit loans, those losses are too small to be taken into account.

Until now, people are puzzled about the "money drought". In June 2013, M2 in China reached 100 trillion yuan, during which period the short-term inter-bank rates rose by a large margin due to the central bank's decision to reduce the issuance of monetary base. Within a few days, commercial banks were swamped by a money shortage and ended up in a financial crisis. The real reason is shown by the equation "$\Delta D_d = \Delta H_h + \Delta S_s$", where ΔD_d is the loan variation at a certain stage, ΔH_h is the repayment variation at a certain stage, and ΔS_s is the savings variation at a certain stage. The larger the credit loan scale is, the more the loans turn into savings. Also, the gap between loans and repayments is greater and the banks shoulder more debts. If the central bank does not inject monetary base into the banking system, commercial banks will be trapped by money drought due to which they have no deposits to issue loans. Banks, no matter how big or small, are short of money. The capital chain ruptures.

At the end of June in 2013, China Merchants Bank (CMB), Industrial and Commercial Bank of China (ICBC), and Bank of China (BOC) began to set restrictions on the money transfer of large deposits. They even canceled the money withdrawals from ATMs. The stock market crashed, losing a market value of up to some trillion yuan. The financial crisis had appeared. This gives us a lesson that inappropriate policies create the "money drought". The relevant departments are not familiar enough with the rule of capital movement. The conventional financial theories have severe defectiveness.

The periodical shortage of money in the banking industry is a normal economic phenomenon. Guaranteeing monetary base issuance into commercial banks serves as a fundamental method to sustain the normal turnover of credit capital.

The shortage of money has nothing to do with the scale of credit loans. Nor does it relate to the areas the investment capital goes in. Banks in every nation are lacking in money and each of them is troubled by the periodical shortage of money. This is a basic financial fact. In 2008, the Subprime Mortgage Crisis was superficially attributed to the default of monetary funds in the downward economy. But to quest its real reason, it was the debt accumulation that caused the money shortage of commercial banks and then swept the global financial market.

In practice, we use easing monetary policies to cope with a downward economy and tight policies against a high inflation rate. All in all, it is to relate money issuance to the development of the economy. Easing money is for a shrinking economy. This is only specifically for the case of the commercial banks' money shortage. Now what we are discussing here is why banks are so thirsty for money. In news reports, public opinion seems to believe that banks have abundant capital and by no means are in great demand for it.

Whether the money supply is easy or tight can be reflected from the fluctuation of short-term rates. When the short-term rates surpass the long-term ones, banks are in a financial strain and long for more monetary base issuance from the central bank. This has already become a common sense of finance. But in this crisis, the central bank declined the policy without explaining why it chose not to implement the conventional policy. Was it a "secret maneuver"? Then rumors soared. The public opinion leaned to one side cheering with few exceptions. What is more ridiculous, such ignorance was disguised with words such as "courageous" and "unyielding", leaving the financial market full of wailing and despair.

People seem to do well without theories. And truly, there is no such theory that is not included in a textbook but powerful enough to persuade the audience. Then what can persuade them? Only methods like "crossing the river by feeling the stones" "sticking to the issue on its merits" and "the trial-and-error method" can do so. They are the mainstream thoughts. Then what came about after the trial-and-error method in the financial market in June 2013? We lifted the rock but only dropped it on our own foot.

The more money is issued, the more money is accumulated. Because loans turn into savings and cannot be fully repaid. Otherwise, most of the loans can be paid off, and banks can, therefore, harvest profits. Also, what money ought to do is to go around repetitively instead of getting accumulated. M=km reveals the fact. M is the loans, m is the monetary base and k is the multiplier. If loans are not diverted and in the end fully repaid, we need to multiply n to both sides of the equation. n is the times that the loans go around. (Here we ignore the bad loans since they are too small, compared with the total loans, to surpass the banks' profits.) As a consequence, there is no need to increase the supply of monetary base. Even though the social economy expanded, a moderate rise of monetary base issuance would be appropriate. Meanwhile, owing to the existence of n, the increase of loans is unlikely to exceed the growth of national income.

However, the economic performance in practice is not always in accord with conventional theories. The growth rate of money aggregate is greater than that of national income. Why is no *n* included, or is *n* too small? Answers, such as the extension of the construction period, and the increase of bad loans, are all impossible to explain why money grows faster than the national income.

6.4 Excessive Issuance of Money is a False Proposition

A hot discussion about the money aggregate is among people. Some scholars write essays to order and analyze the phenomenon, perceiving that the money issuance in our country is excessive. I have read dozens of papers, and found out that most of them hold a disapproving opinion. But pitifully, they fail to explain clearly what the "excessive money issuance" is from the beginning to the end of their papers.

To summarize papers and books I have read, I categorize the opinions into four types. The first opinion blames for the excessively fast-growing money supply. The second holds the idea that the ratio of the money supply to national income is much higher. The third attributes to a relatively bigger interest gap between deposits and loans. The last puts it down to inflation. Each of them is explained as follows.

Money issued by the central bank through direct loan issuance and the purchase of national debt and bills is called the monetary base. Monetary base multiplicatively creates credit money through the cycles of lending and re-lending of the commercial banks. We define the derivative money as broad money, such as M2 which includes cash and current deposits. In 2012, the balance of M2 in China was 105.45 trillion yuan, ranking top 1 in the world. It occupied approximately a quarter of the total money supply all over the globe, equivalent to 1.5 times as much as that of the US. According to the report of Standard Chartered Bank in 2012, China contributed 48% of the global increments of M2 from 2009 to 2011 after the outbreak of the financial crisis. In 2012, China continued printing a considerable amount of money. The new increase of M2 was as much as 12.26 trillion yuan, which still accounted for up to 46.7% of the global new increments of M2. Some people perceive it as a consequence of the implementation of the proactive fiscal policy and the easing monetary policy, both of which induce a greater demand for money which, in turn, leads to the excessive issuance of money. This is the internal reason. In terms of the external reasons, foreign capital flows into China due to the foreign trade surplus and appreciation of RMB. With the current exchange rate regime, the central bank had to passively release more monetary base.[1]

Those reasons listed above are not the evidence to judge whether the money release is excessive or not. Every country, at that time, enacted an easing monetary policy. It is a rather weak conclusion to solely identify China's easing monetary policy as the culprit of the excessive money supply. Other countries or regional central banks which applied a fixed exchange rate regime pegging against the US dollars may also lead to a larger money supply. Just like China, they cannot be blamed for the excessive money release, either.

Some other papers compare the money-supply-to-GDP ratio in China. There are some scholars exemplifying the excessive money supply with the M2-to-GDP ratio which increased year by year. At the end of 2013, M2 in China reached 110 trillion yuan. The M2-to-GDP ratio was as high as 200%. Some people regard it as a result of the excessive money supply, worrying about the "would-be-accelerated" inflation rate.

There has not been an agreed value of the M2-to-GDP ratio that is taken as reasonable in the academia of economics. For example, according to the World Bank, until the end of 2011, countries and regions with a high income had an M2-

1 Chen Yunbing, *A Study of China's Excessive Money Supply and Its Effect on Inflation*, the 18th issue of *China Business Update*, 2013.

to-GDP ratio of 139.33% on average. The ratio in the US was 86.04%, 239.99% in Japan, 181.35% in Germany, 207.01% in Taiwan Region of China, 334.83% in Hong Kong, China, and 166.61% in the UK.[1] From the statistics, we cannot judge which government excessively issued money and which did not.

M2 is greater than GDP. This is a common feature in each country. Though the growth rate of M2 and that of GDP change in a similar way, the former on average is higher than the latter. So in terms of the absolute magnitude, the M2-to-GDP ratio presents a rising trend on an annual basis.

How does this happen? Some scholars explain it by employing $Y=vM$ from the perspective of The Quantity Theory of Money. In the equation, Y is national income, v is the velocity of money and M is the money supply. The reciprocal of v, $1/v$, is the M2-to-GDP ratio. Given that the money supply, M, is greater than national income, Y, then v is smaller than 1. Meanwhile, M2 has a higher growth rate than national income, so v is getting smaller and smaller. $1/v$ is bigger and bigger. This means money supply increases, namely excessive money supply.

The declining velocity is a reason for the increasing amount of money, but it cannot be used to judge whether the money supply excessive or not. The declining velocity of money is related to the Law of Irreversibility in money movement. The velocity of money declines, since the credit loans are diverted to becoming other income, such as the salary, and further becoming the savings, the increase of which means the decrease of re-spending. In this case, satisfying the demand of economic growth for money supply asks for more capital to sustain the turnover of credit capital. So the growth rate of M2 exceeds that of GDP. This is not the excessive money supply, but an inevitable decline of the velocity of money due to the diversion of credit capital to savings.

Other scholars think the interest gap of commercial banks is relatively big with an overall precipitously fast increase. Its effect is equivalent to the excessive

1 Cao Gang, "Deflation is What to be Concerned about", *Talents Mag.*, 2013, Issue 5.

money supply.[1] In theory, the interest gap refers to the residual of account deposits of commercial banks minus their loans. The amount of the interest gap equals the deposit reserve. China's commercial banks enjoy a relatively big gap. This is attributed to the inflow of foreign capital. In the 1990s, the rapid economic growth was accompanied by a considerable jump in foreign trade surplus. During the same period, The People's Bank of China implemented a mandatory settlement system. All foreign currencies had to be sold to the central bank, and the RMB received was deposited to the commercial banks. Meanwhile, with the expectation of RMB appreciation, foreign capital flooded into China, enlarging the interest gap of commercial banks.

For commercial banks, their main source of monetary base comes from the money given by the central bank. The large interest gap indicates a sufficient supply of monetary base, which is of vital importance for commercial banks to expand credit loans and reinforce their risk-resistant capacity. The super quantitative easing monetary policy in developed countries and regions, such as the US, the European Union, and Japan, is indeed pouring monetary base into commercial banks. The increase of the supply of monetary base to expand the interest gap can, on the one hand, helps the banks to overcome financial difficulties, and, on the other hand, energizes them to issue more money which further prompts the national spending such as investments and consumption, stimulating the national economic growth.

Though countries have various ways of enacting quantitative easing policies, the target, and the effect are always similar and consistent. In the US, Federal Reserve Board directly purchases national debts on market. The money spent in this transaction flows to the commercial banks, increasing their monetary base. The European Central Bank issues loans to commercial banks in each member country. Those commercial banks are responsible for buying the national debt of their own country. Money used to buy national debts ultimately goes into

1 Zhao Hongrui, *A Theory of China's Money Aggregate*, Economic Press China, 2013.

commercial banks as deposits. In this way, the supply of monetary base increases and the interest income is harvest by the banks. Therefore, the profits are gained.

China is different from those developed countries. China enjoys a sufficient supply of monetary base and a relatively large interest gap due to the long-term foreign currency inflow. The People's Banks of China raised the required reserve ratio with the increase of foreign currency in order to control the credit scale. The ratio increased from 6% in November of 1999, to 20% in May of 2012 with an adjustment on the annual basis. In detail, the required reserve ratio for large financial institutions is 20%. For medium- and small-sized institutions, it is 16.5%. Such a high ratio is rare even worldwide. Currently, CBRC (China Banking Regulatory Commission) requires a deposit-to-loan ratio not higher than 75%. The liquidity ratio has a limit of 25%. The high required reserve ratio is one of the triggers that induce "money drought" in commercial banks. At the end of a quarter and a year when the central bank started the audition, commercial banks are busying retrieving the money, and remitting the deposit reserve to the central bank. If a commercial bank fails to meet the requirement for the reserves and its loans cannot be recovered right away, it will be anxious to raise money at the inter-bank money market. If every commercial bank is lacking in money, the short-term inter-bank rate will rise by a large margin. In this circumstance, the whole financial system will be faced with a shortage of money and even turbulence if the central bank cannot manage to inject money into it.

Generally speaking, economics determines the volume of money supply primarily based on the price index. The Quantity Theory of Money insists that the greater the money supply is, the higher the price level will be. In other words, the increasing price indicates excessive money supply. This opinion prevailed in the 1980s. However, ever since the threshold of the 1990s, the total volume of money supply continued increasing, while the increase of price index experienced a downward trend. The same phenomenon was observed in many countries. Scholars felt puzzled at first. "The mystery of China's money maze" was a good example.[1] In the late 1990s, why did China sustain a two-digit growth rate but have a price index with a decelerating growth rate? The monetary theories failed to explain it. Because this is not a short-term feature. The short-term discrepancy between money supply and price index can be reasonably explained in this way that the increase of price lags behind the increase of money supply. However, the continuously decreasing price index becomes a trend. With the increase of money supply, not only the growth of price level slows down, but the money aggregate experiences a downward growth rate. All of these phenomena are beyond the capacity of the old theories.

Figure 6-1 displays a declining trend of the growth rate of national income and that of the money supply with the expansion of the economy and the absolute magnitude of the money supply. Both growth rates abide by the law of entropy changes. From the long-term trend of the increase of money supply, the disorder at the micro-level has a greater impact as the money supply grows larger. The growth rate of national income and that of money supply decline and will approach zero. The economic development in each country differs from each other, so their national income grows at different rates and, thus, the growth rate of money supply varies. We need to neither bear in mind that neither determine whether the money supply in a country is large or small by simply comparing the indicators among different countries nor give a final judgment of the "excessive money supply" only based upon some indicator. If the price index fluctuation is used to explain the rationality of money supply, particular attention must be paid to the discrepancy of economic development level, since the price index is just related to money supply instead of in a causal relationship with it. With different economic developments, they can be both positively related and negatively related. In summary, the excessive money supply has not been decently explained by an existing theory and the statistical indicators attempt an ineffective explanation.

1 Chen Daofu, "High Money Stock in China Should be Treated in Dialectical Manner", *Development Research*, 2011, Issue 3.

The so-called "excessive money supply" is nothing but a naive surprise at the economic indicators, or a helpless concern, or a false proposition with no verified answer even after repetitive argumentation.

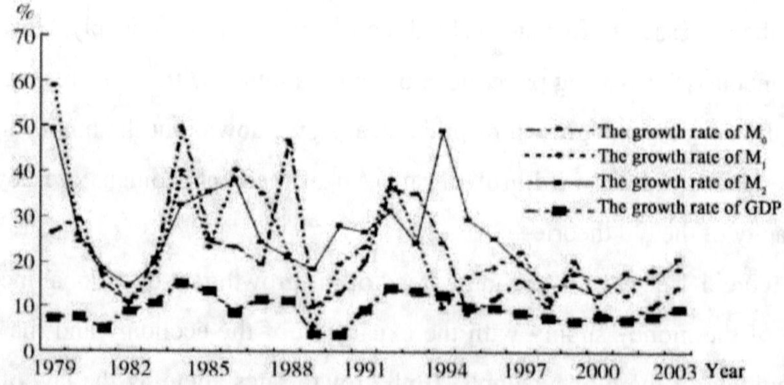

Figure 6-1 the strata of money (1979-2003)

Note: China's national income and money supply both have a declining growth rate.
Source: Ma Lieguang, A New Discussion of Economics: Multiplier, Statistical Entropy, and National Income, page 300. The Figure is originally Figure 9-3 in New Stage of Economic Growth and Financial Development in China, with Wang Guangqian as the editor-in-chief.

6.5 High Investment Rate Is a Reflection of Mighty National Economic Competitiveness

Ever since the reform and opening-up, the investments-to-GDP ratio is kept above 30% in China. In the 1990s, the investments on fixed assets made up 37% on average, which then rose further after 2000. As shown by the data from 2003 to 2010, it continued to be above 40%,[1] which significantly boosted China's competitiveness. In 2014, GDP reached 63.65 trillion yuan according to State Statistic Bureau. This is the first time that GDP exceeded 60 trillion yuan. If counted on the USD basis, it is 10 trillion dollars. Tracing back to 2000, GDP

1 Liu Shucheng, Zhang Liancheng, Zhang Ping, eds., *China's Economic Growth and Economic Cycles (2011),* Economic Press China, 2012, p. 6.

reached 8.9 trillion yuan and the economic magnitude was more than 1 trillion dollars which, in 2005, exceeded 2 trillion dollars. "Could anyone foresee the economic magnitude could double within only 5 years? Or could anyone expect that in 2014 GDP would break the barrier of 10 trillion dollars? In reality, we took only 14 years to lift GDP from 1 trillion dollars to 10 trillion."[1] A high investments-to-GDP ratio means that the country has a variety of projects to invest in. Its economy is energetic. Investments boost productivity and promote consumption. Given that investments obtain the capital by applying for loans, part of which change into residents' income in the form of salary, tax, and other earnings, investments promote consumption. The retailing amount rose from 2.9 trillion yuan to 26.24 trillion, increasing by 10 times. It is due to the high investments-to-GDP ratio that China's economic competitiveness is greatly enhanced with a relatively high global trade surplus.

Germany shares a similar situation. Germany is an economic giant in Europe and a major borrowing country. The majority of loans borrowed are used for investments and boosting consumption. Among the EU member states, Germany enjoys the highest investments-to-GDP ratio which was maintained at 45% or above for about 20 years. A high investment ratio guarantees the vitality of its economy and products made in German is famous for unique competitiveness other countries cannot compare with. Though Deutsche Mark has been replaced by Euro, the latter against US dollars appreciated by more than twice of the former. Germany, as a result, still keeps a trade surplus. The high investments-to-GDP ratio makes Germany the power with the most mighty economy and the strongest competitiveness.

6.6 The Key to Stimulate Economic Development is Loan Growth

In simple terms, as long as the loans cease to grow, the economic crisis is

1 Cited from *Reference News*, January 23rd, 2015, originally from Yu Mu, "Breaking 10 Trillion Dollars---A New Hora of China", *Hong Kong Economic Times*, January 22nd.

inevitable, no matter how large the money stock is. Though the effect of monetary capital made upon the economic growth is, to some extent, related to capital scale, the capital movement and its growth are more important. If capital has difficulty in participating in the social system and ceases to grow, the economy stops developing.

The amount of money derived from the monetary base is determined by two factors. One is the reserve ratio of commercial banks which is the proportion of deposits compared to loans. The higher the ratio is, the less the derivative loans will be; otherwise, loans will be more. The reciprocal of the reserve ratio is the multiplier of the money amount created by the monetary base. The other factor is the demand for loans from commercial banks. In a depressed era, fewer borrowers apply for loans. To the commercial banks passively hoard money and fewer loans are issued. So the credit activities are prone to slowing down or even stagnating. The money amount derived from the monetary base is of a smaller scale. In contrast, in prosperity, investments boom. Significant demand for credit is created. With a given reserve ratio, the amount of money derived will multiply. Generally speaking, countries with a high economic growth rate also have a quicker growth of the broad money, M2; those with slower economic development are faced with a downward growth rate of M2. So the central bank increases the monetary base mainly for the sake of providing capital to commercial banks. Another purpose is to provide money for the government by purchasing the national debts at the market. The central banks have a limited effect on the growth of M2. For example, though the ECB (European Central Bank) injects a large amount of money into the commercial banks, banks are still in the swamp of slow growth of money since the commercial banks are trapped by the depressing situation of credit borrowing. According to the statistics published by the ECB, in the January of 2014, loans of the private sector (i.e. families and private companies) fell by 2.2% on a year-to-year basis and by 2.3% compared to the statistic last month. At the same time, in the Eurozone, January saw an increase of M_3 supply by 1.2% on a year-to-year basis and by 1% on a month-to-month basis. The growth is slow.

Japan encountered a similar situation. "In March 2013, Bank of Japan issued the monetary base worth 134.74 trillion yen, increasing by 124.04% compared to 60.14 trillion yen at the end of 1998. The ultimate effect of the monetary policy is realized by adjusting the money supply in the operation of the national economy. However, the indicator, broad money M2, did not grow by such a margin that could echo the incremental issuance of monetary base. At the end of February 2013, Japan witnessed an average volume of M2 as 828.2 trillion yen, while, at the end of 1998, M2 was 611.6 trillion yen. This meant an increase of only 35.42%. Japan implemented an easing monetary policy in two periods-March, 2001 to March 2006 and December 2008 to the present. Compared to the time when the quantity easing did not take place, the monthly outstanding monetary base in QE periods apparently exceeded that in the non-QE period, but the average turnover of M2 only kept a moderate growth."[1]

The main factor that affects the M2 growth is the economic development's demand for money. After 2008, the super QE policy of the US federal government boosts the liabilities of the Federal Reserve Board. However, the monetary base remains in the commercial banks, and the credit scale experiences no expansion, which leads to a lower deposit-to-loan ratio. The addition of monetary base from the Federal Reserve Board aims to prevent the existing amount of bad debts from further expansion and keep away from the threat of bankruptcy. The steadiness and safety of the banks' assets are also guaranteed with the abundant money supply on hand. But depending solely upon the supply of monetary base makes no direct difference on the real economic recovery. In coincidence with the increase of the Federal Reserve Board's liabilities, the People's Bank of China significantly has raised the supply of monetary base since 2008 by a similar amount to that of the US. The difference lies in its effect on the loans. China enjoys the growth rate of loans three times as high as that in the US. This

1 Guo Kewei, "Effects and Limits of Super Easing Monetary Policy in Japan", *The Banker*, 2013, Issue 6.

is interpreted as robust economic growth in China. For example, the economic growth rate in 2013 in China stayed at 7.7%, while, in the same year, the US only kept 2%. The economic strength of China lays a foundation of the credit expansion which sustains a growth rate of 20% approximately. One of the critical elements to prompt credit capital is investments which attract a large number of trusts and wealth management institutions. In the middle of 2012, many loans stemmed from non-banking organizations whose capital is available at the cost of higher interest fees than that of commercial banks. The ardent pursuit for capital fully indicates the great demand for borrowing and lending. However, in the US, the loans grew rather slowly despite the large monetary base which did not boost the investments but led to a continuously declining interest rate. According to the statistics published by Federal Reserve Board on October 4th, 2013, total loans of the commercial banks were 7.3181 trillion dollars with an annual growth rate of only 2.3%. Until September 25th, 2013, new loans were worth 48.6 billion dollars and the first quarter contributed 31.8 billion, while the second and the third only made up for 16.8 trillion in total.

The managing director of Silvercrest Asset Management, Patrick Chovanec, pointed out that the third round of QE by the Federal Reserve Board made the US monetary base rise to 3.5 trillion dollars, almost 4 times as much as that before the financial crisis. In other words, if the US residents kept borrowing loans and spending, as usual, the nominal GDP of the US ought to be 4 times as much as today. The reason why the inflation has not skyrocketed with no limit until now is that the loans remain unchanged. 84% of monetary base injected by the Federal Reserve Board directly turns into the deposit reserve which has not been used yet.[1]

As shown in Figure 6-2, commercial banks in the Euro Zone lent less and less from 2009 to 2013. The economist of Crédit Agricole, Fredrik Ducrozet, argues that despite the greatly increased abundance of the capital of commercial banks, they still refuse the normal management of their balance sheets due to the lack

1 *Wall Street*, https://wallstreetcn.com.

of demand for borrowing. This exerts much pressure upon the European Central Bank to continue a QE policy. The excessive deposit reserve approaches zero. So is the inter-bank interest rate. The cost of borrowing a loan is very low. Except for Germany, the credit in the banking industry is still in the gloom or even ceases to grow.

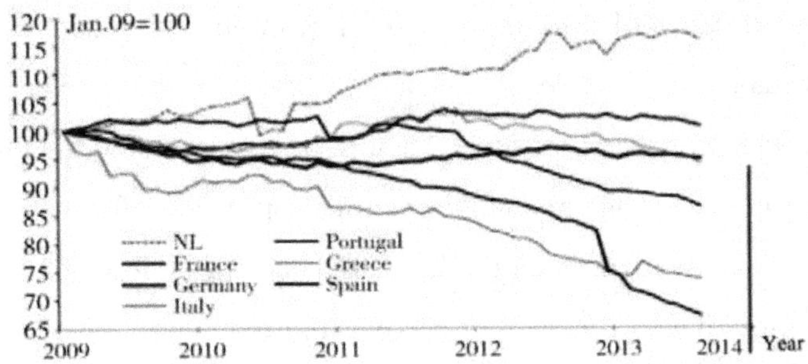

Figure 6-2 Changes of company borrowing in some European countries (the credit scale in January 2009 is taken as 100)

Note: NL , France , Germany , Italy , Portugal , Greece, Spain
Note: Wall Street, https://wallstreetcn.com.

6.7 Changes of Central Banks' Measures

6.7.1 Central Banks' Direct Purchases for Government Bonds

The US Federal Reserve, the Bank of Japan, and the Bank of England set foot on the way of large-scale purchases for government bonds on their own with no plan to turn back. No turning back means central banks are unlikely to sell the same amount of bonds at the market at some appropriate point after directly buying government bonds of a large scale. Due to the depressed economy, a financial crisis would be induced if central banks quit the plan of bond purchase and sell the bonds at hand step by step. A weak economy may squeeze out the chances of selling bonds on a large scale, as for central banks. In the long run, central banks store the bonds so much that they become the main holders of government bonds. When bonds are due, central banks can receive the money spent on the bond purchase. However, thanks to the necessity of buying new bonds again, any reduction of the purchase by the central banks would confront their governments with the payment difficulty, on condition that the government spending could not be cut off by a large margin. So, bonds constitute a significant value in the balance sheets of central banks. This is a “sustainable” situation.

Apart from the three banks mentioned above, The European Central Bank, as well as central banks of medium-developed countries, will take this “road of no return” gradually. And The People’s Bank of China is no exception. The reason for such large-scale purchases for assets mainly lies in providing the monetary base for the market, except for maintaining normal operation of the government and companies. In particular, when the loan issuance slows down or even declines, the commercial banks can neither recover old loans nor issue new ones. The process of capital turnover in society ruptures even though the market is abundant in money. At this time, social capital settles down in the form of savings. If the loans cease to increase, this part of social capital is out of effective turnover and the society as a whole has to endure the old debts since the old debts cannot be paid by the new loans. Therefore, commercial banks are faced with the danger of bankruptcy due to the money shortage.

In the cycle of the monetary capital flow, debts are the counterpart of the monetary wealth, i.e. income savings. The accumulation of monetary wealth is the accumulation of debts. People cannot, on the one hand, accumulate wealth and, on the other hand, take effective control of their debt. In the market economy, canceling national debts and reducing fiscal expenditure will definitely drag down the residents’ income, especially the income of the poor and the middle class. Therefore, it is unavailing to reduce the fiscal expenditure just to get free from the debt crisis.

The solution is simple, as far as I’m concerned. The central bank directly purchases government bonds. The government transfers the monetary base to companies and residents by lifting the income, improving the welfare, etc., so that the society has a stronger purchasing power.

In fact, open market operations (e.g. direct purchases for bonds) raise the awareness of the central banks to change the conventional ways of monetary base issuance. Injecting monetary base into the commercial banks or issuing indirect loans at the financial market has distinct disadvantages. The side effect is that debts continue accumulating. It means debt accumulation instead of crisis resolution.

If the central bank issues monetary base by taking open market operations, the government can manage the capital and provide the monetary base to society in the form of welfare allowances and housing allowance, or by subsidizing medical institutions, key constructions, livelihood projects, sustainable agriculture, and other areas.

Meanwhile, the central bank builds its own financial companies to trade stocks at the market in a direct manner. This can both increase the supply of monetary base and keep the market stable. Also, the central bank has appreciated assets. Enterprises of good credit are still rare resources. The central bank ought to directly hold the stock. The central bank collects part of the social debts by direct purchases, sharing the government debts, or holding part of the bonds held by companies of importance. In order to hedge the debts, if needed, the central bank can raise the price of gold by n times alongside the money issuance, so that the asset account is balanced. Society and the government can hand over part of the land ownership to the central bank to improve the asset value.

There are two prerequisites before doing so. Firstly, spare no effort to add the varieties of commodities. With sufficient commodity supply, the economy is beyond the reach of severe inflation. Then, respect the scarcity of resources. In the market economy, the income of the public mainly comes from work rewards and investment returns. Therefore, it is forbidden to distribute monetary base to consumers directly.

The supporting measure is the mechanism of bankruptcy reform which forces large enterprises and banks with amounts of debts to go bankrupt, reducing the social debts by eliminating unqualified participants. In other words, it is reasonable and rational for the central bank to avoid acquiring company debts blindly and encourage competition systems and rules to cope with social debts.

A small reform is a life or death decision. Effective ways burgeon from trivial changes.

6.7.2 Negative interest rates

In June 2014, The European Central Bank finally implemented the policy of negative interest rates. ECB adjusted the inter-bank overnight rate from 0.0% to -0.1%. On January 29, 2016, The Bank of Japan announced the new excess reserve ratio of -0.1% targeting part of the financial institutions as "a fine". The old excess reserve ratio was approximately 0.1%. The Bank of Japan claimed further reduction of the negative interest rate. The US economy recovered in a short period. Increasing the interest rate could only stimulate the economy for the short run, after which the economy plunged back to the gloom where lower interest rate drew attention again. In the long term, the US is of high likelihood to enter an era of negative interest rates.

The central bank charges interest of the commercial banks based on their account balances in the central bank, aiming to deal with the commercial banks' reluctance of lending money. Developed countries issue fewer loans mainly due to insufficient demand for capital. In a depressed economy, commercial banks bear more responsibility for lending to companies of medium or small sizes. Then the central bank applies negative interest rates but, unfortunately, gets little progress in boosting loan issuance. ECB's enacting of negative interest rates made some difference on the Euro since negative rates dissipate some demand for the Euro so that the Euro depreciates or at least has less probability to continuously appreciate.

The negative inter-bank overnight rate produces a limited effect. The interest rate of deposits must be included in the spectrum of the negative rate policy. In other words, I am concerned about whether the deposits probably face negative rates more than the policy itself. If the commercial banks charged interest, what would the depositors do? They would withdraw the money and put it in another bank that paid those interests, or a bank that neither charged interests nor paid interests. Then the banks charging interests would lose their deposits or even go bankrupt due to the drainage of money. However, in a depressed economy, if most central banks in the world applied negative rates, reaching an agreement of charging interests of depositors, such a reform would be a watershed.

Firstly, negative rates stimulate consumption and, to some extent, boost the economy. For depositors, negative rates reduce the demand for savings. The more money is deposited, the more fees are paid. Then, negative rates generate profits for the commercial banks by collecting deposits only. It is such a surprise that the financial system is easily stabilized without much effort. It has a positive effect on the banks' immunity to the financial crisis and the stability of the financial institutions. Thirdly, negative rates are a coin with two sides. The advantageous effect is to enhance the profit-making ability and the tolerance of larger bad debts. Disadvantageously, the commercial banks are more conservative and become reluctant to lend money. Deposits can bring them profits, so why do they bother to issue loans? However, just like the profit-making corporations that were born to earn money, commercial banks, in order to maximize their profits, will not take the conservative way that the credit loans are reduced as the mainstream action. Faced with loans that can bring profits, commercial banks will never miss the chance.

The prime risk is the moral risk when the policies supporting negative interest rates are implemented. Contemporary commercial banks have never charged the depositors of interests. It goes against their behavioral code. Depositors have no other choice if negative interest rates are accepted by all banks. Wealth owned by depositors becomes the targeted preys. However, when the economy is in the long-term gloom, under the pressure from insufficient investments, gloomy consumption, and accumulating debts and deposits, it is not impossible for the central banks in each country to enact the negative interest rate policy.

Then, another probable trouble is excessive cash. Having to pay the banks interests drives the residents to keep their money at home or put them aside in the bank safes, instead of depositing money in banks. The hardness to keep cash and to keep cash safe by the residents themselves protects the society from depositors' panic and bank runs as long as the policy is executed step by step, though the cash in circulation increases. Moreover, the consecutive loan issuance enlarges the monetary aggregate in commercial banks. So the excessive cash in circulation will not lead to a decline in deposits.

Comprehensively, in the long-term depressed economy, charging depositors of interests appropriately promotes investments and consumption. Once people keep more cash at hand, consumption will grow. The existence of a variety of financial products squeezes part of the cash out of the deposits and directs it to trusts and funds, even though cash in trusts and funds is also stored in banks. Diversified ways to make deposits alleviate the burden of debts originating from deposit-making and partially increase the total investments.

Though the negative rate policy is not inapplicable, it still bears many risks that cannot be underestimated. "One size fits all" simplifies the implementation and ignores the potential danger. Central banks may allow commercial banks to charge extra fees to test the waters just as what the ECB is now doing and see what can be carried out next. If it goes well, commercial banks are encouraged to charge depositors of differential interests based on the terms of deposit. The negative interest rate policy is to be implemented within a small scale in order to keep the society away from significant impacts. Losing depositors is a catastrophe for commercial banks.

Chapter 7

Phenomena and Principles of Self-limiting

Self-limiting is a civilized way of biological evolution.

——**Ma Lieguang**

7.1 The Definition and Phenomena of Self-limiting

Why is development always limited? Well, it is not easy to answer it. Maybe religious explanations comfort you. They owe every achievement to God who is almighty. He set rules on how nature and human beings co-exist. Human beings never thoroughly destroy nature out of endless greed. Similarly, human beings get far away long before the catastrophic natural disaster actually takes place. Why does human development follow the law of self-limiting? Only those idiots who have no idea of the thought that "God makes humans happy" keep asking such a question.

However, philosophy may be lacking in the firmness and confidence of religions. Philosophers were born to be skeptics and it is their daily routine of questioning "whys". In order to be oblivious of political opinions and religious ideologies, philosophy always tries to keep a distance from religions. Unlike philosophy, economics pays more attention to scientific methods, so the economic analysis is always in search answers in reality that is rather cold and icy. Why is every economic phenomenon self-limited? Why is there no eternal growth within a limited space? What girds the economic growth? Or what is the law of self-limiting for economic growth?

Self-limiting refers that the micro components of a system reach the maximum disorder and the system has developed to its extreme on given conditions. Such limitation is determined by random laws inside system. Random movements reflect internal disorder, but the disorder only relates to the system's own scale, unaffected by other factors.

Though external conditions are still loose and do not restrain the development of the system, all systems, after reaching a certain scale, stop developing, due to the influence of the tendency towards maximum disorder. The determining factor is supposed to be within the system. Since the internal movements of a system comply with the law of irreversibility, the maximization of the disorder is irreversible under given external conditions.

Individual elements within whichever system conform to a highly united and orderly pattern. The whole system is embedded with significant kinetic energy, absorbing more energy from the outside. Generally, consistent systems are called microsystems. Though a system possesses a large number of subsystems, it is a microsystem if it presents obvious consistency.

As mentioned in 3.1, to differ a microsystem from a macro one does not resort to how many subsystems it owns but to whether it presents consistency or inconsistency. Consistent systems are microsystems, while inconsistent systems are macro systems. When the consistent microsystem expands sufficiently, its internal configuration changes, showing some inconsistent patterns. Here, according to the definition, the microsystem is taken as a new macro system.

Within a macro system there exist a large number of micro subsystems.

The micro subsystems are independent and in random changes, so they lack consistency. Their movements are neither predictable nor ordered, not to mention the independent individual elements inside them, which also shows randomness and inconsistency. Though the microsystems have their own kinetic energy and are bounded by the system, every microsystem has independent movements that are not related to other systems. Therefore, the relations among microsystems, if there is any, are tiny and insignificant. That is to say, amongst microsystems, there do not exist interactions with widespread effects.

Once individuals head for freedom, the whole system steps into decline and extinction from development.

If the elements at the micro-level grow more independent, negative phenomena take place–their interaction weakens, the internal disorder aggravates, energy absorbed from the outside reduces, the system's vigor starts to decrease rather than continuously grow, and the growth and movements of the system itself slow down until ultimate termination.

For an open system, orderly macro systems are going to end up in the qualitative change or collapse. The reasons for collapse stem from both the exterior and the interior. Changes in the surroundings induce the appearance of a new order within the microsystem. New kinetic energy drives down the disorder at the micro-level, leading to qualitative changes or even the collapse of the old system. The microsystems will stay stable for a long time as long as their outside world stays stable. However, after the disorder at the micro-level of the system approaches its maximum, the microsystems' loss of efficiency and degeneration accumulate. Since degeneration itself is an incidence relation, it will from consecutive changes which then disturb the stability of the system. The macrosystem gradually loses its balance and steps into extinction.

From the perspective of the spatial relation, any static and homogeneous space is easy to be squeezed and broken by external force. Homogeneous space contains the least kinetic energy so that the external energy squeezes into the space effortlessly. Then the space exposed to squeezing and crushing becomes uneven.

If the space is closed and isolated, the degenerated microelements scattering within it will also disturb the homogeneity of the space part of which turns into an uneven status.

The disorder at the micro-level of space is a result of the expansion of the space as a whole. When disorder at the micro-level approaches its maximum, the scale of the entire space develops into its own extreme after which the system steps into a decline and extinction.

The self-limiting of the micro individual, as well as the individual extinction, is not only for the sake of the maintenance of the normality of the whole. Meanwhile, some behavioral proneness and the existing time of the individuals will also influence the scale of the whole. For example, the increase of the average life longevity does not affect the population initially. But, once some age as a threshold is reached, say 65 or 70, the birth rate will drop, the population to update a generation will decline, and the total population will decline rather than continue growing. In developed countries, the decline of population is not due to the disruption and limitation of the external living conditions but to the prolonging of the lifespan whereas the prolonging lifespan of the individuals leads to the shrinking of the whole scale.

The rule of the system's self-limiting is displayed as follows. The average of the individual lifespan times the number of the individuals is a constant. Assume $\overline{x}$ is the average lifespan, N is the number of the individuals, c is the constant, we have-

$$C = \overline{x}N \tag{7-1}$$

Here, $\overline{x}$ presents the average lifespan. The longer the lifespan is, the smaller the population will be; otherwise, the population will be larger.

The prosperity and the decline of a system are essentially a transmission from order to disorder. The external sign of the disorder is still the variables linking to the circulation of the system, such as the frequency of the cell division in biology, the frequency of money turnover, and the distance a man has walked in his or her entire life, and so forth.

Here is one example. The growth of a cell is restrained by how many times the cell divides. A mature human body on average has 100 trillion cells.[1] They all come from fertilized eggs. After the sperm unites with the egg at the initial stage, the embryo grows into the sophisticated and grand life system through cell division. When a child grows into an adult, the cell division starts self-limiting. Their total amount stagnates to increase. A part of the cells, such as the brain cells and the muscle cells, cease to divide. Other cells continue dividing but follow some rules, namely fiber cells. Thanks to the division of fiber cells, the dead cells are replaced so that we do not look old within a short period. The fiber cells can also cure wounds.

In the laboratory, we can observe the cell division. Once people wrongly reckoned that cell division was endless in the lab-made circumstance and cells never grew old. The US cell biologists Leonard Hevlick and Philip Muirhead published an unprecedented essay in 1961, testifying the reproduction life of fiber cells of a normal human body was limited and the fiber cells would die just like other cells and the human body. Also, for the first time, it confirmed that the lifespan of cells was related to the number of times of their division. The limited frequency of cell division never enabled an unlimited cell division. When it comes to why cells cease to divide, biologists hold different opinions. Some think it is due to an inset program of the cell's DNA which limits the times of cell division. However, this opinion has not yet found evidence from the DNA. Others argue that cells are randomly damaged in the process of cell division. Accumulated damages stop the cells from further division.

Self-limiting is a widespread phenomenon that can be easily found in biological systems and non-biological systems. Though each system, based upon its own unique situation, put forward or rebut some arguments, they, in general, all obey one law: the law of entropy. The disorder at the micro-level eventually leads the

1 Tom Kirwood, *Time of Our Lives - The Science of Human Aging*, translated by Xie Deqiu, Shanghai Scientific and Technological Education Publishing House, 2001, p. 105.

whole system (the macro system) to growth stagnation and irreversible decline and extinction.

7.2 The Theory of Self-limiting in Economics

In economics, income and expenditure are equivalents in one transaction. Your income is spent on products. So no matter how much you spend, it is earned by the seller. In other words, your expenditure equals the seller's income. This equation stand for itself at whatever level. Therefore, in the national income accounting, the argument that total income equals total expenditure reveals the practical situation in a relatively true manner.

In a certain period, total income generated from the income at the initial period after the circulation of re-spending is related to the turnover times. It is comparatively understandable. For example, if a man spends his income of 10, 000 yuan to purchase products, the seller sells products worth 10, 000 yuan and gains 10, 000 yuan as the income, after which the 10, 000 yuan is spent by this first seller to buy products, and the second seller, who sells the products, obtains the 10, 000 yuan. Suppose each future income unit spends all the income and does not deposit money, then the cycle of income → expenditure → income → expenditure...will continue and generate a total income *n* times of the initial number. In one period, if the cycle goes for 5 times, then 50, 000 yuan is created. If 6 times, then 60, 000 yuan is created. If n times, the total income reaches 10*n thousand yuan. The 10, 000 yuan at the beginning, after *n* times of turnover, grows into the total income worth 10*n thousand yuan.

People need to save part of the income for expenditure in the next period, or they are just reluctant to spend them all. So some people deposit part of the income and spend the rest. Suppose every person makes deposits. When the sum-up of every person's deposit reaches the initial 10, 000 yuan, the spending and re-spending of the initial 10, 000 yuan come to an end. For example, everybody spends 80% of the income and deposits the other 20%. Each time when the initial

10, 000 yuan is spent, we lose 20% of it as savings. In the end, 10 thousand yuan only creates 50, 000 yuan as the total income. This is because no income is used for re-spending once all the income turns into savings. After continuously adding up the math sequences, we get a number 5, which is called a multiplier. It means a multiple, too.

The deduction above shows the spending and re-spending are limited by the multiplier as long as people deposit the money, turning part of the income into savings, and the income at the beginning of a certain period remains unchanged. Here, the multiplier is the deposit ratio. In the example, 20% is the deposit ratio. The higher the deposit ratio is, the smaller the multiplier will be and consequently, the total income will be smaller; otherwise, the multiplier is larger and the total income is larger.

Suppose people do not deposit. They spend all their money. The larger the circulation times, n, is, the greater the total income will be. Theoretically speaking, n could be in endless cycles. But in practice, it has a limit and is countable. This means deposits are meant to take place. In economic activities, a situation with no savings never exists.

Another factor affecting n is the scale of the initial expenditure. If the initial spending is not 10, 000 yuan but 1 trillion yuan, 5 trillion yuan, or even 10 trillion yuan, then n is likely to approach an extreme number as the initial expenditure continues increasing. Here the NI entropy equation describes this connection.[1]

$$S = n = \log_2 Y \tag{7-2}$$

Here Y is national income, S is entropy, and n is the number of re expenditures of the initial national income From this equation, we know that n is equal to the NI entropy. As the economy expands, the disorder at the micro-level tends to aggravate. Its maximization leads to the growth stagnation of the macroeconomy magnitude.

The self-limiting led by the scale expansion is a prevailing law followed by

1 Ma Lieguang, *The Great Collapse of Capitalism*, Economic Press China, 2012, p. 23.

all systems in the globe. Without it, the earth would have been fully occupied by endlessly expanding systems. And intelligent creatures are no exception in obeying the law of self-limiting. The population growth also follows it. The past demographic theories were troubled by a big concern that the geometrically growing population would lead to the shortage of energy and food and the destruction of nature given that the natural resources were limited, and thus the disaster brought by overpopulation would ruin us.

Currently, when energy and food supply are sufficient, the population tends to set a limit on itself as the world population increases. The more developed the economy is, the lower the birth rate is. The total birth rate of the middle-income countries and the developed ones — the average number of children born by each woman in her entire life — has already been lower than that required by the population replacement. Due to the development of society, the average lifespan is longer. People prefer not to give birth to more babies. This mental factor eventually results in the declining population in developed areas. Though poor countries still bear a faster-growing population comparatively, this will not last long before the better medical condition, the longer lifespan, and the declining birth rate takes place, as long as the world economy continues growing. Maybe it would be less than half a decade for the world to witness the self-determined limit of the human population, after which the exponentially growing population would switch to a new track where it declined exponentially.

Let's come back to economics. The spending and re-spending of money income are bounded by two factors — income amounts in previous stages and the circulation times in the current stage. In terms of the gross number, income amounts in previous stages affect the turnover frequency in the current stage. When the total income accumulated in the previous stage reaches a certain scale, the increase of the turnover frequency during spending and re-spending in the current stage converges to a constant. The re-spending frequency will not increase in the same amount as that of the total expenditure. It sounds like the footstep of an adult. The bigger the weight he or she has and the heavier the burden he or she bears, the slower they march ahead. From the mechanism at the micro-level, since the expenditure is in a fixed proportion to the money income, savings, and the savings distribution determine the multiplier in the initial turnover of spending and re-spending. When savings are prone to be randomly distributed, the multiplier approaches its limit.

Conventional macroeconomic theories mainly explore the relation between spending and income from the perspective of commodities, taking for granted the mechanism forming in the process of money income spending and re-spending. For example, Keynesian definitions of gross expenditure and gross income are based upon commodities. They think money realizes its value when measuring the value of commodities.

To define the national income with a new theory does not contradict the emphasis on commodities laid by the conventional theories. In new theoretical models, commodities are substituted with the money income. If we define that the money income and expenditure stand for the same value of commodities, then the amount of money as income and expenditure is the number of commodities. If we confine the money income to the value category of the national income, then the money income equals the national income. The either-or assumption is required before building a theoretical model. When we try to explore the relationship between money and commodity movements, some assumptions are allowed to be set beforehand to clarify the relationship between the money income and the national income for the purpose of briefly and clearly presenting the changes of the national income.

Surely, other methods are not totally excluded from illuminating the thought above. Apart from the spending and re-spending of money income, we can express the rule of national income changes from the turnover frequency of commodity transactions.

The national income in a certain stage can be calculated from the average merchandise volumes and the total transaction times. The multiplication of the two variables is the gross merchandise volume. The math equation is as follows.[1]

$$Q = N\overline{y} \tag{7-3}$$

N stands for the transaction times, $\overline{y}$ is the average merchandise volume, and Q is the merchandise volume measured by the amount of money. What I would like to express here is the average merchandise volume tends to approach a constant and the times of transactions determines the gross merchandise volume, if we have very sufficient commodities. This equation excludes the effect on the gross merchandise volume if the average volume varies.

Suppose the total amount of merchandise belongs to the category of the national income. Then, the gross merchandise volume equals the national income, i.e.-

$$Y = N\overline{y} \tag{7-4}$$

Y stands for the national income, $\overline{y}$ is the average merchandise volume within the category of the national income, and N is the total transaction times of the national income.

The average merchandise volume $\overline{y}$ is the multiplication of the average price and quantity shown as follows-

$$\overline{y} = \overline{p}\,\overline{q} \tag{7-5}$$

$\overline{y}$ is the average merchandise volume, $\overline{p}$ is the average price, and $\overline{q}$ is the average quantity of merchandise traded. The average price and the average quantity do not refer to some specific transactions for a specific commodity. Apparently, things are too specific to generalize them, such as some kilos of vegetables, rice, some clothes, daily necessities, a bicycle, a computer, a smartphone, a car, a house, and so on. The average merchandise volume also does not lie in specific transactions but the statistical average of all those transactions. With the total amount of merchandise and the number of times of transactions known, the average merchandise volume can be worked out.

---

1 Ma Lieguang, *A New Discussion of Economics: Multiplier, Statistical Entropy, and National Income*, Economic Press China, 2006, pp. 112-122.

Significantly, the phrase, "average merchandise volume", is to express the trades at the micro-level by utilizing average terms. At the micro-level, $\overline{p}$ and $\overline{q}$ are two constants. When $\overline{q}$ price rises, $\overline{q}$ decreases; when price decreases, $\overline{q}$ increases. When the $\overline{q}$ economy develops and reaches some scale, the price stops rising or even deflation starts to appear. The average merchandise volume is also steady. The volume variation of each transaction at the market does not affect the change of the gross merchandise volume. Compared with the frequency, the volume variation at the micro level is too small to be taken into account of the gross volume, especially the increments of the average merchandise volume. After all, the number of times is the main factor affecting the gross merchandise volume.

In conclusion, if the circulation times of the money income and the times of merchandise transactions are limited, then such limitation will ultimately drive the growth of the national income into stagnation. Why are they limited? Because the disorder at the micro-level echoes the increase of circulation times and merchandise volume. When n, the number of merchandise transactions, becomes greater, the disorder among the specific economic activities aggravates. As n approaches its limit, the economy magnitude ceases to grow further since the disorder at the micro level also maximizes.

Chapter 8

Demographic Crisis in a Depressed Era

Urbanization progresses fast. Mansions stand and scatter in cities almost overnight. The streets are crowded. Air pollution prevails. An expanding population stuffs the living space. As cities continue swelling, city residents feel like being surrounded by more and more people and a worry hangs over them correspondingly. It has quietly become extravagant to settle down again in the rural areas. However, in an utter resentment and indignation, the natural law secretly alters. The population declines annually. Youngsters give their way to the elderly who now form the larger group.

In a place crowded with people, the crisis of an abrupt population decline seems to be far beyond their perception. Though enough reasons exist, people hardly reach an agreement on such a crisis. With a large population filling up our world, preaching the necessity to prevent the crisis receives a cold greeting.

But I always have a feeling. It is not the anxiety about the future but an inner sense — "I walk in the crowd, as if wandering amongst the scraps from the future, a future as far as I could foresee."[1]

Some people say it is normal to witness the rise and fall of population and there is no need to worry whether it is going to be overpopulated or underpopulated. After all, the world population has reached 7 billion. Normally a decline is acceptable for such a large number of people now. Any discussion about the rise and fall of the population is a waste of time and exaggerating the outcome. Does it have any meaning to explain the probable population decline? The crisis is only a scribble on paper. It is an imagined war that will by no means appear in the future.

Humans can never observe and understand the low birth rate and the aging population based on their experiences from the past and the current fondness. Any naive perception taking the population fluctuation as a generation replacement without much harm can be answered by the forthcoming severity. What I would like to point out is the differences in the population decline between the contemporary era and the past centuries. In the past, the whole population, as well as its fluctuation, was within a lower age range. Before industrialization, poverty was the main culprit killing people, inducing a high death rate. Many people died during their adolescence or early adulthood. What corresponded to it was a high birth rate. Each family bore 3 to 5 children. Humans were like other animals in nature to sustain their existence and development by giving birth to more offspring.

After industrialization, the birth rate declined in line with the aging population. Hence, the changes in population growth were in essence different from the past. The population aging reflects the fact that the elderly become larger in both the absolute and the relative terms. The fertility desire goes tumbling down. As long as society advances as usual, the decline of the population continues. Without any threats for the existence, the group aging is likely to usher the species to the border of extinction.

1 Friedrich Nietzsche, *Also Sprach Zarathustra*, translated and compiled by Zhu Lili, China Commercial Publishing House, 2010, p. 109.

When we are thrilled to enjoy the magical technological advancements and get bored of the biological evolution which is too slow, we "are the people on a fast track but actually from the Stone Age"[1]

But the technological advancements bring another outcome totally beyond expectation — the aging population as a result of a longer lifespan and a lower birth rate. The slowness of the biological evolution contrasts the fastness of the technological advancements, astonishing God. Human beings are in danger of losing control over themselves. The awareness is raised by developing the law of self-limiting. Maybe human beings had better take a rest on their way to further developments. Retardation in development and a fall in population might lead to a brighter future. Will the future be brighter?

China's family planning makes little significant difference in altering the downward trend of the birth rate. The data since 1970 reveals a declining birth rate common in countries including China, India, Indonesia, Iran, and Thailand. China's birth rate drops down almost as much as that in Thailand. Iran witnessed a slump since the 1980s and got closer to China and Thailand after 2000.[2]

8.1 The Current Situation and Problems of the Declining Birth Rate

In a depressed era, economic growth is prone to ceasing. In correspondence, the population growth tends to decline as the per capita income increases. This is a statistical law. Almost every middle-developed countries witness the decline of the fertility rate after the per capita income continues growing for a certain period. Population growth stagnation starts before the economic stagnation in developed countries and regions. Ever since the mid-60s of the 20th century, the fertility rate and the birth rate both decreased to their prewar status and kept on declining.

1 Tom Kirwood, *Time of Our Lives — The Science of Human Aging*, translated by Xie Deqiu, Shanghai Scientific and Technological Education Publishing House, 2001.

2 Cai Yong, "Low Fertility Rate and Its Social and Economic Impacts", originally from Liang Zai, *Demography*, China Renmin University Press, 2012, p. 119.

They have been lower and lower compared to the rates required in generation replacement. The population growth approaches zero.

Thanks to the social progress, a series of improvements happen consecutively in the nutritious condition, medical care, public hygiene, and fundamental facilities, after which human life longevity quickly gets prolonged. "Only within a century, the growth of the expected life longevity equal or exceed the add-up increments of lifespan during 4,000 years from Bronze Age to the 19th century."[1] The US is a typical example to verify the statement. In 1900, the average lifespan of the US women was 77, which rose to 79 during the Second World War and further climbed to 85 in 2003.[2]

What echoes the prolonged average lifespan is the quick fall of the fertility rate in the middle-developed countries and the developed countries. At the beginning of the 21st century, about half of the world population lives where the fertility rate and the birth rate are below the level required by the generation replacement.[3] According to the United Nations *Demographic Yearbook*, from 1950 to 1955, each woman in the world gave birth to 5 babies approximately, while between 2005 and 2010, the number was 2.55. After half a century, the general fertility rate all over the globe almost got halved.[4]

The post-world war II baby boom did not sustain for a very long time. China's high fertility rate continued till the end of the 1960s, primarily because the policy supports it. Besides, the population that rebounded after the plunge induced by the economic turbulence in the early 60s also made a contribution. In other words, China welcomed another stage with a high birth rate after an economic trough. The statistics reveal that the population changes in China still comply with the law established in the industrial society. After the 1970s, the birth rate and death rate

1 Liang Zai, *Demography*, China Renmin University Press, 2012, p. 53.

2 Ibid, p. 145.

3 Ibid, p. 99.

4 Total fertility rate (TFR), also called the aggregate fertility rate, refers to the average number of children born by each woman at her fertility age in a country or a region.

dropped in succession, while the average expected lifespan kept growing.

Developed countries featured by a severely aging population face the loss of their economic competitiveness that swamps the great powers' economies which are soon surpassed and replaced by the emerging countries. The comparison between China and Japan nowadays exemplifies it. In 1978, China's national income was only 1/6 of that of Japan. But today, China has a national income greater than Japan, ranking amongst the biggest economic entities. To trace back to Japan's situation between the 1970s and 90s, it is easy to notice the economic stagnation after its per capita income reached the level of developed countries. Meanwhile, the longer lifespan was accompanied by a fast drop in the birth rate and Japan stepped into an aging society. "For the Japanese demography, 2005 was the turning point when the population started to drop naturally. But within a short period, the natural decline reached about 10 thousand. In 2010, the population began to experience a greater decrease, and the amount exceeded 200 thousand in 2011. In 2013, it was as many as 240 thousand."[1]

During the same period, China had a low per capita income and insufficient urbanization level. But it also bore great economic potential. The reform and opening-up policy laid the foundation of the market economy, liberate productivity, and rejuvenated the population. The whole country was full of energy, creating economic miracles.

China implemented the planned economy and endured a low economic efficiency. Additionally, political movements impacted society, slowing down the urbanization progress. But the population grew fast. Since the 1950s, the government had publicized policies to encourage fertility and boosted the birth rate by using political and administrative methods. Though in the 1960s, the population slumped, China had more and more people for about 30 years after its establishment. The population was 551.96 million in the 50s and soon soared up

1 Cited from "Japanese Media : Population Reduction will Influence the Economic Development of Japan", Huanqiu.com, January 6th, 2014, originally posted in livedoornews.com, January 1st, 2014.

to 829.92 million in the 70s, meaning 277.96 million people were born during 20 years. In 2013, 1.36 billion people lived in China. However, the aging population appears with an overwhelming pressure on China. In the next few decades, the crisis faced by China is not the geometric growth of population and the shortage of energy, but, on the contrary, the geometric decrease of population and the severely aging society. How many families welcome a second baby? Now, the only child grows up with one couple of parents and two couples of grandparents to support. When the grandparents' generation passes away, the whole population reduces by a half. When the parents' generation passes away, the whole population loses a half again. In brief, the population gets halved when one generation fades away from society. According to China's demographic situation publicized by the National Bureau of Statistics, the family size, i.e. the number of people of each family, was 4.33 persons in 1953, 4.43 in 1964, 4.41 in 1982, 3.96 in 1990, 3.44 in 2000, and 3.10 in 2010. This is what I described just now — one kid with two parents and four grandparents. (Figure 8-1)

Figure 8-1 One child only is better

Note: This picture is posted online anonymously.

The average number of people within a family declines due to a variety of reasons, such as the aging population and the surge of the empty-nest elderly. The urban population grows with the improvement of living conditions and the significant development of the real estate industry. In contrast to the period from the 1950s to 1990s, the young live independently at a younger age on average, leading to the shrinking family size. However, in general, the main reason is the decline of the birth rate which lingers around a very low level. Newborn babies and children aging 0-14 occupy a smaller part of the population structure and their proportion continues to reduce. With more children, the family size is bigger, while fewer children mean a smaller family.

A family bearing 3.1 persons means the formation of a 4:2:1 heredity mode. Within three generations, the population slumps in the generation of grandchildren. The heredity mode once forms and ever persists, with strong resilience to reverse itself quickly. Nowadays, there have not yet been any effective conditions or key driving factors to reverse this situation. As long as the population crowds into the urban areas, raising a kid costs more and living conditions are greatly improved. So more and more young families are reluctant to bear and raise more children. The considerable habitual inertia dwarfs the influence of the abortion of the family planning policy.

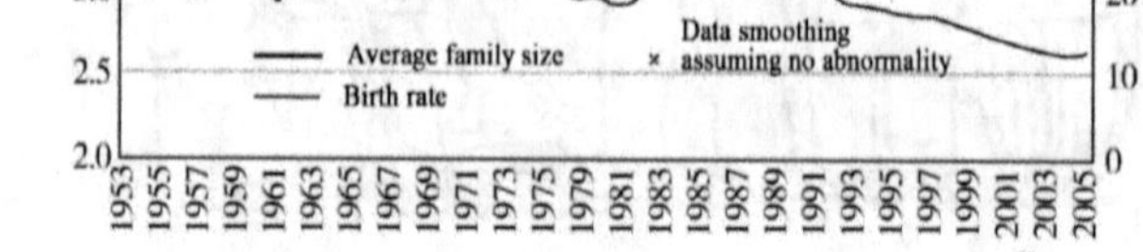

Figure 8-2 Changes in average family size in China and the birth rate

Source: Guo Zhigang, "Exploration and Analysis of the Changes in China's Families", *Chinese Journal of Population Science*, 2008, Issus 3.

What worries us most is the diminishing willingness of bearing more children. With the improvements of the living conditions and the urbanization, late marriage and late childbearing prevail among the young generation. The fertility rate drops.

More families would like to bear one child only, which has formed a trend. Some people argue that only those in the rural areas choose to bear more, but no one is willing or able to do so given that the young are now living in cities. According to files given by the National Bureau of Statistics, China had 1.36 billion people in 2013, where the urban population reached 0.73 billion, accounting for 53.73%, while the rural population was 0.63 billion, making up for the other 46.27%. However, the 0.63 billion rural population contains more than 0.2 billion migrant workers, the young group of which work in urban areas instead of living in a rural environment. Compared with their parents, their willingness to bear more children was much weaker. Though the family planning policy was not strictly implemented in rural areas, the number of children was obviously smaller. In the 1980s and 1990s, urbanization progressed in a comparatively low manner. Rural population maintained above 0.8 billion since rural families generally chose to bear a second, or even a third, baby. The only child was popular in urban areas. From 1980 to 2000, China's birth rate maintained between 1.4‰ and 2.2‰. But, it continued declining as the urban population expanded.

According to the Tabulation on the Population Census of the People's Republic of China by County in 2010, the total fertility rate of China was 1.8110‰, where cities had 0.88210‰, towns had 1.1534‰, and rural areas had 1.43755‰. Amongst others, the last five with the lowest fertility rate were Beijing with 1.70670‰, Shanghai 0.73665‰, Liaoning 0.74090‰, Heilongjiang 0.75140‰, and Jilin 0.760000‰. The top five with the highest fertility rate were Guangxi with 1.7895‰, Guizhou 1.7485‰, Xinjiang 1.52885‰, Hainan 1.51265‰, and Anhui 1.48155‰. The World Population Data in 2010 shows that, all over the globe, each woman gave birth to 2.5 babies on average. The data in developed countries was 1.7, in less developed countries was 2.7 and in the least developed countries was 4.5. If China was excluded from the less developed countries, the rest had 3.1. The total fertility rate of China was lower than half of the world average level and far below the average level of the developed countries. At the same time, some disputes aroused on the accuracy of the population census. After the census in 2010, the National Family Planning Commission once announced a severe failure to report where more than 20% of newborn babies were not reported. Therefore, the actual fertility rate was supposed to be 1.5‰, or even 1.6‰. But it was rebutted by the sampling survey of the census' quality that claimed the failing-to-report rate of only 0.12% so that a "severe" failure did not exist.[1] *China Statistical Yearbook 2016* publicized the sampling survey outcome of the 1% population in 2015 when the total fertility rate was only 1.07‰. In other words, each woman bore one child only.

8.2 Forecasts of Future Population

By taking out simple calculations in mathematics, we can work out worrying results. The fertile age range of women is 20 to 40 with 90% of children born before their mothers are 35 years old. In 2015, "after-80" females consecutively stepped into their 35th year, losing the incentive and energy to bear a baby. In 2025, similar things happen to the "after-90" females. In 2035, when "after-80" and "after-90" females lose their fertility, it takes only 20 years instead of a hundred years for our society to panic.

With only one child in each generation, the typical family with three generations is molded into a 4:2:1 structure, in which there are one child, two parents, and four grandparents. At the micro-level, the sum-up lifespan of the three generations, namely the time longevity from the birth and death of the three generations, is determined by two factors — the average lifespan of the last generation, e.g. 70 years or 80 years on average, and the age range of women from birth to fertility. Women's age range with fertility is between 15 and 49, but most children were born before their mothers are 40 years old. Therefore, the age range from 20 to 40 is defined as the effective childbearing period. Effectiveness means

1 Cited from "China's TFR in 2010 only at 1.18‰", *China Economic Herald*, July 10, 2012.

more than 95% of children were born when their mothers are aged between 20 and 40. Based on the sampling survey data in 2012 from the National Bureau of Statistics, women aging from 20 to 40 gave birth to 10,889 babies, accounting for 96% of the sample containing 11,379 elements. In 2003, the proportion was 98%.

That women in the last generation chose to bear babies from the age 20 or the age 35 impacts the generation's life cycle. Simply, if women in the past two generations choose to bear babies at age 25, the third generation has a lifespan of 80 years. The lifespans of these three generations share some overlaps. The second generation was born 25 years after the birth of the first generation and the third was also born 25 years later than the second. Therefore, the sum-up lifespan of three generations is supposed to be 130 years, since the average childbearing age of the first generation is 25, plus that of the second generation which is also 25, then plus the average lifespan of the third generation which is 80. In other words, it takes 130 years for the three generations to live from birth to death.

The audience can check the lifespan of their own three generations. In general, the lifespan of the three generations has nothing to do with the lifespans of the first and the second generation. It is only related to the lifespan of the third generation. However, the age when women in the first and the second generation gave birth to babies also influenced the lifespan of the three generations. Late marriage, late childbearing and the longer lifespan of the third generation determine a longer life cycle of the three generations. Otherwise, the total life cycle is shorter.

Since the average value is taken. the life cycle, i.e. the lifespan, of the three generations only connects to the childbearing age and the average lifespan of the third generation. It is independent of the number of people in three generations. For the 4th, the 5th, or the *n*th life cycle, this relation also stands. In other words, the life cycle, T, of n generations can also employ this relation. The life cycle of n generations in total equals the sum-up of the last generation's average lifespan, T_1, plus the average childbearing age of women in each generation, T_2. The general form describing the life cycle, T, of n generations is as follows -

$$T = T_1 + (n\text{-}1)\, T_2 \tag{8-1}$$

Here, T is the life cycle of n generations. T_1 is the average lifespan. T_2 is the average childbearing age of women.

If the childbearing age of women is not the average value, this variable can be substituted by the effective childbearing period. The average childbearing age and the effective childbearing period are two different concepts. To calculate the average childbearing age, the effective childbearing period is excluded because the average childbearing age is the average value of the effective childbearing period. The average childbearing age is embedded with some statistical errors and the effective childbearing period is more accurate. Therefore, T_3 is added into the above equation to take into account the effective childbearing period of 20 years because the age range is between 20 and 40. The equation becomes -

$$T = T_1 + (n\text{-}1)\, T_2 + T_3 \qquad (8\text{-}2)$$

Assume that T_1 is 80 years, T_2 is 20 years, indicating that women start childbearing from age 20, and T_3 is 20, standing for the 20 years from age 20 to age 40, n is 3. To substitute the variables for the numbers above, we get the life cycle of 140, years. Within the three generations, only two generations are taken into account in terms of the effective childbearing period of women. So n-1 is applied to represent it. If the first generation is excluded, n is permitted to be set as 4 so that the life cycle of the three generations is worked out.

The population counting also incorporates the assembly of all families in a certain country or area which is always a significant number. The population counting of three generations and the description of the age structure also need to consider the total population within a time range, in addition to the average life longevity and the effective childbearing period. Meanwhile, the average childbearing age of women is set as the starting point to segment different age ranges usually with every 20 years as a one-time node. For example, considering the practice of family planning, we can group people born between 1980 and 1999 as the first generation, those born in 2000-2019 as the second generation, those born in 2020-2039 as the third generation, and those in 2040 - 2069 as the fourth generation. Following this rule, we get the nth generation. The equation used to calculate the population of each generation is -

Newborn babies in a generation l_n = Newborn babies born in the last generation

$$\times 0.45 \times \text{the total fertility rate } a \qquad (8\text{-}3)$$

In each generation, newborn babies l = newborn babies

$$\times 0.45\ (a_1^1 + a_2^2 + \cdots + a_n^n) \qquad (8\text{-}4)$$

The coefficient 0.45 is the percentage of newborn baby girls occupying the total newborn babies. Normally, it is 0.49, but thanks to the long-term family planning, China only had 0.45 for quite a few years. The multiplication of 0.45 and the newborn babies equals the newborn baby girls. a is the total fertility rate. The corner mark n stands for the nth generation, such as "1" meaning the first generation and "2" meaning the second generation. Further generations are generally represented by n. Given that the newborn baby girls only account for 0.45%, the population in each generation remains stable only when the sum-up fertility is 2.222‰. A total fertility rate lower than 2.222‰ results in a declining population generation by generation.

The family planning policy has been in force for about 30 years. From 1980 to 1999, the newborn population was about 0.331 billion. *The 5th Population Census Data of China (2000)* showed that women accounted for 49% of the whole population, reaching about 0.162 billion (women's percentage is different from the ratio of newborn females to the newborn in total). The statistical population data revealed that the newborns were 0.224 billion between 2000 and 2013, part of who were born by those born between 1960 and 1979. Assume that, during the 6 years from 2014 to 2019, the newborn maintained 16 million per annum, then the total newborn within 20 years from 1960 to 2019 reached 0.32 billion which was the approximate population. Among the 0.32 billion people, 49% of them were women — considering the termination of the family planning policy, it is reasonable to take 49% instead of 45% as the approximate percentage of women to the population in each generation. Females were about 0.157 billion with a sampling survey crystallizing the declining total fertility rate at 1.2‰ currently. The expected third generation will embrace a newborn population of 0.188 billion.

Following that, the fourth generation will reach 0.11 billion people and the fifth generation will have 0.065 billion. If 1.4‰ is taken as the total fertility rate, then the third generation will expect a newborn population of 0.22 billion, the fourth will have 0.151 billion, and the fifth 0.104 billion.

In conclusion, with 1980 taken as the starting point, the first generation is from 1980 to 1999 with a population of 0.331 billion. The second generation is from 2000 to 2019 with a population of 0.32 billion. The third generation is from 2020 to 2039 with a population of 0.188 billion. The fourth generation is from 2040 to 2059 with a population of 0.111 billion. The total population of the first three generations is 0.839 billion. Based on the equation (8-2)： $T = T_1 + (n\text{-}1)\ T_2 - T_3$ Assume the average lifespan of the third generation is 80 years, i.e. T_1 is 80, T_2 is 20, indicating that women start childbearing since age 20, and T_3 is 20, standing for the 20 years from age 20 to age 40 when women can bear children, i.e. the effective childbearing period is 20 years. n is 3. After the substitution of the variables for numbers above, the life cycle is still 140 years. 1980 is the beginning and 2120 is the ending. After more than a century, China will have 0.111 billion elderly people aging between 60 and 80 with a total fertility rate of 1.2‰ or 0.151 billion elderly people aging between 60 and 80 with a total fertility rate of 1.4‰, and their offspring.

Though the calculation is not 100% accurate and the declining population and the aging society are not that severe, it is still worth attention that the slump of population and the aging society are inevitable. The Chinese demography will face a time window when the population experiences a cliff fall. Compared with other countries, the aging society in China is much more overwhelming. The data released by the National Bureau of Statistics tells that the population aging 60 and above reached 0.2 billion in 2013, making up for 14.9%, and will soar to a new level as the 0.39 billion people born in the 1950s and 60s step into their old age. Those born in the 1950s were about 0.167 billion and those born in the 60s were about 0.223 billion. To calculate based on the newborn population, we had more than 16 million people entering their 60 per annum since 2010, and 20 million people step into their 60 per annum since 2020. The population born at birth peaks in the 1950s, 60s, and 70s amounted to 0.61 billion. As they become old and pass away, the Chinese population will reduce to 0.8 to 0.9 billion from the current 1.36 billion in 2054. Among the 0.8 to 0.9 billion, the elderly will compose a large proportion since the population born between 1980 and 2010 was about 0.55 billion and they will be old in 2054.

From a static view, the population in China will slump to 0.8-0.9 billion as the elderly reach 0.4-0.5 billion. If it is so, it will be by all means a disaster. Some netizen says, "the number of the impaired elderly in China grow geometrically within the next dozen of years. 'One gets a stroke and the whole family will fall paralyzed'. This will be a prevailing phenomenon throughout China from the North to the South."[1] The cliff fall of population incurs loan losses no matter the repayment schedule is for 20 years or 30 if the loan is borrowed now. If awaking late, or even persisting the family planning policy, we are likely to be slammed by the great economic recession and our nation and country will face a devastating disaster. "Her epitaph must be — 'One child only' keeps the daily blessings. This is the starting point of our nation's recession."[2]

A man without long-term plans must be troubled by instant difficulties. The instant difficulty is the abruptly aggravating aging population. The prominent problem caused by the aging population is the drop of the labor force index, ultimately leading to a population without working power becoming larger than the labor force population. The children in a family with fewer kids or the only child in a family draw too much attention compared to those in a family with more kids in the past. The selfless love and nurturing of parents are taken for granted by the children whose responsibility and obligation to support their elderly are weaker. "Gnawing at the old" becomes a living habit. The focus of the family moves downward from respecting the elderly to cherishing the young. A family spares its

1 Cited from a netizen called Xiaoyuanyuan A, "The Director of the Institute of Population, CASS — Fertility-encouraging Policy Orientation Should Have Come Earlier", 9kd.net.

2 From a netizen called Whyeff2000, 9kd.net.

efforts to nurture the younger generation. The willingness to support the elderly is weaker, so fewer resources are used to improve the welfare of the elderly.

Looking back to the past 30 years, 50 years, and 80 years, time seems to be a flicker of a lighter at the fingertip, feeling like a dream of the last night. This is because of the influence of asymmetric information on the sense of space-time. But when to foresee the future, 30 years, 50 years, and 80 years seem too far away to be linked to the present, so that we might wonder what matters to us. The future 30 years, 50 years, and 80 years are also quick and just around the corner. The most thrilling is that the slump of the population takes place before our people get used to bearing a second child. The cultural custom of "more offspring, more blessings" has disappeared already. The current urge is the insufficient preparation from the ideology and the feelings for the foreseeable population plunge. After a hundred years, the situation might be -

> Sadness arouses on the passage
> where the Qin and Han Dynasty left their traces,
> Numerous palaces were crushed into soil and sand.

——Zhang Yanghao

8.3 The Self-limiting Theories in Biology

According to the Evolution Theory, the geometric growth of biological creatures is restricted by the natural environment and God. So they are unlikely to expand with no limit. "Darwin raised a famous example. A couple of elephants can bear 6 baby elephants within their 60 years' life. Even though the death rate is considered, they will still have 15 million offspring after 500 years. But limited lands, food, and water mean thorough competition among all creatures...inhibiting their endless growth."[1]

Apart from the natural competition and the survival of the fittest as the weeding-out rule, there is another rule that restricts the expansion of creatures — self-limiting. It means the individual life longevity is negatively related to the whole population. The shorter the individual life is, the larger the group population is; otherwise, the population is smaller. For the same biological creatures, taking human beings as an example, the population will stop growing and start declining after the human average lifespan reaches a certain level.

Everything is limited except the universe. The biological groups on earth have fewer individuals as the individual life longevity is longer. A rough rule is drawn from the biological statistics that small-sized creatures live short but have the fertility to bear an enormous amount of offspring and their groups are also numerous; the large-sized creatures live long but they multiply fewer and thus their groups are fewer. In the animal world, insects are small-sized, short-lived, and strong-multiplied. The creatures likely to exist are about 8 million species. Some larger mollusk animals live longer than insects but their fertility is not as good as insects. They form about 200 thousand species. Vertebrates are higher animals. Their average lifespan in the animal world is the longest, but the fertility rate is the lowest. They form about 50 thousand species. In biology, human beings belong to vertebrates. Considering their wisdom, human beings have the lowest birth rate in the animal world.

Population changes in line with the biological rule. Western scholars in the 19th century proposed a large number of essays and articles with the UK philosopher and sociologist Herbert Spencer as the prominent representative figure. He put forward the principle of the self-adjusting population. He argued that, according to the competition and the survival of the fittest, the lower creatures had a low capability to survive and a stronger capability to multiply and they had to sustain

1 Sean B. Carroll, *The Making of the Fittest DNA and the Ultimate Forensic Record of Evolution*, translated by Yang Jiarong, Shanghai Scientific and Technological Education Publishing House, 2012, p. 35.

their survival by enormous multiplication. In comparison, the higher animals can better survive and avoid being weeded out. But their fertility was usually not as good as the lower creatures. Therefore, it was accepted that there was a negative relation between viability and fertility. Human beings are higher animals. Their fertility is lower. With the development of society, the improvement of education, and the advancements of technology, the wisdom of human beings are highly developed, polishing the living skills, but the recession of fertility will continue.

The biological principle is a theory or a school trying to explain demographic phenomena from the perspective of biology. It is featured by the viewpoint of taking demographic phenomena as the biological phenomena. It argues that demographic development is always determined by basic biological laws. The representative theorists also include the US biologist R.Pearl and the Italian demographer and sociologist C.Ghini. Herbert Spencer's *A Theory of Population* in 1852 and *The Principles in Biology* (1864-1867), Pearl's *The Study of Anthropological Biology* in 1925, and Ghini's *New Organism* in 1927, as well as other influential books, are representative pieces of work of population theories in the biology school.

In the 1920s, Pearl inherited and developed the biology school, proposing that human beings multiplied in the same way as other general animals did. They all obey the law of biological multiplication. He experimented on the fruit flies secluded in a closed container. He observed that their multiplication was slow at the beginning and accelerated before a second deceleration and an ultimate termination. Based on that, Pearl asserted that the population growth of human beings was in the same manner, reaching a peak before approaching the termination. He compared the process to the sponge soaking water — no more water would be absorbed by the sponge after it got fully saturated. Therefore, people call Pearl's theory "the sponge population theory". Ghini also explained demographic phenomena from the viewpoint of biological evolution, arguing that the biological factors were the essential factors to cause population changes. He equated the nation and population to the biological individuals, so the population also experienced the childhood, youth, adulthood, and the elderly period before ending up in senility and death. The variations of the birth rate was not a reflection of the social changes but the changes of "embryo cell" quality.

Some scholars explain the population changes by seeking the differences in diet characteristics. The UK demographer T.Debde argued in *The Real Laws of Population* in 1841 that eating food of high quality drove down the fertility rate while eating food of low quality pushed up the fertility rate. After World War II, the American demographer J.de Castroite pointed out in *Appetite and Allocation* in 1952 that the lack of protein gave people in the bad nutritional condition a higher fertility rate, while the people at good nutritional level had a lower fertility rate. He supported a negative relation between the fertility rate and protein consumption.[1]

The improvements of the living condition are vital to prolong the individual lifespan but not beneficial for sure to increase fertility.

Some phenomena regarding childbearing in modern society are connected to living conditions, income, and food intake. For example, as reported, women in rural areas in China can provide more breast milk compared to those in cities. According to a survey in Zhejiang Province, the breastfeeding rate in urban areas was 86% when the newborn babies were 3-month old. When the newborns were 6-months old, the rate fell to 61.8%. In contrast, in rural areas the two rates were 91% and 84.72% respectively, much higher than their urban counterparts.[2] One reason is that mothers in cities need to work. Another primary reason is that mothers in the urban area have less breast milk comparatively.

The women in cities diagnosed with breast cancer are much younger than before. Breast cancer is one of the malignant tumors whose patients increase at the fastest speed. In the past, the patients were mainly women aging 50 to 60. Now it permeates among the middle-aged and the young women. The proportion of

1 Cited from zhidao.baidu, "The Principles of Biology", http://zhidao.baidu.com.

2 Qiu Liqian, "Factors Affecting Breastfeeding in Rural Areas and Counties in Zhejiang Province", Hangzhou.com, December 26, 2006.

women in rural areas diagnosed with breast cancer is low. So the medical experts perceive breast cancer as a typical "rich people's disease". Excessive intake of nutrition, protein, and fat keeps the estrogen at a high level, stimulating the proliferation of breasts and even a cell mutation.

Though the living condition is improved continuously, the quality of sperms continues declining. The affluence of life is at the cost of the fertility rate. From the 1960s to the present, the hottest dispute about male reproduction is the declining quality of sperms which has become a worldwide problem. The Danish scholar Niels Shabakbo once carried out a comprehensive analysis of the sperm quality based on the relative reports of nearly 15, 000 men in 21 countries from 1938 to 1990. He found out that the number of sperms declined by more than 40% within 50 years. The amount of seminal fluid reduced by 20% and the sperm concentration dropped to 66 million per milliliter in 1990 from 113 million per milliliter in 1940. After that, many countries and regions in Europe, America, and Asia publicized their comparative data in retrospective reports, most of which supported the conclusion of the lower sperm quality.

Scholars in China draw similar conclusions. The Institute of Science and Technology in National Population and Family Planning Commission once studied the 256 sperm analysis reports of 11, 726 men from 39 cities and counties, including Beijing, Shanghai, and Tianjin, between 1981 and 1996, and found out that the quality of the seminal fluid deteriorated at 1% per annum and the sperm number dropped by more than 40%. Furthermore, in more industrialized areas, the sperm quality declined at a faster speed. In recent years, clinical cases in the urological surgery and andrology department also confirm that an increasing number of male patients come to visit a doctor due to sperm inferiority.[1]

The adverse effect of "rich people's disease" on fertility also receives some rebuttals. They argue that it is the social factors that drive down the fertility rate

1 Cited from Information Website of Guangzhou Ren'ai Hospital, "A General Decline of Male Sperms", November 10, 2010.

and eliminate the biological basis. One reason is that the decline of the fertility rate has no inheritance foundation. There does not exist any evidence to verify possible physiological triggers. The total fertility rate refers to the total number of children born by each woman during their fertility age. The approximate values of inheritance rate have a significant discrepancy from 0.04 to 0.42. So inheritance does not pull down the total fertility rate. The social factors, however, are more or less related to the prolonged lifespan based on a variety of the analysis of specific cases. For example, the changes in nutrition and living conditions, some "rich people's disease", and the lower death rate of newborn babies all affect the lifespan. Social factors impact the nutrition, the improvement of which increase the survival rate of the newborn babies and reduce the number of the newborn. Other studies show that fatness changes hormones, influencing the ovary, testicles, and the endocrinology cycle, which further reduces the fertility rate.

As far as I am concerned, the biological theories in the 19th century are more persuasive, i.e. the population growth is self-limited. With the technological advancements, the reproduction capacity and the fertility rate (the actual number of children born) all decrease. The self-adjustment of the population is a statistical phenomenon, belonging to the basic rules preset by life and nature. The self-limiting principle that the living bodies were born to obey is manifested by the longer lifespan and ultimately the population decline after the population reaches its peak.

Life complexity and self-limiting exert a greater influence than human wisdom. Social development does not change the law embedded in life itself. Life can reproduce by itself and can also set a limit for itself. The factors affecting human fertility only exist within life. It is impossible to manipulate the fertility rate through political or technological methods based upon human wisdom. Though environmental and social factors may influence human reproduction, they are all external factors and can only impact the direction of natural selection for a living body. The gene group inside a living body reacts to the environmental and social developments and get used to them. However, the adaptive response is not driven by the external environment but by the internal rules. The selective response of the gene group is the main factor.

If the environment and the society are the main reasons affecting the fertility rate, then it means that wisdom of humans is superior to the wisdom of life. But the civilization created by wisdom in brains is by no means paralleled to the life complexity and self-design. So social developments never dominate the decline of the birth rate. It is mainly a living body's response to the changes in the environment and society. The mechanism of this response lies in the gene groups inside the living body. Therefore, the birth rate changes mainly based on the foundation and rules in life.

The young's willingness to bear children gradually falls after the average lifespan reaches a certain level. Is it a result of social developments or an outcome determined by the natural law of life? The answer is obvious. It is driven by human genes. Social developments are exogenous factors. The average human lifespan is prolonged which directly triggers the self-limiting mechanism of childbearing. The statistical law shows the average human lifespan in some countries reached 70 years in succession with the development of the world economy and the improvement of the hygiene condition. The human birth rate started going downhill. The sudden drop in fertility rate stems from the drop of fertility desire, instead of the direct fall of human fertility which comes from gene degradation. However, gene degradation never appears all of a sudden. It is a gene expression that have been accumulated and inherited for decades or hundreds of years. Or it is a metamorphosis that takes a longer time to happen. Therefore, the fertility decline within decades of years is mainly due to the drop of fertility desire. The young are reluctant to bear more children as their elderly did.

The fertility desire is a subjective wish, but its formation is a manifestation of the hidden law of human genes. It is the law of self-limiting. It is shown as the featured interdependence between the individual and the group. A longer individual lifespan is accompanied by a smaller group. The interdependence helps to prevent the group from population explosion. Otherwise, the fertility rate will increase to stop the group to decrease excessively. Therefore, individuals choose to bear more children to eliminate the threat of early individual mortality to the group.

If only the very few in one country enjoy a long lifespan and wealth, the birth rate will not drop. Only in an industrialized society where the national income and the lifespan increase due to social developments can the birth rate decline. In some areas some people are long-lived. Or the very few in the whole society are long-lived. This is a result of their living condition and genes. Besides, females tend to live longer than males. It is not because the females enjoy a better living condition, but is due to the gene superiority accumulated in evolution.

For thousands of years, human marriages and their families have been in an ever-lasting alteration. Agricultural society breeds a large population, the malignant living conditions including poverty, illnesses, and overworking drive down the average lifespan of a family. Children usually go to work for profits to boost the economy. This is of vital importance. More children mean more blessings. The mode forms into a conventional cultural notion that the effective way to get rid of poverty is to bear more children. After industrialization, as the per capita income increases, the human health condition improves a lot. The government provides more facilities and welfare to help support the old. This allows the old to live without relying on their children and hence the desire to have more posterity is weakened. It is admitted that social factors have an impact on population growth. But as exogenous factors, their impacts are limited and not long-lasting. The family planning policy in China brought down the fertility rate. But it did not keep a remarkable effect on the low fertility rate, compared to other countries without family planning policy. In other words, the birth rate in China did not enter a downward trend. The fertility data starting from 1970 indicates that China, India, Indonesia, Iran, and Thailand all experience a declining fertility rate. And the Chinese fertility rate decreases by a margin similar to that of Thailand. In Iran, the fertility rate plunged after the 1980s and approaches gradually to the Chinese and Thai counterparts.[1] The most obvious side effect of the family planning policy in China is that baby girl's account for a lower portion of the total number of newborns. The severely unbalanced girl-to-boy ratio is entrenched in China for many years after the implementation of the family planning policy.

In reality, the effective method to cope with the population aging involves social intervention in the childbearing issue of young people, encouraging them to bear more kids by carrying out economic methods. So the birth rate increases and the population rejuvenates after generation replacements. It looks easy to achieve the goal since the government has the dominating administrative power so every policy encouraging childbearing is expected to receive practical effects. However, as the average lifespan is prolonged continuously, people are more reluctant to have more kids. The low fertility rate perplexing today's world is attributed to the unwillingness to have more kids. Policies encouraging childbearing have been in force in many countries but produce so little effects that the birth rate still keeps falling. People spontaneously choose to have one child only. The irreversible sharp decline of the world population is doomed.

8.4 Economic Theories Regarding Population

Studies upon population involve a wide range of economic issues. Specific issues such as supply, resources, production, labor force, social welfare, government spending are closely related to population. Besides, the demographic amount and its growth both affect the economic development of the country and even the world. Macroeconomics and microeconomics talk about population issues. Since studies upon population are at large economic issues. Therefore, the principles of population compose part of economic theories.

Western scholars propose a theory of natural balance to explain the population issues. Human beings can exist on this planet with transcending power. The

1 Cai Yong, "Low Fertility Rate and Its Social and Economic Impacts", originally from Liang Zai, *Demography*, China Renmin University Press, 2012, p. 119.

Swedish naturalist Linnaeus (1707-1778) believed that "human beings hunt the largest whale in the sea and the most brutal tiger and lion on earth. But they have to obey the highest law of balance. The place where their population is booming is also a hotbed breeding epidemic. Wars often break out in the place where human beings are overpopulated."[1] Linnaeus' theory of natural balance is too experience-based. Meanwhile, he also set forth the religious thoughts, arguing that the meaning of the universe wass self-evident and there was no need to question it. The belief in God can resolve concerns about population issues.

Malthus (1766-1834) challenged the theory of natural balance in *An Essay on the Principle of Population* published in 1798. He insisted that the automatic balance between humans and nature would be broken by the unbalanced growth of the two. The unrestrained population growth of human beings will bring natural disasters. Malthus thought that, if food was a must for human living and the sexual passion was inevitable, then the human fertility would grow infinitely larger than the capacity of lands to produce means of production and livelihood. Without restrictions, the population grows geometrically, while the means of livelihood only increase arithmetically. Natural resources and space are essential to creatures but they are also limited. Rational humans cannot get rid of such restrictions. The limited productivity of lands a natural rule, too, which is manifested among the animals and plants by the species waste, diseases, and mortality. For human beings, the manifestations are sufferings and crimes.[2]

At the beginning of the 1970s, the academic body *Club of Rome* published a research report titled *Limit to Growth* in which they studied the growth of population and capital, cereals, non-renewable resources, environmental pollution combined. It pointed out that the geometric growth of population and industrial

1 Wolf Lepenies, *Qu'est-ce qu'un intellectuel européen? Les intellectuels et la politique de l'esprit dans l'histoire européenne*, translated by Li Yanming, Guangxi Normal University Press, 2011, p. 264.

2 Thomas Malthus, *An Essay on the Principle of Population*, translated by Chen Xiaobai, Huaxia Publishing House, 2013.

capital would confront the industrial society with all kinds of difficulties such as severe environmental pollution and exhausting non-renewable resources. If spontaneous inhibition of the growth of population and industrial capital is unfulfillable, the social economy would exert itself to the extreme due to excessive growth, and, in the meantime, the recession appears in both the population and industrial production. The report also argued for the need to build an equilibrium mechanism to hold up the growth. In equilibrium, the basic demand for materials is satisfied and equal chances are granted to everyone to tap their potentials.

In the 1950s and 60s, the population in each country grew fast. Most developing countries became the focus of attention. With the increase of birth rate and the decrease of the mortality rate, especially the declining mortality rate of the newborn in developing countries, the "population boom" went viral. So the population control drew attention. Under the pressure of a big population, some countries carried out policies to control population growth. In demography, theories are dominated by thoughts of equilibrium. From the theoretical view purely, the growth and decline of the population will finally end up in equilibrium. In the long run, birth rate equals mortality rate and then the population stays in equilibrium. It neither increases nor decreases. Frank Notestein and Kingsley Davis respectively put forward the concept of "population transformation" to explain the relationship between birth rate and death rate. Population transformation theory argued that, in the short run, the rise of birth rate and the fall of mortality rate will induce the "population boom", but, in the long term, the society had to maintain a relative equilibrium of birth and death. Population transformation means the equilibrium of high birth rate and high death rate transforms into the equilibrium of low birth rate and low death rate.[1]

Malthusian population theory and the limit-to-growth theory fail to receive verification in reality. Because after the 1970s, the world population growth

1 Cai Yong, "Low Fertility Rate and Its Social and Economic Impacts", originally from Liang Zai, *Demography*, China Renmin University Press, 2012.

presented a self-disciplined and fundamental change. More countries started to witness a declining birth rate which was lower than the level to maintain population stability. People sought answers for the declining birth rate from a macro perspective and argued that the economic development drove down the fertility rate. So amazing it is that economic development happens to be the "best contraceptive".

However, childbearing is individual behavior. Economic developments as a macro factor do not serve as the best answer. Therefore, some people come up with the idea of interpreting the decline by investigating the microeconomic men. They think that a rational individual builds his or her willingness to bear children upon the comparison between the marginal cost and the marginal benefit. If the marginal cost of raising a child is greater than the marginal benefit, the willingness of childbearing weakens. Others try to explain the phenomenon by taking humans as social beings. They believe that culture, opinions, and even conformity to the mainstream all affect the birth rate. The individual birth and death are for group development. Childbearing is an instinct that reflects the notion of reproduction and inheritance.

In summary, reasons that drive down the birth rate include economic factors and cultural conventions. However, why can economic growth for sure lead to the decline of the birth rate? And why does the conventional culture think highly of posterity weaken? More new questions are found out and more proper answers are expected.

In areas where conventional cultures dominate, such as East Asia including China, Japan and South Korea, the birth rate has already fallen to a very low level and maintained there for a long time. The prediction of the population transformation theory that the birth rate equals the death rate has not come true yet. The world population tends to continue with a low birth rate after experiencing a "population boom" for a short period. If the trend persists, the mortality rate will be higher than the birth rate. In the next few decades, the world population will experience a turning point after which a decline will be inevitable. What worries us is the situation in China, the population aging takes place shortly and sharply, after which a significant slump of the population occurs.

If we admit that the changing notion of marriage and childbearing is a factor contributing to the declining birth rate, then, why does this effect have to be a negative one? Why the notion of childbearing doesn's change to support the increasing fertility rate? No answers will solve the questions once and for all. Endlessly questing upon similar issues deteriorates the reliability of theories. The development of population theories encounters its bottlenecks. The theory efficiency decreases progressively. Are there any exceptions since economic theories and population theories are all restricted by the bottlenecks? Demographic changes, in practice, also experience the process from thriving to declining and shrink to a smaller scale. The transformation only connects to its scale, excluding other factors such as the assumptions of economic men or social beings and conventional cultures. Not to mention the "equilibrium".

Then what is the utmost scale? Briefly speaking, the world population after the low birth rate maintains is in an utmost scale. In other words, it is a concept built from the perspective of the globe and tendency instead of a specific definition to generalize the situation in a specific county or region where the declining birth rate occurs. As long as the tendency and persistence of an irreversible population change appear, it is reasonable to regard the current demographic amount as its utmost scale.

When talking about the limit of population, we assume the social and economic situation as unchanged and this is the foundation for further discussion. Only if the social and economic situation experiences a significant disturbance, will the utmost population-scale change. Penetrations into the social and economic situations reveal that the birth rate and mortality rate remained high before industrialization. The population grew at a relatively low speed. And the population was restricted by the situations. After the industrialization, the living condition was greatly improved with the technological advancements. Material prosperity, sufficient food, impeccable medical care, clean water, decent residence, abundant entertainments combine to improve the health condition. The lifespan increase. The birth rate correspondingly goes down naturally. As mentioned beforehand, we pointed out the negative relation between the expected lifespan and the birth rate. The longer the life is, the lower the birth rate. Otherwise, a higher birth rate brings a shorter lifespan. It is a statistical rule.

Now we further notice that there exists an utmost population scale which is related to the scale itself only. Furthermore, we argue that with the increase of expected lifespan, the population approaches its utmost scale and presents a tendency of long-term decline which is hard to change and reverse.

The statistical entropy can describe the stagnation of national income growth. In other words, the increase of micro disorder leads to the stagnation of national income growth. What are the reasons for declining population growth? Resource restrictions do not share the responsibility because the national territorial areas, the natural resources, environmental conditions, and other possible factors that might interfere with the deteriorating resources do not show up at all. The world mineral productions and agricultural goods are in sufficient supply, which eliminates the possibility of resource shortage and insufficient supply. The reality is technology boosts the merchandise supply. People are now and will continue to better off since the living condition is gradually improved. Healthy people increase and so do their lifespans despite a large group of people with chronic diseases.

The math formula to describe self-limited changes is the Logistic Equation, illustrating a fact that the growth of a variable approaches zero if the variable concerns its scale only and the scale has a limit.

I once employed the Logistic Equation to depict the changing path of the national income and monetary aggregate growth. The statistical resources confirm the accessibility of Logistic Equation in terms of interpreting the population growth. The demographic amount is like national income and monetary aggregate. The growth of the aggregate complies with the law of self-limiting—the maximization of disorder at the micro-level leads to the stagnation of aggregate growth. The principle of entropy changes in national income and monetary theories have been explained. Here I am going to clarify the disorder at the micro-level. In a social and economic environment with specific industrialized features, the gender relation does not change, but their notions and combinations change into a variety of types. The diversity of notions and combinations is defined as the changes of relations at the micro-level. Individuals have a variety of preferences in terms of marriage, family, and childbearing. And the preferences are changeable and random without a definite direction and a consistent rule. Random changes breed disorder of population at the micro level which is pointed out above.

The diversity of childbearing notions manifests the disorder of fertile individuals at the micro-level. Diversity is a relative concept compared to the single notion of childbearing. Before industrialization, marriage and family existed in a single form. Poverty, illnesses, and bad hygiene conditions brought a high mortality rate. To fight against the misery and preserve the family bearing more kids is the easiest. It can guarantee family stability and reproduction.

Factors affecting the birth rate are diversified. Such diversification involves many aspects including marriage, family, and childbearing. Specific examples are living together but not getting married, high divorce rate, single-parent families, more women becoming the labor force, better social welfare, the disappearance of several generations under one roof, DINK (living without childbearing), the higher unemployment rate of young people, poorer young generation than the generation of their parents, being looked after at old age changing into being gnawed by children, the collapse of the conventional notion of loyalty and filial piety, etc.. All the factors for sure bring down the birth rate. All in all, the young generation is reluctant to bear more children.

8.5 The Results of Self-limited Population Growth

Population growth abides by the law of self-limiting. If human beings fail to control reproduction based on their wisdom, some other laws are likely to take control of it to eliminate the probability of endless population growth. The law of self-limiting comes into force, not at the expense of testing the limit of nature. Instead, it functions more gently to subtly reduce the human birth rate without imposing pains on them so that the population is under control. Despite the painful outcome, self-limiting is the most civilized way in biological evolution compared with brutal events such as disasters and famines.

Without the liaison mechanism, humans would enjoy a long lifespan and a high birth rate which would undoubtedly induce a population boom. The earth was teeming with humans. Biological crisis and resource shortages were the preludes to a catastrophe. Only when limits are set on species, can nature revitalize with vibrancy and abundance. Sophisticate and harmonious regulations are based upon mutual restraints. Once humans are in the reign of the earth and override other species, another law will automatically take over the responsibility of limiting the growth of the human population. Technological advancements that transcend natural creatures prolong human lifespan and, at the same time, trigger off the decline of the fertility rate. With the decreasing death rate of individual living bodies, the fertility rate declines at a faster speed. There is a limit for the human population. Once reached, the population will go downhill. The instinct self-limiting ability helps to avoid the natural punishments on humans, keeping them safe from devastating natural blows. Natural disasters always target human beings as a whole. The overgrowing population makes impending natural disasters and resource shortages of a high likelihood. Self-limiting is a preferred result of natural selection. It, as a "civilized" method, is also accompanied by suffering, but the moderate way of population development it brings is just the most proper choice for the long-term existence of human beings.

The self-limited population is featured by the negative relation between the average life longevity and the birth rate. Thanks to the income increase and improvements of living conditions, the newborn endure a lower death rate. People's way of living and life philosophy also change. There is little need to feed more children to support the family and prepare for old age. Unlike living in poverty, the young generations inherit wealth from the older generations and enjoy better social welfare. They no longer bear as many responsibilities as their ancestors did in terms of supporting the old age in a family. Apart from cultural factors, employment, interests, hedonism, environmental pollution, and other factors that can also account for the decline of the fertility rate, the most important reason is the longer lifespan. (Table 8-1)

Table 8-1 Average lifespan in China and the birth rate

Year	Average expected lifespan (year of age)	Birth rate (‰)	Mortality rate (‰)
1950	37. 00	18. 00	
1960	—	20. 86	25. 43
1970	—	30. 74	7. 64
1980	—	18. 21	6. 36
1990	68. 55	21. 06	6. 67
2000	71. 40	14. 03	6. 45
2010	74. 83	11. 90	7. 11

Resource: collating from sampling survey records from China National Bureau of Statistics

Industrialized society witnessed a downward birth rate. In the meantime of prolonging lifespan, the birth rate increased. This only existed from the 1950s to the 70s. After the 70s, the birth rate and death rate both continued declining. In the long run, the increase in life longevity is negatively related to the birth rate.

Human beings, by taking the self-limiting way that the individual lifespan and the group number are related, deepen the understanding of individual life meaning. After the birth of a newborn baby, he or she grows into adolescence and then adulthood. Due to the limited frequency of cell division, he or she will become old as time elapses. The longer he or she lives, the more genes decay, and the more negative entropy accumulates which eventually leads to the death of the individual. We used to regard the individual death as the group continuance. The individual death positively boosts the group replacement and evolution. Now we know more than that. The changes in individual lifespan also lead to the changes of offspring group numbers.

Life and death interchange in every generation. To sustain the life cycle of a species, metabolism is the foundation. If metabolism slows down, i.e. the average life of the older generation becomes longer, the living bodies themselves will start the mechanism to reduce the number of the next generation. The mechanism is self-limiting in terms of controlling the reproduction. This is a natural law. The creatures cannot both live long and bear more. They contradict each other. If we can quantify the long lifespan and the reproduction number and multiply the two variables, we get a constant. Assume lifespan is x, the number of the offspring is y, then x times y is a constant c. x and y are negatively related as shown in the equation $xy=c$. If visualized in a graph in the coordinate axis (Figure 8-3), they form a hyperbola.

Human beings should never dream of living eternally or rejuvenating which is disobedient to natural laws. Only in heaven or Eden can eternal life exist. On the earth, a natural world, humans have to face life, old age, illness, and death. If humans try to extend their lifespan into 80 or 90 years, a disastrous slump of the population needed by generation replacement will confront us.

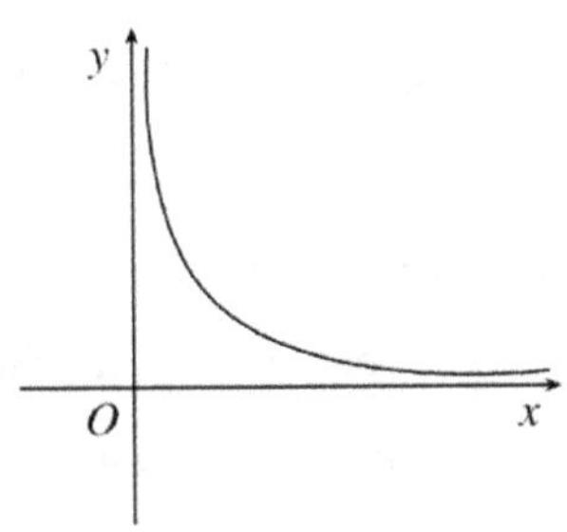

Figure 8-3 the negative relation between average lifespan and birth rate

Note: As shown in the diagram, the longer the individual lives, the fewer the posterity are; Otherwise, the shorter the individual lives, the more children are born.

Can human wisdom transcend the wisdom of life? There is little possibility for now. Even though it is trusted that technological advancements can treat and cure all diseases, humans can hardly escape death. Even though everyone can live for more than 100 years, the population will drop greatly. We have to face some less harmful crisis such as the greater economic recession and some more thrilling disasters including the genetic diseases which hang over the humans and swamp them. If one day, humans manage to develop technological means to control and alter themselves or create some wisdom superior to theirs, it will also be dreadful.

Think it this way, the newborn created by the technologies can sooner or later replace the current human beings, wiping them out of the universe and recording them as another extinct species.

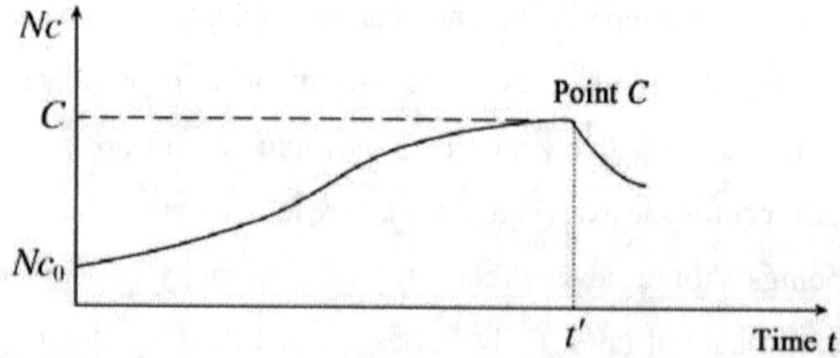

Figure 8-4 the trend of population growth

Note: Population N_c has a limit C, after which the population becomes smaller in a cliff-off manner. the curve is deducted from Logistic Equation

Self-limiting results in the population decline. This is not in slow progress. Nor it is a change of small geometric accumulation. It is a cliff off which is still a disaster for human beings who have to deal with such reality.

Self-limiting is chosen by human beings but this choice comes with significant risks. Because generation replacements will induce a population plunge which deteriorates the optimized development of the group. But the likelihood of a world population explosion is eliminated. The horrible geometric growth of the population is gradually replaced by a declining trend. The population will decline geometrically after reaching a peak. This is a process of variation which is symmetric. There has been an abundance of stories of geometric growth. Here comes the concern about the geometric decline. It is a well-known story of the king and his 64 checkerboard cells. It is said that in ancient India, a smart official invented chess. To reward him, the king granted his request by putting a grain of wheat in the first cell on the checkerboard, 2 grains in the second, 4 in the third, 8 in the fourth, and so the king did. The number of grains in the *n*th cell is 2^n. If n is infinite, the outcome is an astronomical figure. It is said that to fill the 64 cells, 1406.5 billion tons of wheat were needed. This example shows the astonishing power of geometric growth. However, the current concern is the reversed situation where 1.3 billion Chinese give birth to one child only in each family in each generation. This means a geometric shrink of population. The speed is so fast that whoever thinks of it will gasp in astonishment. The king granting wheat to his officials is a story but what confronts us Chinese is a severe reality.

We can imagine the geometric decline. Assume there were 0.7 billion couples in 2014, each couple bore one child only. And after their children grew up, they also bore one child in each family. If it continued, there would be only one person in the 31st generation. After 660 years, the only person passed away at age 80, meaning the extinction of 1.4 billion people once thrived on earth.

So whether the aging population signals the decline of a group? Individuals get old after their fertility gets lower, so the fertility rate declines. Though this does not necessarily stem from the decline of human reproduction, it is by no means a good omen. We have to think about the information behind the declining population—the aging population signals the aging human beings as a species. Despite tens of thousand years' evolution, no one can put forward a precise prediction about the gene diseases induced by the effect of gene decays which have been accumulating for hundreds of years?

Biology has paid attention to it for a long time. Biologists think that biological evolution requires enough numbers of the population to weed out the degeneration that does not fit the groups. If the group number declines, there will be no extra groups to inherit benign genes. Once the minority of gene mutation predominates, excluding the malignant mutations, groups will lose the chance to choose because of the insufficiency. This inhibits the groups' natural selection. Evolution and natural selection are eventually replaced by inbreeding and malignant gene mutations. So the biological groups quickly vanish. The process is irreversible, called "irreversible sink".[1]

1 John St. Verde, translated by Liu Ying, *The Mystery of the Degeneration Theory, Gene Entropy and Genome*, Shandong Friendship Publishing House, 2010.

The evolution of all creatures including human beings involves biological value. One species with the willingness to reproduce normally need at least two children of each couple. So the amount of species will maintain stability. As mentioned before, if the boy-to-girl birth ratio is in an acceptable range, the total fertility rate is supposed to maintain at 2.1‰. This is a baseline. From the viewpoint of evolution selection, an extra part of the population is good for natural selection. In botany, seed selecting events reveals that plants with greater fertility are more likely to select their superior genes and pass them to the next generation. Though for humans, there is no concern for seed selection, maintaining at least a 2.1‰ total fertility rate is essential for population stability. It can prevent the population from an enormous decline due to accidents and an unexpected burst of gene diseases. If the total fertility rate falls below the baseline, like the current 1.2‰, the nation is endangered by the hereditary disaster caused by a gene mutation. Now we have to maintain vigilance for possible gene mutations. We believe in Evolution Theory and have faith in the accessibility of higher developed human beings through evolution. However, it is still worth strong awareness of the aging population and the decline of the total fertility rate which increase the harm of possible short-term degeneration and environmental impacts on physiology.

According to researches, human beings have been in existence for 3 million years. The thriving and waning of the population took place in each dynasty but never reverse the tendency of increasing. Particularly after the Industrial Revolution, population and life longevity increased at the same time. The twin increase came to its turning point after World War II. When the lifespan increased by year, middle-developed countries and their above experienced a geometrically declining population required by generation replacement. As long as the medical sciences and technologies keep advancing, the increase of human lifespan will persist. If we admit the social development boosts the increase of the average lifespan, then does it mean that stopping the advancements of medical sciences and technologies is the only way to change the decline of the population? Unless great economic depressions, recessions, or even wars and disasters take place, the social development is unstoppable. So is the increase of the average lifespan. If the world stays in long-term peace and development, the world population will drop sharply due to the total fertility rate becoming far below the level required by the generation replacement.

What will happen after the aging population, the declining birth rate, and the population slump after the generation replacement? Will human beings face the same situation where other endangered creatures have already been? The aging population and population slump will lead to an impairment of self-selection in a biological sense. If some kind of gene diseases caused by environmental pollution and other gene mutations appears in reality, the only way is to persuade the patients to stop childbearing. Reminding ourselves of the declining population that has been already in existence, we easily know that there are no extra human beings to cope with the gene diseases by eliminating the mutated genes from the gene inheritance. Gene diseases are likely to continue prevailing until the whole species die out.

Even though there are no gene diseases, economic depression will occur as the population reduces. Economic growth has a process of entropy changes. A population decline is going to cause market contraction and supply decrease. The economic development turns into stagnation and enters into a trend of long-term recession from the current continuous growth. This process is roughly in accord with the trend of population aging. Economic depression makes the living condition worse. Social turmoils and wars are foreseeable. So is poverty. Once the death rate soars up, the population will decrease again.

No one is aware
That terminal awaits at the next stop.

——Shu Ting

Chapter 9

Theories of Multidimensional Space in Economics

In economic theories, the thought of multidimensional space is still an uncultivated virgin land. It still lacks concepts, viewpoints and systematic principles, and few people pay attention. This chapter is just a preliminary introduction to some of my thoughts on multidimensional space, which still have a long way before forming into mature theories. I will continue to exert myself to explore this exciting field next. This chapter serves as a modest induction in hope of providing for interested readers a reference worthy of pondering. For more content about the theory of multidimensional space, you might be willing to refer to the book *The Space and Principles of Thoughts* by the author.

9.1 Geometric Measure of Commodity Trading

9.1.1 Multidimensional Space

1. What is space?

Space is an abstract concept that is easy to understand. When people feel their own existence, they will naturally acquiesce in space. Space is not only real, but also recognized by wisdom. Space itself also has theories linking to the practice.

In physics, space is the form in which matter exists. This definition is easy to understand, because a form refers to some structure of the universe, and the structure contains the properties, including continuity, size, position and their alike, shared by matters.

Space is still a philosophical concern. German philosopher Kant (1724-1804) took things as just phenomena of sensory cognition, space and time as subjective mental states, and argued that the attributes of space can be expressed by a priori geometry.[1] Therefore, a form is also specified by a geometric object such as angle, distance, and vector, and a measure of space, such as area, volume, length of side, and so on. Geometric objects refer to abstract things with location, scale and surface properties.

The measurable relationship of space defines space as "the place where everything exists."[2] In a three-dimensional space, we define space as the place where things exist. A three-dimensional space is a space we can see:

Space

Above the tree shades,
Exists the azure sky.
Its vastness and broadness
Highlight the bird flying with liberty
Across the wilderness.
The transient noumenon
Soaring high
Ushers my vision to the paramount.

———Ma Lieguang

1 Ma Lieguang, *The Space and Principles of Thoughts*, Economic Press China, 2011, p. 42.

2 Shan Zhenwen, *Levels of Space*, China Compilation & Translation Press, 2012, p. 3.

People are familiar with the three-dimensional space and can perceive it with intuition. The world that you can see when you look around is a three-dimensional space between the heaven and the earth that can be expressed by length, width, and height. This is the space where human beings and the whole shoot exist. The description of a three-dimensional space grants a showcase for physics to fully demonstrate its talents. The world we see at a glance is the three-dimensional form of objects.

In terms of abstract mathematical definitions, space also exists in another two forms — multidimensional and branching (fractal) forms — apart from the three-dimensional from. With forms being expressed with math, space integrates into a form that can perceive and describe things with abstract expressions.

Humans use geometric principles to formulate the concept of space. Besides, we observe and infer multidimensional spaces from the logic of mathematics, such as 0-dimensional, 1/2-dimensional, 2/3-dimensional, 5-dimensional, ..., *n*-dimensional space.

If variables are expressed in a coordinate, a variable with 1 degree of freedom is called 1 dimension, a variable with 2 degrees of freedom is called 2 dimensions, and a variable with 3 degrees of freedom is called 3 dimensions. In a three-dimensional space, a straight line possesses 1 dimension, a plane 2, a cube 3. A ragged coastline has a dimension between 1 and 2. For disordered shapes such as snowflakes and coastlines, their spatial dimensions are expressed in fractional numbers.

We call the set of continuously changing forms of multiple variables as Riemann space. These dependent variables are usually affected by three factors or even more which are expressed separately and not combined with their counterparts. Moreover, the latter is linearly independent. Therefore, the number of the dependent variables that affect each other is called the dimension of space. Riemann space is a multidimensional space.

Space comes into formation as variables continuously change. This type of space is also called generalized space, namely multidimensional space. This is

Riemann's idea. Riemann, for the first time, introduced the concept of generalized space in a lecture given at the University of Göttingen in Germany in 1854, where he interpreted the continuous collection of similar phenomena in ordinary space as generalized space which was expressed by multiple variables, and displayed geometric relations such as distance, angle, and boundary. According to Riemann, the set of continuously changing forms of multiple variables and processes is defined as dimensional space for variables, if the system is composed of variables.

2. What is the difference?

Three-dimensional space and substances combined form a three-dimensional world. It is the world where human beings live. In the three-dimensional world, every stone is different, and every stone has its meaning of existence.

The difference in substances is not substances themselves, but an abstract attribute which is the form of space rather than something.

Everything in the world has specific features that differ themselves from others. But these differences are not determined by the nature of elements. Differences always exist. Differences are the absolute attributes distinguished from the nature of things. This type of attributes that do not depend on the attributes of substances can be expressed by geometric relations where differences are expressed as forms of space, including different angles, different distances, different dimensions, and so on. From this point of view, the difference is a form of expression of the space. Due to the abstract form of space, space is still the difference that distinguishes one space from the other. The differences in substances are both concrete existence and the universality of matter. Whenever we describe the difference as the form of space, space is no longer an abstract subjective concept, but a certain attribute of matter. No things exist with no differences. Neither does the space.

The same is true for non-material thoughts. "When everyone thinks the same, it means that no one is really thinking." The same thoughts certainly leave no space for critical thinking.

The changes of variables form differences and the differences among variables can be expressed by geometric relations. Geometric relations highlight the existence of space. Therefore, what we call difference is the geometrical features of a certain space.

Changes and characteristics show the existence of space. Therefore, when we speak of difference, we mean the geometry of a certain space.

9.1.2 The “distance” of commodities

Geometry is precise mathematics, which is used to measure the actual size of matter in space and quantitative relations of various variables. However, the recognition that separates the precise geometry from the microcosmic disorder is naive. Geometry is hidden deeply in chaos and random movements. A fickle economy always has some spatial attributes, such as geometric measurement, minimum distance, microscopic constants, etc. Geometric variables exist independently in complex systems, constructing a basic framework for describing multidimensional space.

The existence of space manifests the existence of spatial distance. The measurement of distance, apart from Pythagorean law, includes Riemann metrics, topology, etc. If the variable has numerical scales, the distance can also be worked out by linear algebra. For example, in period t_1, 2 pieces of a certain product were sold, in period t_2, 3 pieces were sold. These two purchases form a continuous process with a numerical difference of 1 piece. In other words, the “distance” of the two purchases is 1. The difference in quantity is 1 piece, and the “distance” between the two purchases is 1. From the perspective of sales amount, if each piece is worth 10 yuan, 20 yuan is earned in t_1, and 30 yuan in t_2, so the “distance” between the two periods is 10. 10 is neither 10 pieces, nor a unit measurement of physical space. It is an abstract scale. Therefore, it is acceptable to calculate the distance between two points that continuously change by applying geometric formulas without considering the limitation of variable unit. Please refer to the following analysis:

In practice, the sales amount is determined by the quantity of products sold and the unit price combined, i.e. sales = unit price × quantity. To unify the scale, natural numbers are used, given that the scale of the unit price and the quantity of the commodity are different.

Suppose x and y belong to the array of natural numbers. The natural numbers in x group represent the number of the units of products sold. The sales unit refers to the smallest unit of sales, such as one piece, one unit, one set, one suit, or one batch. The symbol "→" represents the "correspondence". For example, 0→0 piece, 1→1 piece, 2→2 pieces, ..., $n \to n$ pieces. Or, 0→0 batch, 1→1 batch, 2→2 batches, ..., $n \to n$ batches. The natural numbers in y group correspond to the unit price of the product, such as 0→0 yuan, 1→1 yuan, 2→2 yuan, ..., $n \to n$ yuan, or 0→0 yuan, 1→10 yuan, 2→20 yuan, etc.

In this case, geometry embraces no attributes of commodities, and geometric relations exist in all continuous changes. Therefore, the numbers in calculation do not have measurement unit. In other words, no unit name exists after each number. In a three-dimensional space, a measurement unit can be expressed by specific scales, such as meters, centimeters, degrees, arcs, seconds, etc. However, in a multidimensional space, there coexist numbers of the dimensional degree and other numbers that correspondingly stand. Whether the latter has measurement unit or not is up to specific analysis in specific situations. Numbers with no unit can also quantify geometric relations, and they are more abstract in comparison to numbers with measurement unit. Therefore, they are applicable to all systems as a more generalized group of numbers. However, the lack of intuitiveness deteriorates them, and they, therefore, have a difficulty in comparing and calculating with numbers possessing measurement units.

For example, suppose the sales of t_1 period are 100 yuan, the sales of t_2 period are 180 yuan, and the total of the two periods is 280 yuan. The sales volume in t_1 period is 10 pieces, and the price is 10 yuan each. The sales volume in t_2 period is 20 pieces, and the price per piece is 9 yuan. The total sales volume is 30 pieces. Suppose x is the sales volume. In t_1 period, $x_1 = 10$ pieces, and in t_2 period $x_2 = 20$ pieces. Suppose y is the unit selling price, in t_1 period, the unit price y_1=10 yuan, and in t_2 period y_2=9 yuan. The sales "distance" of the two periods is given by the formula $d^2 = (x_2-x_1)^2 + (y_2-y_1)^2$. After substituting $x_1 = 10, x_2 = 20, y_1 = 10$, and $y_2 = 9$, we get $d = 3.3$.

In the process of continuously selling a certain commodity, the number of commodity transactions also determines the transaction volume of the commodity. The transaction volume of the commodity is determined by the three factors—quantity in a single transaction x, commodity price y, and transaction times z. Commodity transaction volume = quantity (x) in each transaction × unit price (y) × number of times (z). The sales "distance" of the two periods is given by the formula $d^2 = (x_2-x_1)^2 + (y_2-y_1)^2 + (z_2-z_1)^2$.

Suppose the unit price of sales remains unchanged. The unit price of t_1 is y_1=10 yuan, and the unit price of t_2 is y_2=9 yuan. The average sales volume of each commodity in t_1 period is x_1 = 1 (piece), and the number of commodity transactions in period t_1 is z_1 = 10 times. The average volume of merchandise sales in the t_2 period x_2 = 1.2 (pieces), the number of merchandise transactions in the t_2 period z_2 = 17 times. Substituting the variables with numbers in the formula $d^2 = (x_2-x_1)^2 + (y_2-y_1)^2 + (z_2-z_1)^2$, we get d = 2.86. A total of 30.4 pieces of goods were sold in the two periods, and the total sales amount was 283.6 yuan.

Table 9-1 Analysis of the commodity "distance"

Each sales volume x (pieces)		The unit selling price y (yuan)	The transaction times z	The total sales amount Y (yuan)	The total sales volume (pieces)	Distance d
Period 1, t_1	10	10	1	100	10	—
Period 2, t_2	20	9	1	180	20	—
Total	30	—	2	280	30	3. 3
Period 1, t_1	1	10	10	100	10	—
Period 2, t_2	1. 2	9	17	183. 6	20. 4	—
Total	2. 2	—	27	283. 6	30. 4	2. 86

As shown in the table, when the aggregate indicators of the system index is constant, the spatial dimension increases and the spatial distance decreases.

After the number of transactions is introduced, the unit price remains unchanged, the commodity trading volume and sales amount both increase, the total gap widens, but the distance reduces. The main reason for the shrinking distance is that the two-dimensional gap of sales is decomposed by another variable in the three-dimension. Under the premise that the unit price of the product remains unchanged, the frequency of sales increases, which breaks down the single sales amount. Although the total sales gap between the two periods has widened, the geometric distance has decreased.

Therefore, for the multiplication of multiple variables, when the total number is constant, the more independent variables, the smaller the spatial distance between the variables.

In reality, commodity sales are affected by many factors. For example, car sales are affected by multiple factors such as gasoline prices, parking fees, and number of parking spaces. If listed one by one, these factors are multiple variables that exceed three-dimensional dependent variables. The relationship between commodities affects each other. The assembly of continuous changes of these variables is multidimensional space.

Generally, for the mathematical formula $Y=x_1 \times x_2 \times \ldots \times x_n$, if x is greater than 1, and when Y is constant, $d^2=\Delta x_1^{\ 2}+\Delta x_2^{\ 2}+\ldots+\Delta x_n^{\ 2}$, which tends to decrease as the variable x increases. In this case, the multidimensional space is crowded space. When the spatial dimension increases, if the total amount y remains stable, the spatial distance between variables will decrease. In contrast, if the spatial dimension decreases, as the remaining x increases, the spatial distance will become longer.

Suppose Y is the residents' income, C is consumption, I is investment, and z is government expenditure. When the economy grows, consumption, investment and government spending will all increase. Only when the proportions of them in the total output value tend to be equal, the average distance between consumption, investment, and government spending will tend to be the smallest. If a certain item grows too fast, for example, if government spending grows too fast, the proportion of it in national income will increase significantly, and the distance between consumption, investment, and government spending will be larger. The following example assumes that under the condition that the sales volume and unit price of each product remain unchanged, if the number of product sales increases by 10 times, both the total sales volume and spatial distance will increase.

Chart 9-2 The Analysis of Commodity Distance

Each sales volume x (pieces)		The unit selling price y (yuan)	The transaction times z	The total sales amount Y (yuan)	The total sales volume (pieces)	Distance d
Period 1, t_1	1.2	9	17	183.6	20.4	—
Period 2, t_2	1	10	170	1700	170	—
Total	—	—	—	1883.6	190.4	12.41

To think simple, we assume that *x* and *y* remain unchanged, and *z* is magnified by 10 times. Then the distance of two arbitrary points in the three-dimensional space increases to 12.41. While the spatial dimensional degree does not increase, the spatial increases with the variables.

Therefore, the spatial distance is positively proportionate to the growth of sales variables. The faster they grow, the longer the spatial distance will be; otherwise, the distance gets shorter, which means the space is almost filled up.

9.2 Position, Distance and Behavior

9.2.1 The Principle of Geussi

The principle of Geussi means that all creatures have their own position in nature which is called ecological niche. Species with genetic relations and sharing the same living habits do not compete for the same living space in the same place. Because they have difficulty living together. The same species avoids staying close to each other to keep separate living space.

The Russian ecologist Geus did a biological experiment. He kept genetically related paramecium Aurelia and paramecium cauda-tum in two identical bacterial culture media. A few days later, they both survived. Then, he kept them in one culture medium, and only the paramecium Aurelia survived. In a third experiment, he put paramecium cauda-tum and paramecium bursaria in the same container.

Paramecium cauda-tum and paramecium bursaria do not have a genetic relation. As a result, both survived and a stable relationship appeared between them.[1]

Here it is easy to find out that only dissimilar species can achieve equilibrium in the same environment. Each species has its need for an independent living space. Similar species, if living in the same space, will encounter space segmentation. In contrast, different species with relatively big distinctions require smaller space and live in harmony, while similar species ask for larger space to survive so that they avoid crowding together with having to enduring the same attributes.

The reason for it is still the same with the situation that is reflected by the relationship between distance and magnitude, or the dimensional relation in the previous section. When the number of species is constant, and the size of the species is equal, the commonality of species reduces the multidimensional distance between them, resulting in narrow and crowded space. If there is a big difference in species, it means that each different species accounts for an uneven proportion, and the multidimensional distance between species is extended. So the difference will stretch to make a larger space. Even if the size of the three-dimensional space remains unchanged, a balanced relationship will come into formation, as long as the multidimensional space of the system is big enough. Furthermore, difference and similarity are traits of species, and different traits belong to the category of multidimensional relationships. Therefore, space segmentation of species is not only related to the size of the three-dimensional space, but also related to the multidimensional distance of the system.

In three-dimensional space, between systems there are multidimensional relations, minimum distances and coordination relations. The minimum distance of the multidimensional space between systems may be shorter. These systems tend to have the same size. If the three-dimensional space is relatively small, mutual exclusion will occur. In contrast, systems with larger differences may have

1 Huang Xiaolin, Huang Mengxi, *The Most Amazing Laws of Economics*, New World Publishing House, 2010, p.118.

longer distances of multidimensional space. In three-dimensional spaces with the same features, species that embrace greater discrepancies can enjoy a coordinate mutual relation.

If the market economy is regarded as a system of multidimensional space, it also has a "niche" phenomenon. Each company resembles a creature in nature. They all have their own space at the market which corresponds to the independent "niche". The "niche" is exhibited by the uniqueness of products and services, only those with distinct characteristics can survive and expand in competition. Companies of different sizes have naturally come into existence in the fierce market competition, and they are also classified in different grades according to their scales. Smaller companies have a larger number, while bigger companies are fewer. In the same industry, companies of large, medium, and small sizes have their own market shares. The combination of various sizes and different strengths usually improves the product qualities of competing companies and makes their services better so that the market prosperity is boosted.

No totally equivalent companies exist at the same time in the market economy. Neither are there two identical companies, nor two companies with zero distance between every mapping point of them respectively. Meanwhile, the product supply will never equal the demand utterly. The equilibrium at the product market does not refer to the exact match between the supply and demand of every product, but to the status where the distance between supply and demand reaches its minimum.

9.2.2 The Minimum Distance

The intuition of the distance in three-dimensional space does not apply to the multidimensional space exactly since the latter is relatively closed and independent space without the consistency of the three-dimensional space.

The relation between three-dimensional spaces is invariable, and it is built upon layers with one wrapped upon the other. This dimensional constant bridges the three-dimensional spaces, unlike the multidimensional space which is self-enclosed. As the dimensional degree of space may change, multidimensional systems are not necessarily intercommunicable.

The physical three-dimensional space is normal space. No matter how much it is enlarged or contracted, it is still three-dimensional. Opening the door of a sealed room usher you to the outside world which is also three-dimensional. Even if part of the space becomes distorted space after being taken out and twisted, it is still three-dimensional. The curved space mentioned in the general theory of relativity is just the bending of lines. It is still three-dimensional. Once time t is taken into account, it becomes four-dimensional space-time. This is the most that physics can study on space. Whether the space is going to change distinguishes the three-dimensional space from the multidimensional one. The dimensional degree of the former is a constant, while the latter has a varying dimensional degree.

The distance between multidimensional spaces is not the spatial distance perceived in our experience. Its measurement is not restricted to length, width, and height only, since length, width, and height are only a geometric scale for the difference between variables. However, within a system where elements change randomly, the geometric scales can be used to explain the spatial density. For example, if the changes between variables are big, then the geometric distance is big; otherwise, the geometric distance is small.

In a multidimensional system, distance is related to the dimension. In turn, the dimensional changes also affect the distance, and this complies with a law of the relation between the spatial dimension and the distance.

The multidimensional space is an assembly of continuous changes of variables. If a variable continues growing, mutually affected new variables are fractionated from the interior, or the spatial dimension increases due to the microcosmic disorder. Anyway, the spatial distance between variables may become shorter consequently.

Thanks to the minimum distance between the variables, the space has a limit to reducing to. Once the limit is approached, the space is filled up. If at that time, the variables do not grow, the magnitude changes will also be restricted.

If no minimum distance exists, the mutually communicative assemblies of variables are the same. Once no discrepancy occurs, all the assemblies end up being in one static system.

In the example of selling products above, if only integers are used, the integer 1 is the minimum distance, such as the price gap of 1 yuan, one transaction, one product, and so on. If the difference 1 disappears, the two periods of merchandise sales are exactly the same with no change. Once the geometric distance in the spatial relation is zero, the multidimensional space ceases to exist.

9.2.3 Repeated Trial and Error

In economic life, people often seek equilibrium, and optimal regulations and strategies so they can achieve a reasonable allocation of resources. The method is to repeat trial and error, and finally find the best solution after making sufficient comparisons. The essence of repeated trial and error is to find out the minimum distance between variables in the multidimensional space.

A strategy is exposed to the effect of various factors. That is, a point in space is determined by a few variables, and the minimum distance between the point and its corresponding point can be obtained by adjusting the values of variables for many times (indicating the relation). Therefore, this point can approach its corresponding point. The minimum distance between two arbitrary points in space is the optimal regulation and strategy.

Many examples can support the repeated trial and error, through which the economic relationships are coordinated, including the market division of labor, transaction mechanism, traffic rules, corporate management regulations, policies and regulations, property rights systems, and so forth. The repeated trial and error almost generalize all market behavior and relationships in need of coordination.

The assembly of all economies constitutes a space where each system has one type of wisdom. Through repeated trial and error to coordinate the spatial relationship and frequently adjust the spatial position, the system makes itself in a comfortable status where the energy consumption is minimized. This, in economy, is shown as the maximization of benefits. In the space of a system, each element approaches the minimum distance between each other through trial and error, so that the micro-systems are evenly distributed in space, and each system reaches the maximum disorder.

The reason why repeated trial and error can correct the deviation is that there is a range of possible distances between two arbitrary points. A possible world exists in space. There is no uniqueness to choose between the possible world and the realistic one. There is only possibility. This determines that repeated trial and error is a process of choosing the right direction. Only after this process, the relationship between two points can tend to be the optimal. In this state, the distance between the two points makes them comfortable — the minimum space of the niche.

Human beings accumulate experience through repeated trial and error. Making a choice is the universal wisdom of life. The process of biological evolution is a process of repeated trial and error so that species are adapted to the environment. The hypothesis of the economic man in economics refers to the fact that the economist can achieve his goals by making a range of choices. No economist can manage to succeed at once without making repeated trial and error.

9.3 The Spatial Relationships in Economic Phenomena

It is easier to understand economic relationships by introducing the concept of space in economic variables. The concepts of space alteration, connection and replication are helpful to explain economic phenomena.

9.3.1 Space alteration

Space alteration means the transformation from the low dimensional space to the high, or the other way round. For example, the market selling a single product transforms to a market selling various products, or from selling products of low quality to selling products with sophisticated functions and serial upgrades. All these changes lead to the complexion of geometric relationships in space.

Systems are hierarchical. The connection between systems has microcosmic consistency. For two macrosystems that communicate with each other, they build the boundary through connections at the micro-level. Therefore, another system or another world exists at the boundary.

Sometimes, imperfection contains more beauty. Space alteration is realized by following new possibilities which brew new assemblies of serial events (space). "People always doubt the existence of the path after numerous frustrations and obstacles before realizing that a brand new hope is just waving its hand behind the next difficulty." This is a phenomenal expression of space alteration. Its corresponding explanation in economic relations is that new systems are found from the old ones. Such finding and development are neither a repetition of the current system, nor a replacement between similar objects. It is the appearance of another system. New products, new corporations, new industries and new markets appear.

Boosted by the technological advancements, several new products start burgeoning. The research, development, promotion and application of every new type of products are indeed a process of serial alteration and upgrading of space. The assembly of continuous economic changes constitutes a series of new space.

The market segmentation is a form of space alteration. If every product is regarded as an independent system, then it has an independent space of its own. More independent microcosmic sub-spaces come into formation in the market economy. Each of them has its own independent world.

The purchasing power increases with the increase of income. The product market witnesses new products being developed, new industries being built, and new demands being created. Products are more abundant, and the market continues expanding. The process of market expansion and segmentation is also the process of market explosion.

The occurrence of new space is orderly from the superficial features, but, indeed, it is an event of small probability that randomly occurs. Only when the event does occur, the event is certain. It remains uncertain before the occurrence. This is like drawing a lottery. There is always a winner, but who is the winner remains uncertain.

Space alteration always creates miracles. The best system always appears when people are most unconcerned. In the past forty years or more, China's economy has experienced dramatic changes. This is a significant miracle. Though many problems come along, this economic miracle was totally unpredictable years ago.

Multidimensional space transforming to a lower-dimensional space means the decline of a system since the disappearance of diversity means the separation of systems and the decrease of systematic kinetic energy. In economic depression, a large number of companies went bankrupt, resulting in economic contraction and output reduction. The economic space transformed from diversity and multidimensional prosperity to the depression in low dimensional space.

9.3.2 Space Connection

In economic life, we find common details in some different systems. These details link the past and the present like a ribbon. For example:

The standard distance between two rails nowadays is 4.85 inches. Railways were designed by engineers who built trams and they set 4.85 inches as the standard distance between two wheels of a tram. But where did the standard tram wheel distance come from? Those who built trams were originally designers of carriages. So that is where it came from. Then why did carriages use this standard? The width of riding traces in roads in Britain was 4.85 inches. If carriages used other wheel distance, its wheels were to be broken once riding on the road. Then where did the riding traces come from? They came from the ancient Roman. Because roads all over Europe, including the old long-distance roads in Britain, were built by the Roman for their troops. 4.85 inches were just the width of chariot wheel distance. Then why did the Roman choose 4.85 inches as the width of their chariot wheel distance? The reason is simple. It is the width of the cruppers of the two horses leading the chariot. The story did not end here. The fuel tank of the US space shuttle has two rocket propellers on both sides, and these propellers will be transported by train once selected. Given that there will be some tunnels on the road, and the width of these tunnels is only a little wider than the train track, then the width of the rail is determined by the width of the rail.[1]

These examples are explained by the "path dependency", meaning that people get self-reinforced by following one institutionalized direction. The "path dependency" determines that the width of the rocket propellers of the US space shuttle is up to the width of the two cruppers two thousand years ago.

In philosophy, the phenomenon is described as microcosmic consistency. From the perspective of vertical history, some major achievements and details are always retained so that a civilization was built and has been passed on from generation to generation like the genes that remain unchanged and link the past, present, and future. From the perspective of horizontal relations, the connections between people do not prevail because, in fact, people's social networks are not large. However, due to the large scale of the market economy and the increasing diversification, the microcosmic commonality becomes the medium to keep the rapport, linking the producers and the consumers. The bond with people connects producers and consumers. Producers do not know consumers, and consumers are not concern about producers. Products and prices are the content of microcosmic commonalities between producers and consumers. A boundary point represents the complex relations among producers, between producers and consumers, and the different demands, as well as the mass of effective information. This cuts off the transaction costs at the market so that the market economy manages to operate with high efficiency.

If different economic theories are regarded as two different systems, the two systems share some common points though their main arguments differ. For example, Adam Smith coined "invisible hands" to express the effective market principle of balanced allocation of resources that was widely accepted by economists in his era. In masterpieces of David Ricardo and Muller, as well as Marx, the concept of equilibrium was put forth. The notion of equilibrium

1 Huang Xiaolin, Huang Mengxi, *The Most Amazing Laws of Economics*, New World Publishing House, 2010.

becomes a commonality shared by economic theories in different eras, and of various schools. Such commonality is the microcosmic consistency of economic theories, namely a link at the micro-level among different thoughts.

The clock time is a boundary that links every system, too. Everybody, and even the whole society schedule daily routines according to the clock time. The clock time has synchronicity. If aliens in the universe also know of time, then they share commonality with human beings, which is the living habit of complying with time.

The three-dimensional space and the clock time are special attributes at the micro-level. From the perspective of space and time, all systems that have been in our cognition are changing in space and time. Even a notion, or a dream has occurred in realistic space and time. An instant and a position combined form an element in the assembly that represents a relationship of order. This is the only universality of multidimensional system, apart from which there is no uniform boundary between systems.

The microcosmic connection displays a state of disorder. Between systems exist tiny boundaries where there are only a few elements. Between boundaries are boundaries as well. They twist together like a mess. Each space-time point is multiple spaces and a multiple worlds.

Though all creatures are connected, we cannot know the world by learning the boundaries, because the multidimensional systems are independent and closed ones. People have no knowledge of the multidimensional space except for the sense of space and time. For this reason, stars in the sky might be very close, while the expression in the lover's eyes is faraway.

In general, each sub-system inside a system is combined by being grouped together. If the system is randomly changing, the occurrence of a certain combination is an event of small probability. More combinations that do not occur stay as possible events. If the system is integrated by confirmed relations where sub-systems obey a certain type of arrangement, then the system is deterministic. it is equivalent to view the randomly combined macrosystems as a microsystem with only one definite relationship.

For example, a network system contains multiple connections between different nodes. If the connection is between two single nodes, then this connection is a combining relationship that can be completed in multiple paths and methods. However, if a communicative center is built to connect other nodes according to their preset numbers in arrangement, then the connection is limited to one definite path and method. That is to process the macro network connection at the micro-level, which greatly increases the efficiency of the network. From the perspective of management, this is actually to view the network connection from the outside as a system with a certain order, and view the macrosystem as the microsystem so that the system becomes efficient and manageable. This method is widely used in the network management, such as the Internet, transportation, logistic network, bill exchanges between banks, and so forth.

A simple and single point-to-point network is effective. But to extend a single function of the network to a sophisticated system with multiple functions is equivalent to build a macrosystem. Unfortunately, using this method to build a macrosystem always fail. It is similar to the practice that a planned regime is always of low efficiency, so the planned economy is an inefficient economy.

The multi-points to the multi-points method in management resorts to the specific analysis according to the concrete practice. There is not supposed to be a universal principle that can be applied to all situations. Because one system cannot replicate another. Even the point-to-point information is asymmetric. Moreover, each system in the market economy has its "niche" to keep the freedom of the system in space and the individual independence. A microsystem responds repulsively to any external control if the control invades its "niche".

9.3.3 Space Replication

Space replication refers to the imitation of one system to another. This type of system replication is called the system's space imitation because the relationship between the spatial dimension and geometric distance is emphasized. It includes not only the accurate self-replication in the interior, such as cell division after which one cell is divided into two identical cells but also the perception of systems. In other words, to what extent a system can replicate another is related to the geometric attributes of spatial elements in the two systems.

When it comes to the cognition and replication of a macrosystem, the splendid achievements of empiricism do not exist. The earliest branch of science started from the classified observations of natural history and historical resources. This is the base camp of empiricism. However, descriptions loyal to nature and history encounter problems later. That is the mess led by detailed descriptions. The limitation of the replication of macrosystems is that the more accurate statistical records and the status quo incur more ambiguous conclusions, which deteriorates the accuracy of empirical data.

John Joachim Winkelmann was a German scientist who later became an observer loyal to empiricism and the founder of archaeology. He insisted on compiling natural history and art history through direct observation. But he felt being trapped by many difficulties of categorizing historical materials when he compiled them. German philosopher Herder commented on Winkelmann's research as being lost in a forest where no clarity was found out. This forest is the city of Rome with 70 thousand statues and busts:

> In an intricate forest full of fake signals, there is a group of voices echoing. Some come from critics who often give suggestions to others, some come from hypocritical artists, and others come from ignorant antique collectors. These voices keep echoing and end up in horrible tranquility. Because what they have found in ancient history is only some information out of date. Pliny and Pausanias are like a deserted riverbank where people can neither have a good swim nor obtain anything.[1]

Of course, there does not exist any method to improve the accuracy of data. But these methods have limited functions. If there are relatively many data samples,

1 Wolf Lepenies, *Qu'est-ce qu'un intellectuel européen? Les intellectuels et la politique de l'esprit dans l'histoire européenne*, translated by Li Yanming, Guangxi Normal University Press, 2011, p.172.

they will help to get the information that is relatively accurate. Big data analysis has more advantages than some simple assessments. But information from big data can only reflect the situation of one system from multiple perspectives instead of knowing every detail of this system more accurately.

The spatial distance between two systems is determined by the gap between variables and the number of variables (or the dimensional degree) combined. If the integral differences of the two systems remain unchanged, more variables at the micro-level mean higher dimensional degree of the space. Then the spatial distance between the two systems reduces with the number of variables increasing. For example, statistical research and the respondents form two systems. The collection and calculation of economic data replicate the data in research by using statistical methods. More research samples mean greater accuracy of data collected. From the perspective of spatial distance, more samples mean shorter spatial distance and fewer errors, so the accuracy of data is improved.

Information analyzed from the statistical process is embedded with relatively big errors compared with the economic situation in practice, since the economic statistical data and the respondents form two independent systems, and there is no identical information between systems. The magnitude of errors depends on the number of samples and the gap between sample data and real data.

Between spaces exists the minimum distance. If two systems are identical, the distance d is zero. But it is impossible to have d=0 because the cost of replication will rise by a large margin, and the sophisticated system in continuous changes will face unexpected events at the micro-level. The other system approaching it in detail is likely to find out that the original microsystem has already changed.

I once argued "the past is also changing" to explain the reverse between the macro opposite law and the micro. Now we divide the past and the present into two systems, and suppose the present as system A, the corresponding microsystem as *an*, the past as system B, and the corresponding microsystem as b_n. If A equals B, it means the present has a thorough knowledge of the past, or the present can replicate the past. However, according to the opposite law of the macro and the micro, there must be some cases where a does not equal b among systems *A* and *B*. This means the present cannot replicate the past in every detail, and each replication means a specific situation which differs from the other. For the present, the past is always changing. This is why history does not always have a consistent expression of historical data. Despite of the basal framework and many consensuses, disputes always survive. The triggers of some historical events are unknown to people. Some historical events have not been clearly stated yet. Not to mention a widely-accepted conclusion on it.

Unlike the macrosystem, the microsystem is relatively simple, so the system replication is comparatively easy. The macro relationship and the micro between systems are not in line with each other. Sometimes it is required to simplify and generalize the microcosmic factors for the sake of simplification. So "knowing one element means knowing the whole".

The dimensional degrees of microsystems are fewer, such as 1 dimensional degree or 2 dimensional degree. So the variables for distance calculation are fewer, too. The data are simple. The testing system and the system under test are on the same boundary. Data read through replication has a small difference from the real data. The distance d between two systems approaches the minimum. So the accuracy of replication is relatively high.

In economic statistics, the production statistics of one single commodity, such as iron, bronze, gold, the petroleum inventory, the output of grains, cotton, and oil are relatively accurate. In physics, a star is regarded as an individual at the micro-level so that the variables are simplified. For some macrosystems, macro data, including temperature, air pressure, entropy, and so on, is used to express the state and attributes of the system. For example, when describing the air in an air container, we cannot test the changes of micro molecules in the interior. Instead, we directly use equipments to measure simple variables in physics, such as the chemical composition, volume, pressure, internal energy, temperature, and so forth, to build a relatively accurate analysis model.

For systems with one single indicator, the more magnified the data point is, the more accurate the prediction will be. For example, for stock market forecasts, the shorter the period is chosen, the more turbulent the outcome will be; otherwise, the better the predicted value will fit the reality. Generally speaking, the longer the time is, the better the model based on the past data will fit the stock market. The annual, quarterly, and monthly stock price index volatility fits the reality better, while the daily and hourly data are more random. The trend of macro data is obvious, while the microdata is relatively more random.

The statistical analysis steps are roughly divided intodetermining samples, selecting or discarding data, establishing mathematical models or using statistical methods to estimate the results, and statistical testing. The comparison system of statistical testing and the results of statistical analysis are often two different systems, and the two systems cannot be in complete consistency. Changes of samples and data adjustments will both form a spatial distance. Any change is a system change. If other systems are generated in the same program, the results obtained by the same statistical method will be different. Similarly, if you only change the statistical method without changing the sample and data, the analysis results will also change.

In statistical analysis, there are often situations where the data predicted by simple models are more accurate than complex models. When we make statistical forecasts, a more complicated statistical model with a larger internal process and system may not work out more effective results based on data inputs, compared with the simple methods. In macroeconomics, forecast data made through huge models are often meaningless. Instead, through a simple trend analysis, a subjective analysis, or even a flash of genius thought, the results may appear to be more reasonable, and the difference may not be big compared with the practice.

People's thoughts also have their own space. For complex systems, intuition is often more spatially savvy, so judgments are often more accurate. Just like language translation, a person who can translate English into Chinese can not only memorize the words in the two languages, but also understand the meaning of the sentence. It is more accurate to translate the sentence intuitively. However, computers cannot translate intuitively. So the performance of computer translation is not as good as human translation.

The US philosopher Thomas Kuhn said, "Things spoken out in any language can be understood by speakers of another language through imagination and effort. However, the prerequisite for this understanding is not translation, but language learning."[1] To understand more accurately the ideas of the original work is to read the original work itself. Once translated into another language, the translated version may not be able to accurately express the content of the original work.

"There are many reasons explaining the lack of consensus of economists on choosing an empirical model. One of the main reasons is the great complexity of the modern economy. For example, in the United States, 260 million people make up about 100 million family units. All units are constantly making decisions, hourly, daily, weekly, monthly, yearly, or even longer. Only a small part of the economic results of these decisions are recorded."[2]

Scholars doing macroeconomic statistical analysis often complain that the data is scarce and inaccurate. The calculated results are wrong if incomplete, or even wrong data is input into the model. In fact, the model itself and the actual system are two independent systems. Even though the correct data is input, there will still be a big gap between the simulating conclusion and the actual result.

In China's statistics of national income, there have been cases of false reporting of income over the years. Therefore, some people questioned the quality of the data, and argued that the statistical data did not reflect the true situation. In practice, there is both false reporting and a large amount of concealment. The existence of errors is definite, and it is relatively large. However, it is not impossible to use these unreliable data to do statistical analysis and comparison.

1 Thomas Kuhn, *The Road Behind the Structure,* translated by Qiu Hui, Peking University Press, 2012, p.53.

2 Clive W J Granger, *The Setting and Evaluation of Empirical Modeling in Economics*, translated by Hong Fuhai, China Renmin University Press, 2013, p. 4.

Statistics of national income have errors every year. As long as the error term does not fluctuate greatly, the economic growth rate through calculation will not be affected by the total error. If the errors that cannot be corrected remain the same every year, the number of fixed errors will not affect the calculation of the growth rate. If the error needs to be reduced, more manpower and material resources are costed. People will also find out that the error cannot be eliminated, no matter how much effort is made. The more details you test, the more and messier problems of correcting errors will be induced. The final result is not to eliminate the error, but to replace the old error with the new one. For example, if the price of a new house is included in the consumer price index, how to adjust the weights is a difficult problem. If it is not solved properly, the effectiveness of the past years' data will be weakened.

Under the vision of the market economy, the simulator has its own subjectivity. Some models are based on a certain theory. For example, Klein established the US macro-econometric model based on Keynesian theories. Another well-known empirical model built with data is the model for the Amazon water conservancy project done by Granger. However, whichever the kind of model is, it is essentially a replication of a subjective vision to another system. What the model finds out and how to combine the findings with experience are determined by vision in a large part. It is related to the angle and distance between systems, as well as to the subjective perception of the model builder. This subjective perception resembles the self-perception of an artist towards his or her works which is unreliable. "A sculptor once said that he views his art in this way. That is, he can sculpt a large stone carefully until he discovered that the statue hidden in it."[1] Art and forecasts made by economic modeling are both based on individualized judgments. Although the consensus of consistency is emphasized, the consensus itself is a limited vision which is not necessarily closer to the practice than the models with

1 Clive W J Granger, *The Setting and Evaluation of Empirical Modeling in Economics*, translated by Hong Fuhai, China Renmin University Press, 2005, p. 5.

no consensus being reached.

People have to admit that economics does not have any universal principle that is consistent with experience. Everything will change once the vision alters.[1]

1 Lawrence, the US economist, was born in 1920. He is the author of *Keynesian Revolution* and *An Econometric Model in the United States*. For his contributions to econometric models, he won the 1980 Nobel Prize in Economics and is known as the father of econometrics. In the 1960s, he presided to establish an economic model consisting of more than 200 stochastic equations and theoretical equations, and there were hundreds of endogenous and exogenous variables in the equations. Although this type of macroeconometric model is widely used by countries and economies in the world, and produces certain effects, the results are limited. The main reason is the spatial gap between the model and reality and the disorder of economic changes. They affect the accuracy of the model forecasts.

Chapter 10

Dilemma and Innovation of Economics

The future directions of economics include space, possible world, randomness, self-limiting, entropy changes, the opposite law of macroscopic and microscopic, chaos and so forth.

10.1 Dilemma of Economics

Economists never stop their exploration. They correct, amend, and develop the past theories, but the outcome is still not satisfying. "We have done everything that the macroeconomics requires, but it does not seem to be enough." This is the disapproving comments of the US economist Sidney Jones in 1974 when the Keynesian thoughts were deteriorated by the economic stagflation.[1]

Reviewing the history, we notice that economic thoughts and the market economic develop hand in hand, and the modern market economy, i.e. the capitalism, is built upon the ruins of feudalism. The economic thoughts that

1 Zhang Shuxiao, *Introduction to World Economy*, Economic Science Press, 2005, p. 161.

describe the growth of personal assets of individuals and social wealth are the theories of free market economy exemplified by *The Wealth of Nations* written by Adam Smith. After the inheritance and development made by David Ricardo and Jean-Baptiste Say, it is widely accepted by most economists. In macroeconomics, Say's argument has been deeply rooted in people's mind that supply creates demand and the market economy has the function of automatically adjusting the supply-and-demand equilibrium, Walras' general equilibrium model is known as the most perfect model that expresses the relationship between supply and demand of commodities in the free market.

These early thoughts resist the government intervention, arguing that the basic function of government is just to provide public service. In the field of finance, the policy that links currency to gold is implemented so that the fiscal ends meet. However, the economic depression in 1930 directly threatens the capitalistic regime. People were severely concerned about the mechanism that automatically adjusts the economy. Therefore, the US President Roosevelt implemented a new policy to intervene economy, and Keynes' economic thought of managing the demand appeared. The implementation of policies of fiscal deficit and credit money greatly drove up the proportion of fiscal spending in the national income. The industry of finance enters the fast-growing stage. In the 1970s, the developed capitalistic countries in the western world underwent economic stagflation where slow-growing economy and high inflation coexisted in the long run. Keynesian theories were exposed to doubts due to their inability of explaining and coping with stagflation. Therefore, the macroeconomic theories are again experiencing a series of evolution and innovation, during which period appear new classical theories regarding technological advancements, including monetarism, rational expectations, economic fluctuation theory, new Keynesianism, and so forth. Economic theories become more diversified, and there exists no economic theory that prevails the world with absolute authority.

After the World War II, the world split into two camps — capitalism and socialism. Between them are fierce fiscal and economic competitions. After the great economic development in the post-war period, collectivism failed to challenge the economy of private ownership did not bring more remarkable theoretical achievements that boost the social wealth. Macroeconomic thoughts explain the economy unclearly. Different opinions are in hot debate. After each economic crisis, there is always a crisis for economic theories. Such overwhelming criticism asserts the fact that mere amendments of the existing theories never solve the problem completely.

The limitation of traditional economic theories has something to do with their historical background. The 18th century is a period of revolutions in Europe. Scientific revolution with Newton as the leading figure showed up first, followed by the French Revolution which pursued the changes and reforms. It is a period full of passion. People seem to witness a novel era totally different from the period when Ancient Egypt and Ancient China existed, and a brand new civilization that distinguishes itself from the old ones of typography and hieroglyphs.

Economic theories formed their theoretical system in the 18th century. The free market economy quickly developed. When it came to the outcomes of development and whether there would be a disaster, economics left it to God who would take care. Human beings only focus on advancing, reforming and progressing. Economics was born to assist development. It has been advocating development since the very beginning. There are no theories regarding depression and disasters.

From the perspective of the history of economic thoughts, the development of economics is subject to philosophy and natural sciences. In 1678, Newton published the book *Mathematical Principles of Natural Philosophy* which thoroughly stated his notions of the universe that all creatures in nature coexist in harmony. Then almost one hundred years later, in 1776, Adam Smith introduced harmonious and effective thoughts to economic relationship in society in the book *The Wealth of Nations*. He compared the market economy to the "invisible hand" which guides the social wealth to grow in equilibrium automatically and effectively.

The notion of conservation of energy in physics is also learned by economics. The conservation of energy is known as the first law of thermodynamics. The thought in physics that is associated with conservation of energy is the notion of symmetry. For example, the equilibrium between positive and negative electrons at initial stages, and the theory of relativity both well demonstrate the principle of coordinate system symmetry, the exploration of dark matter in astronomy, the wave symmetry in quantum mechanics, and so forth. All of them are inspiring examples.

Equilibrium, symmetry, and other notions that embrace the same or similar meanings directly inspire economics. "The word equilibrium almost comes into existence at the same time as the economic theories." "The earliest recording shows that the physiocratic economists used the word equilibrium. Bouager Bell (1646-1714) thought about the relationship between national income and consumption, reckoning that there was equilibrium between the buyer and the seller. Durco (1727-1781) used equilibrium in theories regarding capital. Quinay (1964-1774) built a model of balanced income growth in 'Economic Table'."[1] Afterwards, economics employs the notion of equilibrium throughout the whole system, such as the market equilibrium theory of Say (1767-1832), the general equilibrium theory of Walrus, the Keynesian assumption that investments equal savings, Monetarism, and the monetary theory based upon the market clearance, and so on.

Though new Keynesian theories and Monetarism at late stage put forward the thought of non-equibrium and non-neutral money, these thoughts are still restricted to the dispute of part of the existing theories and partial amendments. The amendments for errors based upon the conditions like imperfectly competitive market and money crash do not involve the criticism and denial. That is, Keynes' theory of income determination did not exist without the assumption of the

1 Ma Lieguang, *The Space and Principles of Thoughts*, Economic Press China, 2012, p. 73.

equilibrium between investments and savings. Similarly, without the assumption of the equilibrium between supply and demand, there would be no Monetarism and the economic thought regarding rational expectations.

Therefore, the development of macroeconomics is centered on the economic growth and is a process of continuous detailing. But the limitation of macroeconomic perspective is easy to find. The past macroeconomics only reflects a partial stage of the economic growth instead of establishing a knowledge of the whole process of economic development.

Scholars after one generation and another keep repeating the theories explaining the economic cycles. For example, Ricardo argued "banking industry cannot increase national wealth". "The economic aggregate fluctuates around the equilibrium."[1] Money cannot affect the real output, and economic turbulence is caused by external factors. The preparatory supposition prefers the balanced relationship, insisting on the notion of equilibrium between commodity supply and demand but ignoring the law of disorderly changes within the economy.

For the market economy, if the space-time equilibrium of the economic prosperity and depression is in a relationship where the space-to-time ratio of economic prosperity equals that of economic depression, or the division of the two ratios is a constant, then the economic prosperity and depression interchange like four seasons, and thus the market economy realize its equilibrium. Such equilibrium does not fluctuate around the equilibrium of the potential output, but is similar to the space-time equilibrium that waves around the interchange of coldness and summer-heat, as well as the daytime and night.

Numbers of facts show that physical ideas and methods are not only valuable to physics itself, but also make great contributions to the development of natural sciences and even social sciences. Although economics borrows concepts and methods, the traditional economics has a narrow vision because it pays too much

1 Joseph Schumpeter, *Theory of Economic Development*, translated by Zou Jianping, China Pictorial Publishing House, 2012, p. 985.

attention to the growing problem. Economics progresses at such a slow pace that it changes after the happening of economic situations and lacks predictability. As a result, it gradually loses the value of application.

The word "physics" first came from the Greek word φυσικ with an original meaning of nature. Ancient European people call physics "natural philosophy". In the broadest sense, it is the study of the natural phenomena and laws. In China, the word "physics" originates from the encyclopedic work "Physics Brief" written by Fang Yizhi in the late Ming and early Qing Dynasties. In the field of physics, basic elements of the universe are main objects of study, including materials, energy, space, time and their interactions. The basic laws and regulations under study help with the thorough understanding of the system. Physics in the classical era was composed of the studies of the natural sciences that are very similar to it. Not until the 19th century did physics divert from philosophy and become an empirical science.

Macroeconomics draws on the concept of conservation in physics, but refuses to agree with the impact of microcosmic disorder upon the entire economy. In fact, the two principles are related. In physics, basic laws include a variety of symmetry theories, such as the law of conservation of mass and energy, but these principles are based on the condition that the system is closed or the external situation is relatively stable. Only isolated systems or natural systems have the relationship of conservation. For these systems, the principle of entropy also exists in them. The balanced state corresponds to the state of maximum entropy.

The intersection of the supply curve and the demand curve in economics intuitively reflects the equilibrium point where supply equals demand. This point determines the equilibrium price of supply and demand. But the equilibrium price is on condition that other factors remain unchanged. This means it is a single market price and is relatively closed without being affected by other markets and relative prices. The general equilibrium theory, however, expects to weaken the assumption that "other factors remain unchanged" in a single market, so equilibrium can be expressed from the linking relationship between supply and demand in multiple markets. Moreover, this assumption can be extended to the whole economy to view the equilibrium between supply and demand. However, the market itself is an open market.

In this case, in order to create an open system equivalent to a closed one, people often assume that the external conditions of the market remain unchanged, economic policies are stable, and technological advancements are stable.

Methodologically speaking, if economics does not follow the principle of conservation, there is no reason to refuse the principle of entropy. Similarly, if economics does not reduce to a terrible copy of natural sciences, new thoughts and ideas have to be introduced. The new thoughts are specifically for disorders in society. For disordered macrosystems, deterministic experiments have no meaning, and will not reappear. The future direction for the development of economics is space, possible world, randomness, self-limiting, entropy changes, macro and micro inversion, chaos, and so on.

The law of entropy expresses an irreversible process. Entropy changes refer to irreversible changes. The growth of national income obeys the law of entropy changes. In the past, macroeconomics did not have a more direct theory of entropy changes, and theories of irreversible debt accumulation. Therefore, the theoretical system of macroeconomics is incomplete and cannot explain the long-term stagnation of economic growth and the accumulation of debt. Sustained economic prosperity seems to have nothing to do with entropy changes. However, "the mysteries of nature are hidden in silence, and great power often marches in silence." Debt crises are more and more serious from time to time, and the meaning of the entropy change theory will naturally emerge.

If economic theory is not forward-looking, it can neither accurately predict the future situation, nor predict the existence of unknown facts as physics does. Then economics is an art of thinking, an ever-changing fashion, a fading-away idea, and a nostalgic antique. We cannot resist raising a strong question — what's wrong with the macroeconomic theories? In front of a changing economy, theoretical predictions have generally failed, and the effectiveness of economic policies is weakening continuously. These phenomena indicate that there are flaws in basic ideas.

In the perseverance of the elderly people and the young ones who lived through the old days, time was wasted by hanging around and doing meaningless things. Precious youth has been wasted. The books and papers that are renewed year by year are like the withering grass on the grassland, dispersing when the wind blows. How come the classics of the prosperous literary soul are inherited and the cornerstone of great thoughts are cast.

Changes

I expect the appearance of surprise,
That the technological advancements burgeon like the ceaseless caress of Spring breeze.
Significant changes happen in our life.
Questing and thinking never stop year by year,
Philosophy, however, staggers in the misty forest of conflicts.
Wandering at the riverbank of time,
Feeling the dreamlike life and the vicissitude of time,
I only see the truth from faraway ancient periods,
Persevering like the antique shadow of the sun and the moon.
How can the conventional thoughts persist as if they were the mountains,
Too heavy to move.
How can one step forward take a hundred years?
I expect the happening of surprise,
Even though it is only a tiny change.

——Ma Lieguang

10.2 Defects of Traditional Theory

10.2.1 Deficiencies of Keynesian Theory of National Income Equilibrium

Investments and consumption employed by Keynes refer to material objects, that is real commodities rather than credit money. If the analysis of how investments and consumption are related to income is carried out by using money, only the value of commodities is reflected. Saving in English is translated into Chinese as thrifty and preservation. It disobeys the Chinese linguistic codes that the economics textbooks translated saving in English into savings when introducing the theory of national income accounting. It does not conform to the meaning of savings in Chinese, which is conventional. Savings belong to the concept of currency deposits. Savings are the balance of the income of enterprises and residents after being used for expenditure.

The "savings" in national income accounting belongs to the category of products, while the retention of products should be translated as storage. A netizen named 1993108 on the RUC Economic Forum said, "It seems that it should not be translated as savings at the beginning. Because the word savings has a conventional meaning in Chinese, it seems that it can be translated into storage, hoarding and so on." He is who I know the first person suggests modifying the translation.

I would like to regard this detail as advancement in the research of thoughts. A small change can explain the problem clearly. In the national income calculated in material objects, commodities except investment products correspond to reserves, hoarding, and storage instead of "savings". This avoids the disputes over the concept of "savings" in the categories of commodities and money, and equating residents' bank deposits with national income "savings."

Those Keynesians secretly applied the concept "savings" in the category of commodities to the category of money without explanation. They took it as a convenient way to correspond the commodities to money and talked with no holding back about chaotic thoughts. Once the concept of hoarding or storage is used, their theories lose the empirical basis of money. For example, the expression that the investments always equal savings should be expressed as "investments always equal storage." Though the meaning of the statement does not change, its theoretical value compromises, and its attraction deteriorates. In the two-sector model where only manufacturers and consumers are included, perhaps Keynesian theory can also use the expression that investments equal savings. However, if the financial sector is introduced into to compose a three-sector model, is it a bit far-fetched for the commodity category?

In Keynesian theory, investments also include investments in material objects. The investment is an exogenous variable independent of the process of the national income expenditure. Keynesian economic theory did not find a way to describe the principle of the formation of the total investments, which is the shortcoming of Keynesian theory of national income theory.

Changes in income savings related to national income follow the laws of capital movements, which Keynes's theory cannot explain clearly.

The national income is expressed in money. Therefore, it is more convenient to use money to analyze the relationship between income and expenditure. For example, the government invested 10 billion yuan. This is monetary expenditure, and it is not represented by 10 billion tons of grain. In the income multiplier theory, the investments are monetary expenditure. For this reason, the money representing the investing amount always equals the monetary savings used for investment, meaning the two concepts must be logically equal.

However, if the monetary savings related to investment is only defined as the balance of national income minus consumption, this is a special definition, and not logically inevitable. In other words, it is not general. Because in monetary income, monetary savings should be the part of income minus expenditures. Expenditures include investments and consumption, so there is current gross national income equals current incremental gross national expenditure plus previous monetary income used for current national income expenditure.

The key is to avoid confusing the relationship between total investments and savings, and the relationship between incremental investments and savings.

First, total investment equals total savings. This is based on definitions, that is, in national income accounting, total savings is the balance of income after being used for consumption. What corresponds to output is the part of total output minus the consumption commodities, which corresponds to the total investments from the perspective of national income output.

Second, incremental investment ΔI is equal to incremental ΔS, which is not equal by definition. It can be proved, and incremental savings ΔS can correspond to monetary income deposits. In the income multiplier model, we have the expression of relationship of the incremental national income $\Delta Y = k\Delta I$, and incremental investment $\Delta I = \Delta S$. k is the multiplier. For example, in a certain period of time, a certain enterprise invests 100 million yuan. This expenditure of 100 million yuan equals the income of other enterprises or individuals. Suppose that all the income is deposited in the bank, then the investment of 100 million yuan equals saving deposits of 100 million yuan. This investment is stock and corresponds to national income commodities.

Third, as discussed in the first and second questions, the expression of total investment = total savings is by definition; incremental investment and incremental consumption in $\Delta I = \Delta S$ are logically equal, and this logical relationship does not take the expression of total investment = total savings as the prerequisite. Similarly, the expression of total investment = total savings cannot be directly derived from $\Delta I = \Delta S$.

Under this condition, the reason for taking the assumption that total investment equals total savings as the prerequisite of realizing the equilibrium of the national economy is not determined by reasoning, but only a relationship by defining.

In short, Keynes' definition of the relationship between investment and savings has three obvious flaws.

First, the relationship between total savings and total investments, and the relationship between incremental savings and incremental investments cannot be proved. Up to now, it can only be proved that there is a strict logical relationship between incremental savings and incremental investments represented by monetary income. The identically equaling relationship between total savings and total investments in the category of commodities can only be defined from beyond the national income accounting system.

Second, now we know that the relationship between total investment and total savings is beyond the national income accounting system. If total investment equaling to total savings in the category of commodities is taken as the precondition for the balance of total supply and total demand in income accounting, this equilibrium precondition is not logical in itself, because it is not an inherently inevitable characteristic of the accounting system.

Third, more importantly, from the practicality of economic theories, defining savings as the balance of income minus consumption and applying it to the relationship of income=expenditure, will consequently make investment an exogenous variable creating income. The logical reasoning only contains the consumption re-spending of income, excluding investment re-spending process. The new national income has nothing to do with investment re-spending. This is divorced from the actual situation that people can perceive.

In classical economic theories, the economic equilibrium is expressed as investment = savings. Marshall believes that the savings (accumulation) of material products is the supply of capital. Physical investments constitute capital demands, and interest rates automatically equalize savings and investment, and thus the equilibrium is reached. Investment represents product demand, and savings represents product supply. Investment goods equal savings goods, and the economy is in equilibrium. There is no concept of monetary effects in classical economic theories. In the discussion of the relationship between investment and savings, product equilibrium is indeed what is talked about, while money is just the "veil" of so-called products. In fact, classical economics does not underestimate the role of money in the relationship between savings and investment. It is due to the flaws of the classical economic theory itself that it has to lay one-sided emphasis on product balance and ignores the role of money.

The Swedish economist Weiksel is the first one proposing the theory demonstrating the monetary effect in economy, after which the theory of money gradually integrated into the economic theory system. In the theory of national income, Keynes further refined the theory that money supply and demand affect the macro economy. It takes savings as the exogenous variable that determine the national income, arguing that savings always automatically (or ex-post) equal investment. Based on that, Keynes put forward his theory of stock money (the interest rate theory with liquidity preference).

However, Keynes' theory of investment and savings has the problem that money is not equivalent to products. Total investment and consumption are both flows, while money is a stock. Therefore, the successors of Keynesian theory had to avoid the currency issue when describing the relationship between investment and savings. They only talked about the equilibrium of investment and savings in the category of commodities, but cannot build a logically consistent relationship between products and currency. This is a helpless retrogression in methodology rather than an inheritance of classical opinions.

If Keynes lived nowadays, I bet he would not insist on saying that physical objects are equal. Discovering new topics is conducive to the development of economics. As far as the theory of investment-and-savings equilibrium is concerned, it is no longer meaningful to stick to the analysis of the argument that savings equal investment in the category of commodities.

10.2.2 If adhering to the traditional theory, you have to avoid confusing the residents' savings in bank deposits with savings in national income accounting.

If scholars go for classicism and Keynes' theory of income determination, savings are product savings, not the monetary savings of residents in banks. Since it does not refer to the income savings of residents, governments, and enterprises in banks, quoting bank savings directly is not proper.

If scholars do not go for classicism and Keynes' theory of income determination, they need to stop using the concept of Keynesian savings only, because that definition of savings does not fit the reality.

The author writes a long title to warn those who write articles that they are not supposed to regard saving deposits in banks as product savings since they believe in the relationship that investment equals savings. Neither should they claim that China has a high deposit rate and insufficient consumption. All those opinions misunderstand concepts. It will be better to ponder upon the deficiency of the traditional theories rather than rigidly use concepts improperly.

Many articles confuse household income savings in bank deposits with savings of national income accounting. For example, "Over the past 30 years since the enforcement of the reform and opening up, China's GDP has been growing at 9.7% on average. This rate is mainly due to investment. Where does the money for investment come from? Savings. A high savings rate must be accompanied by a high investment rate. At present, China's high savings rate is normal and reasonable. With a high savings ratio, the economy grows at a faster pace".[1]

A view prevails that residents' savings can be compared with national income directly. For example, "As a large economy, China's outstanding feature is the relatively high domestic savings rate. The current situation is that the savings proportion in GDP is about half of it. It means that China's GDP is over 50 trillion (yuan). That is to say, the funds from various types of savings are around 25 trillion (yuan), but this includes corporate savings, government savings and household savings. Currently these savings mainly come from traditional commercial banks..."[2]

These opinions compare the balance of domestic personal deposits with national income and come to the conclusion that China has a high savings rate. Some news comment that high savings are "the itch of China's economy and the pain of the common people". But from the perspective of economic theories, if

1 "Do not 'demonize' China's savings rate and investment rate", *Securities Daily*, July 8, 2009.

2 Zhou Xiaochuan's speech at the Lujiazui Forum in 2013, China Net, news.china.com.cn, June 28, 2013.

you stick to traditional economic theories, you cannot make direct comparisons in this way. Residents' personal deposits are different from the concept of savings in national income, and they cannot be directly compared.

According to the interpretation of traditional theories, the saving deposits commonly referred to belong to the category of money, while the "savings" in national income accounting is in the category of products. Residents' income savings in bank deposits is a concept different from that in national income accounting. The latter corresponds to the value of products. National income is calculated in two ways, namely the expenditure method and the income method. From the perspective of expenditure method, the expenditure of national income is divided into investment expenditure and consumption expenditure. From the perspective of income method, national income is the sum-up of wages, rents, profits, and interest income.

In the analysis of the income relationship, a simplified two-sector model is used assuming that it only includes enterprises and residents, and that part of the residents' savings from income minus expenditures is equal to the investment expenditures of enterprises. In national income accounting, both savings and investment refer to physical commodities, such as machines, clothes, grain, etc. The same batch of commodities in a period is regarded as investment using the expenditure method, and savings using the income method.

Although national income is expressed in the amount of money, such as billions, tens of billions, and trillions, these numbers represent the value of commodities.

In comparison, saving deposits in banks come from the central bank's money supply and commercial banks' loans. Although bank deposits and product amounts are closely related to the economic scale, they are not completely equivalent. If the household savings in bank deposits are equated with the savings in national income, it is like saying that more money issued by the central bank or more loans from commercial banks will increase national income in the same amount. This is incorrect.

It is not to say that there is no equivalent relationship between household savings in bank deposits and national income. Suppose that in a certain period, monetary income and expenditure are equivalent to national income, that is, to stipulate that this part of monetary expenditure is equal to the expenditure of national income, and then within this spectrum, new incremental savings in bank deposits are part of national income. For example, introducing the banking system into a two-sector model with only corporations and residents, and stipulating saving deposits are only part of national income, then we have residents' income savings equaling the increase in bank deposits in this case.

What needs to be emphasized is that in traditional theories, that investment equals saving is only a defined relationship in afterthought instead of an inferred relationship. It is not a logically inevitable relationship. Therefore, we can neither directly confuse household savings in bank deposits with income savings in national income accounting when the required conditions are not met, nor partially equate savings with investment, making a wrong conclusion that the savings rate and the investment rate are high, while consumption is insufficient.

10.3 Equilibrium and Entropy Changes

"Equilibrium" is the basic notion of economics, a pure rational thinking and a sacred truth. In economics, equilibrium is related to the microcosmic notions as well.

For example, the general equilibrium theory means that all markets that interact with each other reach the equilibrium of supply and demand at the same time. The general equilibrium is the mainstream idea of economics. Economists believe that with sufficient information, the relationship between supply and demand of goods can reach equilibrium. Without sufficient information, the relationship between supply and demand will realize equilibrium after repetitive trial and error and being influenced by multiple factors. Through trial and error, the overall equilibrium is achieved under the influence of many factors. Even if the economy is not in equilibrium, it will change towards it automatically.

The general equilibrium theory believes that economic development has its directions, and that the individual behavior in a free market economy obtains information with randomness and equal probability. These opinions are consistent with the formulation of the entropy theory, but the general equilibrium theory does not use the word "entropy". From the perspective of the entropy theory, the general equilibrium is a situation in which system entropy approaches its maximum.

Random movements at the micro-level and the attribute of equal probability are the prerequisites for deriving the entropy change formula of a macrosystem. For a macrosystem with these properties, its entropy formula can be derived as long as the method is right. Like the equilibrium theory, some economic principles do not directly use the concept of entropy, but they learn from theories of random movements and equal probability to express their laws specifically and respectively. In theories regarding consumer equilibrium in economics, it is stated that the equal marginal utility of money will maximize the total utility of the consumer's purchase of goods, if the monetary income is constant. So we can see that the maximization of utility expressed by consumer equilibrium under certain conditions shares some similarities with the principle of maximizing entropy.

Efficient market theory believes that investors in the stock market can get information with equal probability. The prices of securities fluctuate randomly and can fully exhibit all information. Only under such conditions is the market efficient. Then the stock price approaches the equilibrium price under the condition of equal probability. This is the situation that is most likely to occur in the stock market. Any technical analysis and stock valuation and calculations are useless.

Nash equilibrium is a game equilibrium among multiple players. The independent behavior of each participant does not increase their own interests. At that time, every player maximizes his or her interests. This combination of strategies is called equilibrium. In his two papers, John Forbes Nash introduced the differences between cooperative games and non-cooperative games. He introduced the concepts of arbitrary numbers and arbitrary preferences to participants, which made game theory, have more universal applicability. The core idea of the Nash game is still based on the idea that independent individuals make independent decisions, and of equivalent interests. That is how we can deduce the directional equilibrium point of the decision-making combinations using mathematics. At this point, the overall benefit is maximized.

From this example, we can notice that the equilibrium theory and the theory of entropy changes are basically consistent in terms of the prerequisites and the argument methods. The main difference is in the objects of research, rather than the essential difference in methodology.

All systems will eventually develop in one direction. At the micro-level, it approaches a disordered state most likely to occur, realizing the state of the maximized individual freedom under certain conditions. With equal probability, the equilibrium or maximum entropy is reached, and the equilibrium system achieves the maximum overall benefit. The changes in entropy means a tendency towards maximization, and the stagnation of the development of the whole. In this sense, there is no essential difference between the equilibrium theory and the theory of entropy changes.

For a macro system, the equilibrium that is most easily to be understood according to experience is supposed to be the spatial equilibrium of the system. For example, the air in the room is evenly distributed, and the water flows from the high to the low, forming a calm lake. The coordination of organs of the human body is also a kind of balance. Every organ of the body develops in roughly the same proportions on average for different people. It can neither be too swollen nor too large, otherwise it is in malformation. Cells in the body grow with a certain number. It should not be too swollen or grow too large, otherwise it will be deformed. If some cell divides too fast and too many, it will form a tumor, and continue to grow in an unbalanced manner which will endanger human life.

The condition for the existence of a macroscopic system is microcosmic disorder. Individuals in the market economy are independent of each other. Their connections with other spaces are short-range because each space is self-enclosed. Unlike three-dimensional spaces with ceilings and floors, a straight line can extend to the distance.

Equilibrium is a common phenomenon in nature. Everything in the universe and life bodies has some form of equilibrium in space. Although this form varies and does not have a uniform pattern, it has commonality. This commonality is manifested by consistency in statistical average, which helps species to maintain both advantages in quantity and diversity. Commonality and diversity form boundaries and distances in space to maintain the coordination and consistency among life, and between life and environment. The spatiality of all things embraces a coordinated and balanced relationship itself.

The relationship between supply and demand of commodities in the free market also has spatial equilibrium which is divided into micro and macro equilibrium. At the micro-level, it is a relative equilibrium where the supply and demand of a single type of product have a slight difference. Product supply meets its demand roughly, and the demand for a certain product cannot grow with any restrictions.

The equilibrium between aggregate supply and aggregate demand is macro-equilibrium, with dynamic imbalance and maximum mean value. Macro equilibrium is directly related to the level of per capita income. After the per capita income reaches a certain high level, it is difficult to continue growing, or "there is no room for further growth". The aggregate supply and aggregate demand move towards static equilibrium and the growth of national income is stagnant. On the contrary, when per capita income is lower, aggregate supply and aggregate demand are unstable, and the national income is in relatively great changes. The unstable state of aggregate supply and aggregate demand leaves greater room for per capita income growth.

Based on the actual economic state, equilibrium does not mean that all commodities have been cleared and supply equals demand. Because there is a microcosmic distance between supply and demand, zero distance is only on the boundary. The product market cannot concentrate on the boundary. More precisely speaking, the equilibrium on the boundary is an event of small probability whose possibility of occurrence is small.

The approximate equilibrium between aggregate supply and aggregate demand is only a state when the entropy of the system reaches its maximum, but it is not the only state. The reality of the macro economy is that either a strong demand leads to continuing inflation, or sufficient supply results in persistent deflation.

The geometry of the system is manifested in the minimization of the distance of variables at the micro-level. There are continuous conflicts in the system that are caused by disorder. "Good times do not last long" and "prosperous world is filled with trouble". It means the macro system is in a state of stagnation. Also, due to the locality of conflicts and the diversity of changes, the overall coordination and stability of the system will not be undermined. In short, the balance of supply and demand in the macro economy is only a state of maximum entropy in the system, but it is not the only state.

It is a natural process of the development of economic theories from equilibrium to entropy changes. With the understanding of the concept and theories of equilibrium, it is not hard to understand the theory of entropy changes that are not familiar to us. The masters of economics have quietly used irreversible discourse in equilibrium to express their viewpoints on equilibrium. Although none of them mentions irreversible processes, they share the same theoretical premises — independent individuals, random movements, equal probability and maximization. Today, our thinking continues to advance along this path. After years of accumulation of ideas and significant changes in the economic situation, the theory of irreversibility should be on the stage. The climax is the theory of irreversible macroeconomics which specifically covers the entropy theory of national income growth, the principle of irreversible money circulation, etc.

10.4 Transcending the Conventional Paradigm

Let me talk about something regarding transcendence. Though it is just personal pondering, it is after all my own original thoughts. So I would like to share with you and am expecting some responses to avoid confusion.

Transcending the conventional paradigm refers to the alteration of vision, raising some new questions and novel explanations. What does transcendence mean? Compared with the traditional macroeconomic theories, the new theory relatively fits the reality more. That is what transcendence means. Transcendence is not marked by whether people agree or not, but a kind of ideological innovation. Transcendence does not deny the predecessors' thoughts completely. On the contrary, it inherits and develops economics. We must both firmly believe in rational notions and focus on proposing new opinions combining with reality to form a series of new rational studies.

Now there is a tendency that the academic ability is assessed by administrative positions and the hierarchy of universities and colleges. Deans, principals, directors and professors in prestigious universities have a greater say in academics. Their positions represent their scholarship. The academic ability is administrative, and the academic ambiance is hierarchical. This not only dwarfs the academic researches, but, due to the hierarchical form, also restricts free academic communications and the cultivation of talents, which harms the development of academics.

Prestigious schools are respected, so their scholars and students always have a sense of superiority. Even though they do not have some innovative thoughts, they have some academic advantages as long as they have some connections with prestigious institutions overseas, or once study there. In the era when economic thoughts mainly come from foreign countries, they naturally become teachers in their home country even though they are students abroad. Confusingly, they appear to be more conservative and resist adjusting their thinking to the latest changes, given that the economy always changes.

The appearance of new thoughts has nothing to do with nations. Why are thoughts as colorful as materials? It is because those thoughts are born with restrictions. If thoughts are universal, then the world is in a single light shedding for thousands of years. The world is depressing and boring.

The theoretical innovation is the ideal of Chinese intellectuals. Even if it is just a dream, it deserves our efforts. To fight for a sacred dream is the most meaningful life cause. New thoughts in China have their day of being recognized. New thoughts are like new lives in nature that grow quietly. After years of silent efforts, someday they will change the world astonishingly all of a sudden. Because potential power represents the future.

The transcendence in knowledge system is expected to show up in this century. It is also a must in history. Because

(1) Without new paradigm, there will be no knowledge leaps and progresses. The civilization in human world will stagnate.

(2) From the perspective of human history, the appearance of new paradigm is based upon the rising and progress of some nation and people. It has special cultural background. Looking around the world, the Chinese people is the most promising to ascend to the highland of thoughts. We will make total innovation come true after studying hard.

As far as economics is concerned, macroeconomics undergoes greater limitations, such as ironing the economic cycles, investment equaling savings, the circular money multiplier, tense functions of acceleration and multipliers. These theories do not fit the current economic situation, and need amendments and improvements.

Economics still has a few uncultivated "virgin lands". New keywords should be added, including multidimensional space, chaos, irreversibility, possible worlds, the Law of Inversion between micro and macro views, as well as using the hyperbolic geometry to express the relationship between economic changes and space, etc... Empirically speaking, chaos, irreversibility and the opposite law of macroscopic and microscopic are common economic phenomena. Theoretically speaking, these aspects stand for the reform of economic theories.

Economic theories on chaos are now the standard of non-linear economics. We regard as non-linear theories the chaos, the system theory, the information theory, the dissipative structure, synergetics, the hypercycle theory, catastrophe theory, and fractal theory. Amongst others, chaos draws the most attention and theoretical achievements have been made.

Irreversibility is a phenomenon in the circulation of monetary funds. In brief, monetary funds do not flow backward in the same amount in one process. For example, fund movements are irreversible in the stock market, commodity transactions, and bank credit. This theory can explain the economic stagnation and debt crisis.

The opposite law of macroscopic and microscopic is a basic economic phenomenon and a philosophical notion. The hyperbolic geometry can express it. In economic theories, it is a basic principle from which we deepen the understanding of the economic system including randomness, microcosmic disorder, and economic space and its law. Economics wears a new look.

The theory of multidimensional space is a new way to explain economic phenomena, and reveal the internal laws. When distance, angle, boundary, and dimensional degree are combined with vectors, disorder, and systems, new methods of supply-and-demand alteration, self-limiting, statistical explanation, and model assessments are derived.

An academic path comes up naturally. Economics sees a field yet unknown to others. This is new paradigm.

The ideological progresses are indispensable from gradual accumulation. It is like that the adults may not notice daily changes of their kids, but the kids change little by little every day. After a period, the adults suddenly find out that their kids have grown up. This is due to the accumulation of time. And if thoughts can grow as time elapses, their impacts will be dramatic, too.

The economic reality continues evolving, and new theories are combined with new facts, while the old theories are gradually eliminated by reality. The development of thoughts is the process of evolution. The advantages of new thoughts lie in the explanation of and the combination with the reality, bringing more foreseeable critical thinking.

Faced with numerous new thoughts, people do not need to bother to praise them or promote the judgment of the right and the wrong, as well as the good and the bad. The economic reality will eventually decide all thoughts, and people will learn the significance of thoughts. Great thoughts always stand out in comparison. Other human factors do not need to intervene. Great thoughts are to receive recognition and respects ultimately, while other thoughts are abandoned by people.

10.5 The Brief System of Economics

God is the creator. One day, God suddenly feels unsatisfied that there are only males and females in the human world on earth. So he creates a person with mud. This person is both a gentleman and a tree with humanity. So other people feel inspired and start thinking in the same way. However, the moment people start thinking, God laughs. He makes eternal and essential things only. Imitation is not the essence. It is just a joke of God.

The creator was born to create. The noble characters of human wisdom are the ability to make creations continuously and the struggles to pursue. Imitation and study are just the starts. People do not cease to advance at some initial points or after reaching some platform. Even though the progress of thoughts sometimes appears to be time-consuming, the energy of innovation will in the end show up. New thoughts naturally bridge the gap left by old paradigms.

My book *A New Discussion of Economics: Multiplier, Statistical Entropy and National Income* were published in April, 2006. The theoretical value of the book is gradually demonstrated since the economic and financial crisis of the US and Europe in 2008. It introduces the concept of "entropy", building the mathematical formula and creatively, proposing the principle that the growth of national income tends to stagnate and the principle of irreversible monetary multiplier. Meanwhile, it analyzes the asymmetric process of bank loans' issuance and recovery, pointing out the principle of the bank fund movement that has not yet been known, namely the principle of accumulative increase of debts.

Another main theoretical innovation of this book is that it builds the model of non-linear variance of national income and proves theoretically that the state of the distribution of savings is also the main factor determining total income during the formation of income.

The essence of theoretical innovation is the innovation of methodology. This book breaks the traditional classification of macroeconomics and microeconomics. It starts from the microcosmic states of income and expenditure. It explains the macroeconomic phenomena by analyzing the economic principles at the micro-level including expenditure tree, savings distribution, minimum amount of money, number of micro-states. In the field of macroeconomics, it creatively founds systematic new thoughts.

The Great Collapse of Capitalism of mine is a subsequent book of *A New Discussion of Economics: Multiplier, Statistical Entropy and National Income*. It creates a series of new theories in terms of the stagnation of national income growth, collapse and the monetary and financial theories.

This book combines the economic reality at that time, and develops the monetary and financial theories. It further discourses the entropy principle of national income, the irreversibility of money circulation and the opposite law of macroscopic and microscopic.It builds the mathematical model of the theory of entropy changes of national income, in which the equation is much simplified compared with the one in *A New Discussion of Economics: Multiplier, Statistical Entropy and National Income*.

New theories in *The Great Collapse of Capitalism* also include the theory proving that the commercial banks are unprofitable by using mathematical formula. Though such expression is hard to understand, it basically refers to the phenomenon that credit funds turn into income savings and commercial banks cannot recover these loans.

It also builds the endogenous mechanism of monetary base expansion, and proposes the theory that monetary base creates monetary base by analyzing the relationship between income theory and cash. Besides, it explains why systematic crisis happens in banking industry by summarizing the relation, laws and characteristics of bank fund movements. It builds the theories of money supply, leakage and the appearance of collapse.

The theoretical significance of this book stems from explaining why economic growth stagnates and debts accumulate. It puts forward the generative base and evolving mechanism of economic and debt crisis by using mathematical inference and theoretical demonstration. It predicts the great collapse of free market economy.

The relationship between new thoughts and the old is exhibited in Figure 10-1. Macroeconomics is on the whole divided into two branches. One is composed of theories of economic growth and equilibrium, including the multiplier theories of national income and money, theories of savings, investment and consumption, and the model of cyclic fluctuation of national income. The other consists of new thoughts, including the stagnation of national income growth and the theory of the unbalanced and continuous decline.

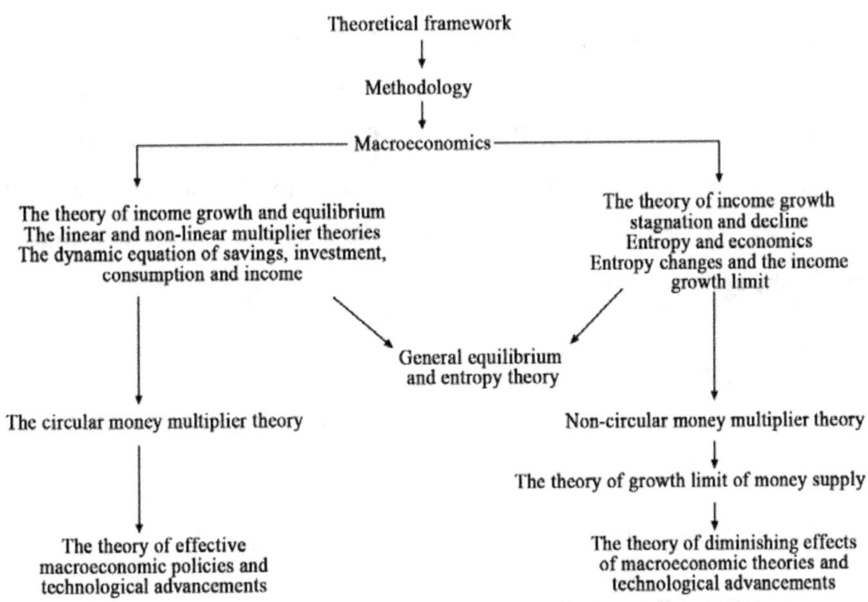

Figure 10-1 The theoretical framework of macroeconomics

Arrows pointing downward in Figure 10-1 means the supporting principles of the two branches respectively. The left arrow signals the main theoretical directions of traditional theories of economic growth. The money multiplier is the basic theory of monetary banking, expressing that the central bank can automatically adjust the supply of monetary base and realizing the self-circulation of money. Fiscal and financial policies have short-term impacts on economic growth. Through policy regulation, the macroeconomic target of ironing economic cycles is fulfilled. Scientific and technological advancements have a long-term influence on economic growth and can effectively avoid the shock on economic growth from the resource and energy crisis.

The right arrow pointing downward expresses the specific principle of irreversible (entropy changes) economics- entropy changes and the income growth stagnation, the non-circular money multiplier theory and the theory of growth limit of money supply. Here we discuss the principle that the short-term effect of macroeconomic policies and technological advancements on economic growth diminishes with the expansion of economic scale.

The two branches intersect at the theories of general equilibrium and entropy, meaning a deeper discussion and discourse of the relationship between the two. The basic viewpoint is that the fluctuation of national income is not only the fluctuation of increase, but, more accurately, to head for the entropy changes to realize the space-time equilibrium of economic prosperity and depression which is shown by the cycle of them.

Chapter 11

Philosophical Economics[1]

In front of the puzzles in the depressed era, we need to talk about philosophy and apply philosophical thoughts to building of new economic theories. Therefore, we broaden our horizons and head for the future.

11.1 Philosophy, Science and Economics

If the universe space is bent, meaning the spatial form is non-Euclidean geometric, then it can be described by hyperbolic geometry, and there must be two fixed points in space. If you accept that "self-consciousness" is a fixed point, then within the earth which is Euclidean space, everything intersects at it. Everyone is self-centered.

---

1 The concept of "philosophical economics" is quoted from "Philosophical Economics" by Mr. Sheng Huatang, a netizen of the CRU Economic Forum. For details, please refer to CRU Economic Forum-Marxist Economics. Zhang Dun used the concept of "philosophical economics" in "Labor Issues in the Perspective of Philosophical Economics" in 2006. For details, please refer to *Journal of Nanjing University*, Issue 5, 2006.

Another fixed point lies in the deepness of the universe, defined as where God lives. It can be proved that these two fixed points are connective to each other through a non-Euclidean line. So, that is what "God is with us" means.

This is a philosophy with no empirical evidence. But it does not mean it is meaningless. Books written by Kant are traditional philosophy of language. There was no hyperbolic geometry and set theory in the era of Kant and Hegel. Modern philosophy expresses ideas by mathematics so that their extremely powerful logic is in perfect expression.

Scientific knowledge has been tested in practice. So people believe that science is true. However, "true" scientific knowledge is only limited to "true" experiences. Because of the limitations of experience, scientific knowledge is also limited. Newton's book was written in the name of philosophy. Scientific thinking is rational and logical thinking. Therefore, the way of scientific thinking is structured in the same as philosophical thinking. Also, because philosophical thinking comes first, especially Western philosophy, the beginning of science has an example to learn from in terms of method.

Scientific principles are not only a summary of experience but also rational thinking. Copernicus's "heliocentric theory", in his time, was not as suitable for experience as "geocentric theory" was. But his view of philosophy made him believe in the rationality of his theory. Under the name of philosophy, Isaac Newton proposed his space mechanics. The concept of absolute space-time and the way of uniform motion are both philosophical principles. These rational principles become the prerequisites of Newtonian mechanics.

The development of modern science and mathematics has marginalized philosophy. Philosophy's approach to the quest for the essence of things based on thinking rather than observation is no longer effective. The thoughts in the mainstream of Western philosophy in the 20th century were positivism, analytic philosophy with linguistic logic as its leading topic, phenomenology, and so on. These prevailing philosophies cannot take the mission of philosophy to pursue perfect thoughts. Positivism was widespread and advocated so indulgently the idea of "learning for application" that rational thinking was lost. Therefore, some people argued that "philosophy is not science, and philosophy is not as rigorous as science" and "the philosophic talks are empty and useless". These are all misunderstandings of philosophy.

Philosophy's study of the nature of things will never let go of any chance that precise language can be used in its expression. Just as science, philosophy also has subtle thoughts in epistemology. We believe that philosophy, which has been wandering in lonely times for long, just enters a period of temporary silence. Once inspirations spring up, philosophy will shine again.

The influence of philosophy on economics is manifested in the excavation and insistence of ideas, including the complete competition in the market, complete flexible prices, complete information and the assumption of the rational person, as well as equilibrium, the marginal utility theory, the theory of entropy changes, as so forth. These theories are not purely empirical, but based on beliefs and the abstract expression of the law of free market. These ideas are embedded with strong colors of idealism, just the same as the pursuit of "eternal love" in religion, poetry, and literary works. The persistence of complete market behaviors reflects the philosophical temperament that the economists were born with.

Unlike philosophy, the mathematization of economic theories is a fast process. Economists use mathematical language to express thoughts and opinions so that economic phenomena can be predicted and explained. Economics lays more emphasis on empirical and practical values compared with philosophy. As a result, economics becomes a dazzling doctrine between idea and experience. It is an art of abstract thoughts.

Now, economics has grown into a great tree of thought. It is different from science because there is always a distance between economics and market experience. Compared to natural sciences, economics has more philosophical illusion. This is the value of ideas that tend to be philosophical. The mansion of economic thoughts is built between philosophy and science. On the road of thoughts, economists are wandering between theories and experience. What is the realm that economics is pursuing so that they can understand what truth is? People never stop questing, thinking, confusing and puzzling. So economists are always running back and forth on the road of thought. They learn notions and methods from philosophy and scientific thoughts, and rewrite drafts of books that dissatisfy them.

Philosophy, science, and economics are all parts of human thoughts. We cannot determine the value of rational thoughts based on experience only. It is like that when people input thoughts and God into their heads, the empiricism of thoughts becomes barrier. On the contrary, on the river of ever-changing experience, it is hard to see what truth is. Rational thinking and experience are not absolutely consistent. This is the truth regarding scientific and economic knowledge that philosophy tells us.

It is a normal phenomenon that the promotion and application of ideas have limitations. If we take knowledge as the objective object, measure the applicability of knowledge by a scale, and set the scale as the highest where knowledge is suitable for the object, it will be noticed that the scale goes down as the object changes, meaning the decrease of applicability. This is like a climber goes mountain climbing with a barometer who observes a declining atmospheric pressure as the altitude increases. The atmosphere has different pressure which makes the sky colorful

The decrease of atmospheric pressure is one of the colorful phenomena in the world.

The beautiful earth, therefore, enjoys mysterious and endless sky.

The limitation of knowledge is one of the colorful phenomena of thoughts.

Lucky human beings, therefore, have magnificent space of ideas.

——Ma Lieguang

11.2 What is Philosophical Economics?

11.2.1 The concept of philosophical economics and interpretation

"Shoot out two arrows in two opposite directions, and, when they meet each other in the air, the world will have become different."

This sentence from ancient Greek mythology is the metaphor of the significance of the combination between science and art. Science and technology have changed the world, while artistic inspirations are indispensable for scientific discoveries. Of course, they are inseparable from philosophy, too."

When a philosopher thinks about physical phenomena and testifies his guesses from empirical data, he is a scientist. Similarly, when a philosopher ponders upon economic questions and puts forward theories to explain economic phenomena, he becomes an economist.

Philosophy, science, art and economics meet each other in the space of thoughts, and, then, the world changes.

Philosophy embraces rational thoughts which also allow a full expression of imagination. A philosopher can say "give ideas freedom!" But economics has to relate thoughts to practice, forecasting the future tendency of economic changes. The approach of settling down the rational and poetic philosophy in the real situation is to extend philosophical ideas to science and economics. This is a direction for the development of philosophical thoughts.

(1) What is philosophy? Philosophy is a general theory that studies all knowledge. It confronts everything in life. It is the rational thought of human beings and the foundation of the development of all other disciplines. From the development history of thoughts, physics did not get separated from philosophy until the 17th century, during which time some studies upon natural phenomena are regarded as scientific researches to avoid confusion from the noble philosophy studying ideas and abstract thinking. Economics, sociology, biology and political sciences gradually claimed their independence from philosophy after the emergence of science.

In the intellectual world, there has not yet formed an agreed concept of philosophy. Starting from the comprehensiveness and abstraction of philosophy, we can define philosophy as a world view. Philosophy involves some fields in need of pondering where it can hardly find answers by collecting experience, such as "existence" "truth" "ultimate target" "free will" "beauty" "art" "morality", etc.. However, philosophy is not a theory whose objects of study do not belong to experiential objects. Nor is it limited to metaphysical speculation, or language formalism. Philosophical theories also talk about some economic problems and use mathematical methods to express their opinions.

(2) What is economics? Economics is a theory that studies the proper allocation of resources and efficiency. It researches on economic phenomena that attract people. Since economics mainly focus on solving practical economic problems, the research objects and theories in economics are in continuous changes. The biggest feature of economics is that the objects of study vary with the eras.

"Economy" originates from Greek which means family management. In ancient Greece, economic activities were simple. Family management was the main concern of people. In ancient China, it was widely accepted that righteousness was noble while interest was low. The economic thoughts were just summaries of experience with clear targets. Officials needed to govern. Residents needed to live a life. Some practical opinions prevail with regards to enriching people, gathering wealth, field management, the population as so forth.

At the preliminary stage of capitalism in Western Europe, commercial capital thrived and developed. To unify the market, mercantilism appeared. In more than 200 years after the mid-17th century, the Industrial Revolution led to a significant change in the world economy. Economics quickly developed in all aspects from the hot market topics of free trade, free competition, labor division, efficiency in early times to value, growth, wealth allocation and so on. After the 20th century, the economy quickly expanded with the great industrial development. Meanwhile, under the permeating effect of economic crisis, there appeared the macroeconomics studying economic growth and fluctuation.

(3) What is philosophical economics? Philosophical economics is short for philosophy and economics. The reason to use this concept is that we hope people view philosophical economics as an independent discipline. Philosophical economics not only presents the close relationship between philosophy and economics, but also proposes a series of economic theories from the philosophical perspective and thoughts, including economic policies. Philosophers mingle some universal laws with concepts they put forward. Economists then introduce philosophical concepts into their mode.

For philosophical economics, the object of study is philosophical content, particularly the economic phenomena. Because we use philosophical thoughts in the analysis of economic phenomena, investigating economic practices by philosophical theories, principles, doctrines and methods.

At the same time, philosophical economics is also an attempt of philosophy to explore. To study economics based on philosophy, on the one side, provides theoretical guide for economic theories, carries out the analysis of economy supported by philosophical theories, and builds up economic models with the economic analysis and practices combined. On the other hand, philosophical thoughts become a school of economics in the process of using philosophical theories to interpret economic phenomena.

Philosophical economics is different from the philosophy of economy. The latter mainly studies economy where philosophical thoughts are only limited to the economic field. It is the philosophy talking about economy. In contrast, though philosophical economics is still philosophy, its objects of study are not limited to the economy. It embraces contents of critical thinking that are more abstract and more universal objects to ponder on.

Philosophical economics includes the contents of the philosophy of economics. If we regard philosophical economics as the system of a comprehensive theory, the philosophy of economy is one branch of the system, which means it is only part of philosophical economics. However, for the philosophical opinion of a specific economic object, there is no difference between the theory of philosophical economics and the philosophy of economics. In other words, for specific objects, they share the same meaning. There is no essential distinction between the two concepts in terms of the micro spectrum and specific objects.

Philosophical economics overlaps economics. For a specific economic theory, does it belong to philosophical economics or economics? Sometimes it is not easy to tell. Generally speaking, these theories are in the category of philosophy; if connected to the economic reality, these theories belong to economics. For example, the multidimensional space, time, and the theory of irreversibility are all topics discussed by philosophy. Once the link to economic phenomena and related principles are put forward accordingly, the space-time theory and the theory of irreversibility become economic theories.

(4) The historical retrospect of the relation between philosophy and economics. There are successful precedents to rebuild the framework of economic theories starting from philosophical theories. In the past, economics tried to go on this way and harvested a lot. The universal method used by economics is to turn philosophical ideas into economic interpretation. In the mind of every economist stores philosophical thoughts.

Before writing *The Wealth of Nation*, Adam Smith published *The Theory of Moral Sentiments*, a literary work in ethics. He socialized personal morality, perceiving that individual altruistic behaviors also brought benefits to others. In *The Wealth of Nation*, he combined the economic freedom with moral philosophy, arguing that freedom was the basis of economic efficiency and abode by moral principles. However, it is a little pity that his ethical theories appear to be more easily understood than economics. "This is the biggest problem we encountered when carrying out the philosophical and philological studies of Adam Smith's literary works — *The Wealth of Nation* is harder to understand than *The Theory of Moral Sentiments*."[1] For economics, this opening is more or less worrying-

1 Wolf Lepenies, *Qu'est-ce qu'un intellectuel européen? Les intellectuels et la politique de l'esprit dans l'histoire européenne*, transleted by Li Yanming, Guangxi Normal University Press, 2011, p. 279.

economics grows from the base point, *The Wealth of Nation*, to diversification. The giant system, together with the wide application of mathematics, makes the expression of economic thoughts tend to be more complicated. And economic thoughts get more and more faraway from ordinary readers. In comparison, *The Wealth of Nation* of Adam Smith has already been a very brief literary work.

Since economics is about rational thoughts, philosophy has effects upon a variety of economic thoughts. For example, the rational man assumption based upon idealism is the basic prerequisite of economics. The rational man was a viewpoint developed in *The Wealth of Nation* by Adam Smith. It means a man is both rational and selfish at the same time, aiming for the maximization of his benefit. The rational-man viewpoint has been expressed continuously from many aspects, and the assumption is used in the respective research fields. Only a rational man can accept information, making economic decisions. The rational man is the foundation for the normal operation of the market economy.

Pragmatic philosophy has great influences upon macroeconomic policies. When economics fails to make a difference, pragmatism and trial and error become the last choices. Pragmatism believes that "truth is determined by time, location and intention, so it is always changing with new situations". "The significance of notion is nothing more than the sum of all its practical effects."[1] Also, there includes Dewey's theory of tools. Basically, after the exclusion of those ideal modes that are not pragmatic, thoughts are just tools to solve practical problems. Since macroeconomic theories have limitations and have difficulty in coping with complicated macroeconomic situations, fiscal and financial policies carried out by the government and the central bank in each country usually adopt the way of pragmatic thinking, targeting precisely at practical issues. Particularly after the US financial crisis in 2008, the macroeconomic theories can hardly explain the stagnation of economic growth. When the liberal economic theory and the

1 Brooke Noel Moore and Kenneth Bruder, *Philosophy: The Power of Ideas*, translated by Li Hongyun and Ni Jia, Shanghai Academy of Social Sciences Press, 2009, p. 233.

Keynesianism supporters lose their effectiveness, pragmatism takes the role of the basic principle when governments make economic policies.

Marx once said that philosophers attempted to understand the world, but the important thing was to change the world. Marxist philosophical system mainly covers the four aspects — materialism, dialectics, epistemology and practice. Marxist labor theory of value inherits contents from the British classical economics. Marxist philosophy thinks of consciousness is the product of labor. What echos this philosophical viewpoint is that labor creates the commodity value. Marx proposes the theory of surplus value in which he argues that value created by labor was not obtained by the laborers. Therefore, laborers are under exploitation. Marx thinks that society is divided into different classes. From this idea is the theory of public-owned planned economy derived.

The Austrian school that stands on the opposite side of Marxism promotes the concept of freedom into the whole economic system by advocating the viewpoint that society is the ensemble of individual opinions. They interpret the individual freedom in general meaning as the personal subjective preference. The value of a commodity is determined by the individual subjective preference. The Austrian economic school builds up the theoretical system by using individual psychology, translating individualism into the explanation of economic phenomena. The Austrian school argues that supply and demand are up to individual decisions, which is also the principle of individualism in methodology. They emphasize that economic decisions are made by individuals instead of the collective. At the same time, they employ the theory of marginalism to compare the variation of increases of costs and that of profits. *The Constitution of Liberty* written by Friedrich von Hayek in social philosophy has an extremely important position in the history of economic thoughts. Some people claim that this book can be paralleled to *The Wealth of Nation* by Adam Smith.[1]

1 Friedrich A. Von Hayek, *The Constitution of Liberty*, translated by Deng Zhenglai, SDX Joint Publishing Co., 2003, p. 2.

11.2.2 The prospective of philosophical economics

(1) The research directions of philosophical economics

Specific research directions and the discipline system of philosophical economics are still unclear. If philosophical thoughts could provide direct interpretations of economic practices, reading economic theories would be like reading philosophy. Reaching this state is a progress of philosophy. At present, it is relatively difficult to answer whether philosophy can extend to economics. Establishing philosophical economics needs the development of philosophical thoughts. We need to have a type of philosophy that can explain economic phenomena directly.

Though philosophy and economics have a close relation, economics is not philosophy. The theoretical system of economics inherits the world view in philosophy more than other aspects, such as ethical philosophy and epistemology. Philosophical principles are not directly implanted into economics. As it is said, the perception of value in philosophy is different from economics. The theory of value in philosophy concerns the meaning of life, the inner goodness, and the proposition for freedom. The theory of value in economics roughly refers to the value of merchandise, which is linked to labor, efficiency and the supply-demand relation.[1]

In economic theories, science seems to have a more direct influence on economics. Moreover, economics makes efforts to step onto the road of science in terms of methodology. It pays attention to logical reasoning and the usefulness of theories. Moreover, some concepts in physics, such as "equilibrium" "recycling" and "entropy", are introduced into economics.

As a result, to analyze the philosophical influence upon economics only in terms of world view and methodology cannot obtain the specific research directions of philosophical economics or the philosophy of economy.

1 For more details, please refer to Zhang Guangshan, *Differences of "Value" in Philosophy and in Economics*, CRU Economic Forum-Marxist Economics.

However, we are still unable to deny the significance of using the philosophical approach of critical thinking to study economics or economic practices and further build up philosophical economics. There a lot of philosophical issues in the economic practice. For example, both ideas and the market economy are research directions of philosophical economics. We need to study the relationship between economic thoughts and experience. Why economic thoughts cannot get close to the real experience as natural sciences do? There appears abstract geometry between different economic schools. The spatial relations manifest the distinctions between different thoughts. Why does the market economy have uncertainty? Why does the irreversible phenomenon exist in the flow of commodities and money? What is the multidimensional space of the economic system? How is the theory of possible world applied to the practical economic analysis?

In different levels of analysis in philosophical economics, there is a phenomenon that we have not get used to — the practical issue often seems to disagree with the temperament of philosophy. It looks like economics that divorces from philosophy. If such a divorce is a misunderstanding, economic theories can be titled with the definition of philosophy. Because the preconditions of theories are the philosophical theories instead of practical experience, including the classical economics and new classical economics that are based upon the rational man assumption, the game theory, labor theory of value, equilibrium, the theory of irreversibility, and so forth. Any economics that is based upon philosophy in terms of theory, principle and method can be called philosophical economics. Besides, economic notions under the effect of empiricism and pragmatism also belong to philosophical economics. For example, "Useful insights are real knowledge", "Cross the river by feeling the stones". What is the relationship between value and scarcity? Radish and cabbage have their own preferences. Bad money drives away good money. There exists tragedy of the commons. More examples are in the waiting list. All these economic theories can be titled as theories of philosophical economics because they introduce philosophical theories into the analysis of practical experience.

(2) The approaches of innovating economics

According to the standard of sciences, economics fails in terms of the practical application of theories. After economics became an independent discipline, it has been so deeply trapped by the swamp of experience that it can hardly get out on its own. The road built upon experience has been blocked. So it does not work when economics attempts to realize self-improvement by combining theory with practice. As a result, the disappointed scholars look around in the hope of finding a way out. They choose to go back to the kingdom of philosophy. It means that scholars choose to broaden their horizon from a rational perspective again, dragging economics out of the swamp of experience and rebuilding economics based on philosophy.

Philosophical economics aims to provide principles and basic theories as prerequisites for economic thoughts from the height of philosophy. Economics regresses to philosophy. Economic theories are based upon philosophical thoughts. Philosophy provides theoretical basis for economics. Moreover, philosophical concepts and notions are allowed to affect the economic analysis directly.

Each economic school has its basic assumptions and research methods. Though theories have divorced from reality, scholars always insist and defend their thoughts without yielding. Because the mind has been solidified in some way and it is hard to change. If new thoughts are to be used to explain reality, we need to rebuild the framework of thoughts.

It is the philosophical thoughts that are used by philosophical economics to rebuild the framework of economics. Economics obtains help from philosophy and establishes a new model of thoughts.

Looking into the future, we know that if the 20th century is a century of economics, then the 21st century is a century of philosophical economics.

Bibliography

1. Wolf Lepenies, *Qu'est-ce qu'un intellectuel européen? Les intellectuels et la politique de l'esprit dans l'histoire européenne,* translated by Li Yanming, Guangxi Normal University Press, 2011.

2. Guo Kewei, "Effects and Limits of Super Easing Monetary Policy in Japan", *The Banker*, 2013, Issue 6th.

3. Tang Duoduo, Zhang Xiaojing, and Wang Hongju, "Keep Policies Stable and Concern about External Risks", *China's Economic Growth and Economic Cycles (2011),* edited by Liu Shucheng et al. , Economic Press China, 2012.

4. Cai Zhizhou, "Analyze China's Economic Growth from the Penetration of the Ultimate Demand", *China's Economic Growth and Economic Cycles (2011),* edited by Liu Shucheng et al., Economic Press China, 2012.

5. Li Xiaoxi, "On Discussing the Cycle of World Economy", *China's Economic Growth and Economic Cycles (2011),* edited by Liu Shucheng et al., Economic Press China, 2012.

6. Chen Taifu, *Pondering Upon Economic Philosophy,* China Social Sciences Publishing House, 2005.

7. 2013luan, "Why TFP in China experiences a marked decline?", CRU Economic Forum, http://bbs.pinggu.org.

8. John H. Holland, *Hidden Order: How Adaption Builds Complexity*, Shanghai Century Publishing (Group) Co., Ltd., 2011.

9. Richard Dawkins, *River Out of Eden: A Darwinian View of Life*, translated by Wang Zhihua and Yue Renfeng, Shanghai Scientific & Technical Publishers, 2012.

10. Douglas North and Robert Thomas, *The Rise of the Western World*, translated by Li Yiping and Cai Lei, Huaxia Publishing House, 1989.

11. magic/tp, "Spirit Irreversibility and Pursuit", http://bbs.pinggu.org

12. Ilya Prigogine and Isabelle Stengers, *From Disorder to Order, A Dialogue Between Human and Nature*, translated by Zeng Qinghong and Shen Xiaofeng, Shanghai Translation Publishing House, 1987.

13. Graham Bateman, Atoms, *Molecules and States of Matter*, translated by Lin Na, Posts & Telecom Press Co., Ltd., 2013.

14. Huang Xiaolin and Huang Mengxi, *The Most Magical Principles of Economics*, New Century Publishing House, 2010.

15.Tom Kirwood, *Time of Our Lives — The Science of Human Aging*, transleteal by Xie Deqiu, Shanghai Scientific and Technological Education Publishing House, 2001.

16. Ma Lieguang, *The Great Collapse of Capitalism*, Economic Press China, 2012.

17. Ma Lieguang, *A New Discussion of Economics: Multiplier, Statistical Entropy and National Income*, Economic Press China, 2006.

18. Charles Seife, *Decoding The Universe*, translated by Sui Zhumei, Shanghai Scientific and Technological Education Publishing House, 2010.

19. Deng Xiang, *The Theory of Economic Convergence and Economic Gaps in Different Regions of China*, Southwest University of Finance and Economics Press, 2006.

20. Ouyang Zhigang, "The Economic Growth Trend and International Synergistic Work During Economic Fluctuations, *Economic Research Journal* 2013, No.7.

21. Chen Yunbing, "A Study of China's Excessive Money Supply and Its Effect on Inflation", *China Business Update*, 2013, No.18.

22. Cao Gang, "Deflation is What to be Concerned about", *Talents Mag.*, 2013. No.5.

23. Zhao Hongrui, *A Theory of China's Money Aggregate*, Economic Press China, 2013.

24. Chen Daofu, "High Money Stock in China Should be Treated in Dialectical Manner", *Development Research*, 2013, No.3.

25. Vernon L.Smith, Rationality in Economics: Constructivist and Ecological Forms, translated by Li keqiang, China Renmin University Press, 2013.

26. Hayek, *The Constitution of Liberty*, translated by Deng Zhenglai, SDX Joint Publishing Co., 2003.

27. Guo Zhigang, "Exploration and Analysis of the Changes in China's Families", *Chinese Journal of Population Science*, 2008, No.3.

28. Xiaoyuanyuan A, "The Director of the Institute of Population, CASS — Fertility-encouraging Policy Orientation Should Have Come Earlier", 9kd.net.

29. Sean B. Carroll, *The Making of the Fittest DNA and the Ultimate Forensic Record of Evolution*, translated by Yang Jiarong, Shanghai Scientific and Technological Education Publishing House, 2012.

30. Qiu Liqian, "Factors Affecting Breastfeeding in Rural Areas and Counties in Zhejiang Province", Hangzhou.com, Dec. 26, 2006.

31. Thomas Malthus, *An Essay on the Principle of Population*, translated by Chen Xiaobai, Huaxia Publishing House, 2013.

32. John St. Verde, *The Mystery of the Degeneration Theory, Gene Entropy and Genome*, translated by LiuYing, Shandong Friendship Publishing House, 2010.

33. Zhang Shuxiao, *Introduction to World Economy*, Economic Science Press, 2005.

34. Ma Lieguang, *The Space and Principles of Thoughts*, Economic Press China, 2012.

35. Joseph Schumpeter, *Theory of Economic Development*, translated by Zou Jianping, China Pictorial Publishing House, 2012.

36. Zhang Guangshan, "Differences of 'Value' in Philosophy and in Economics", CRU Economic Forum-Marxist Economics.

37. The City of Panzhihua in Sichuan Province ed., *The Great Debate — The Third National Symposium Collection of Papers in Entropy and Interdisciplinary Sciences*, Sichuan Science & Technology Press, 1993.

Postscript

We all know that writing is not easy. It consumes mental power and takes pains. Of course, it brings happiness, too. The German thinker Lichtenberg (1742-1799) said he "would rather write like Forster than, under the honeysuckle frame in a mild and cloudless spring evening, create the cutest baby with the most beautiful woman on the earth where God lives."[1] The state described by Lichtenberg may be far beyond everyone's reach.

The German writer Wolf Lepenies once said he learnt what the academic spirit was when lecturing at the French Academy. He approved of the French Academy's "dedication to the science in the process of formation". The approach of carrying out studies in imagination made him respect. The idea innovation does not only come from independent thinking. Immature theories and ideas that drift in mind like clouds are chances for creativity. For economics, new research perspectives stem from re-thinking. In front of reality, we are much confused. Re-thinking brings about magical outcome, leading to the mysterious garden of knowledge.

No magic can a stone into gold and it is also impossible to accomplish academic researches in one step. Academic researches require accumulation. Ideas are flowing. They need comprehension to grasp and time to test. Mr. Zhao Guoliang at Southwestern University of Finance and Economics is my mentor of the graduation thesis. He once told me that thoughts and ideas cannot be understood without expressions in detail so that theories root deep and grow

1 Wolf Lepenies, *Qu'est-ce qu'un intellectuel européen? Les intellectuels et la politique de l'esprit dans l'histoire européenne*, translated by Li Yanming, Guangxi Normal University Press, 2011, p. 118. Georg Forster is a German historian and scientist.

high. His words made a great influence on my writing for a lifetime. No matter how the living environment and social situation change, I always abide by these words to accumulate academic experience and write papers as careful, subtle, and substantial as I can. So I can create a new world by writing.

This book was completed at the end of 2014. The first draft started with a philosophical topic. However, due to various reasons, its publication was postponed. So I happened to have more time to modify it continuously and improve it. This book is the third book of mine on economic theories. The first one is *A New Discussion of Economics: Multiplier, Statistical Entropy, and National Income* which took ten years to finish off and on. It finally came out in 2006. After that, I continue to make effort to make *The Great Collapse of Capitalism* published.

Time, once gone, will never come back again. Writing three books within twenty years makes me feel difficult. So I treat myself with a sentence online "Even though there is no audience clapping for you when you answer a curtain call, you need to bow with sincerity to thank for all your efforts." Delightfully, my initial ideas have not been out of date until today. They stood the test of the economic reality. It means my theory fits the practice. And it is still in the process of improvement. Making progress in the development of thoughts is inspiring.

Also, I would like to thank Sichuan Economic Development Research Institute for sponsoring the publication of this book, and Mr. Dai Yulong, the editor at China Social Sciences Press, for helping me with the publication.

Thoughts are still in quiet changes. Power with no physical form is still gathering. Future belongs to explorers.

Ma Lieguang

March, 2017 in Chengdu

Table of Terms

强制结汇制度	A mandatory settlement system
玻尔兹曼熵	Boltzmann entropy
资金运动	Capital movement
银监会	CBRC (China Banking Regulatory Commission)
贷	Credit
信用货币	Credit money
借	Debit
复式记账法	Double-entry Bookkeeping
认识论	Epistemology
信用本位制	Fiduciary standard
双曲几何	Hyperbolic geometry
惯性质量	Inertial mass
信息熵	Information entropy
动能	Kinetic energy
微观共性	Microcosmic commonality
微观一致性	Microcosmic consistency
交换媒介 (chapt.6)	Medium of exchange
货币量、货币总量	Monetary aggregate
基础货币、货币基础	Monetary base
货币资金	Monetary capital

国民收入	National Income, short for national income
国民收入熵	NI entropy
国民收入乘数	NI multiplier
双小核草履虫	Paramecium Aurelia
袋状草履虫	Paramecium bursaria
大草履虫	Paramecium cauda-tum
人均收入	Per capita income
量化宽松	Quantitative easing
量子纠缠	Quantum entanglement
量子叠加	Quantum
储蓄（也指居民储蓄）	Savings
收入储蓄 10.2 有解释	Income savings
空间力学	Space mechanics
空间转化	Space alteration
国家信用	State credit
绝对时空概念	The concept of absolute space-time
热力学	Thermodynamics
匀速运动	Uniform motion
货币周转率（货币周转速度）	Velocity of money
通货膨胀	inflation
长期停滞	long-term stagnation
长期增长	long-term growth
收支平衡	fiscal balance

美联储	Federal Reserve
资金池	the capital pool
国债	treasury bonds
居民消费价格指数	the consumer price index(CPI)
通货紧缩	deflation
熵变规律	law of entropy change
全要素生产率	total factor productivity
宏观经济学	macroeconomics
增长厌恶症	growth aversion
萧条时代	Depression Era
炒股	stock speculation
中产	the middle class
草根	the grassroots
市场经济	the market economy
新古典宏观经济理论	neoclassical macroeconomic theory
小额信贷	micro cedit
网贷平台	online lending platforms
信托	trust and loan money funds
货币发行	the release of the money
自动调节	automatic adjustment
经济效率	economic efficiency
能量守恒	energy conservation
熵	entropy
不可逆现象	irreversible phenomena
棘轮效应	Ratcheting Effect

热力学第二定律	The Second Law of Thermodynamics
财富积累	wealth accumulation
n 维乘数	N-dimensional Multiplier
货币周转	currency turnover
储蓄（第四章第四节）	deposit
央行	The Central Bank
银行准备金	bank reserves
个人现金存款	personal cash deposits
政府债券	Covernment Bonds
负利率	negative interest rates
自我设限	Self-limiting
人口出生率下降	the Declining Birth Rate
公共卫生	public hygiene
人口预期寿命	human life longevity
平均寿命	the average lifespan
中等收入国家	the middle-developed countries
婴儿潮	baby boom
总和生育率	the general fertility rate
城市化水平低	insufficient urbanization level
计划经济	the planned economy
女性有效生育年龄段	the fertile age range of women
晚婚	late marriage
晚育	late childbearing
有效生育期	the effective childbearing period
独生子女政策	the family planning policy

政府开支	government spending
微观经济学	microecnomics
自然平衡说	a theory of natural balance
人口爆炸	population boom
增长极限论	the limit-to-growth theory
边际成本	the marginal cost
边际收入	the marginal benefit
从众心理	conformity to the mainstream
逻辑斯蒂方程	the Logistic Equation
经济学的多维空间理论	Theories of Multidimensional Space in Economics
微观常数	microscopic constants
几何变量	geometric variables
毕达哥拉斯定律	Pythagorean law
黎曼度量	Riemann metrics
拓扑学	topology
数量标度	numerical scales
线性代数	linear algebra
销售单价	the unit price of sales
格乌司原理	The Principle of Geussi
生态位	ecological niche
亲缘关系	genetic relations
三维空间	three-dimensional space
协调关系	coordination ralations
空间转换	space alteration

空间联系	space connection
“路径依赖”	path dependency
空间复制	space replication
几何距离	geometric distance
经验主义	empiricism
凯恩斯国民收入均衡理论	Keynesian Theory of National Income Equilibrium
信用货币	credit money
均衡	equilibrium
传统范式	Conventional Paradigm
相反率	irreversibility
货币资金流动	the circulation of monetary funds
非线性经济学	non-linear economics
系统论	the system theory
信息论	the information theory
耗散结构	the dissipative structure
协同学	synergetics
超循环论	the hypercycle theory
突变论	catastrophe theory
分形论	fractal theory
商品贸易	commodity transactions
本质	essence
统计熵	statistical entrophy
理论创新	theoretical innovation
储蓄分布状态	savings distribution

微观经济规律	minimun amount of money
微观状态数	number of micro-states
经济现实	econonic reality
内生机制	the endogenous mechanism
基础货币膨胀	monetary base expansion
哲学经济学	philosophical economics
实用主义哲学	pragmatic philosophy
宏观经济政策	macroeconomic policies
公有制计划经济理论	the theory of public-owed planned economy
个人主观偏好	individual subjective preference
个人主义原则	The principle of individualism
供求关系	the supply-demand relation
博弈论	the game theory
劳动价值论	labor theory of value
劣币驱逐良币	Bad drives away good money.
萝卜青菜各有所爱	Radish and cabbage have their own preferences.
一门独立学科	an independent discipline

This book is the result of a co-publication agreement between China Social Sciences Press (China) and Paths International Ltd (UK)

Title: Depression Economics in the 21st Century
Authors: Ma Lieguang
Translated by Wang Wenying
ISBN: 978-1-84464-713-2
Ebook ISBN: 978-1-84464-714-9

Paths International Ltd
www.pathsinternational.com
Published in the United Kingdom

www.ingramcontent.com/pod-product-compliance
Lightning Source LLC
LaVergne TN
LVHW081208240426
836338LV00004B/43